Football Memories

Football Memories

Brian Glanville

First published in Great Britain in 1999 by
Virgin Publishing Ltd
Thames Wharf Studios
Rainville Road
London W6 9HT

ISBN 1 85227 793 9

Typeset by TW Typesetting, Plymouth, Devon

Printed and bound in Great Britain by Creative Print and Design (Wales), Ebbw Vale

For
Samuel, Bella and Joshie
I Nipoti

'You are nothing but a cuckoo,' Denry pleasantly informed her. 'Football has got to do with everything.'

Arnold Bennett
The Card, 1911

1

'BUGGER BOGNOR,' said King George V, on his deathbed, perhaps apocryphally; but it was in Bognor that it all began: with Bognor Regis Town, with Ronnie and with Pickles. Ronnie was real enough. Sturdy, young and blond, the hero of the crowd as he played his green-shirted, Sussex League football for them, in the autumn of 1939. Pickles may have been my father's typically romantic invention, though, if he wasn't Pickles, he was somebody. Elderly for a footballer, ruddy-faced, going a little bald, wily and shrewd. Pickles, my father called him, and told me he had played for Millwall. At just eight years old, I was hardly in a position to dispute it.

I remember, especially, one heroic moment of Ronnie's. Sprawled on the ground after a tackle, he still managed to lunge out with a foot as an opponent closed dangerously in; to sweep the ball into touch, to the ecstasy of the crowd in the old wooden stand.

We, the family, had been caught in Bognor at the start of the war, and my father, who commuted from there to his dental surgery in London, had decided to keep us in Bognor as a precaution: I; my mother, Florence; and my younger sister, Marilyn. My father came from a Dublin Jewish family and talked with a strong brogue to the end of his days, though not as strong as that of his eldest brother, my Uncle Louis ('How are you, Brian? Nice to hear your sweet voice'), who had left home and a domineering, sometimes violent, father – from Lithuania? Latvia? no one seemed sure – to fight in the Boer War. There, legend had it, he had become heavyweight champion of the South African Army and gambled away his share in a gold mine. Stories were told of his legendary strength: how he had bodily lifted up an offending bookmaker, chair and all, in the Regent Palace.

He, too, was turned into a dentist by his father, or rather a quack dentist, among so many other things, in his time. His last days were spent in Soho, a surgery in Rupert Street with a foot-operated drill, and, usually, a young Gentile mistress. When he was ill, my father and the youngest brother, Gerry, would shoot over from nearby Cranbourne Street in the lunch hour to take his patients.

So we watched Bognor, but talked about the Arsenal. My father did. About the romance of Arsenal. The long-unfashionable London team that had been turned into a power by their incomparable manager, Herbert Chapman, and the masterly inside forward, Charlie Buchan. Except that my father, typically and romantically, got it wrong. It was Buchan, he said, who had brought Chapman to the Arsenal. Buchan, who had once been on their books as an amateur, had become a star with Sunderland, and rejoined them in 1925 on the famous £100-per-goal transfer.

Buchan, said my father, was so skilful, so subtle, so creative, that lesser footballers found it hard to play with him. That was why he won so relatively few caps for England. But Buchan it was – though it wasn't – who had the foresight to persuade the Yorkshireman, Chapman, to leave Huddersfield Town, whom he had turned into a Championship team, and come south to London.

Quite wrong, of course; the truth was wholly the reverse. It was Chapman, when he came to Arsenal from Huddersfield, who persuaded Buchan to rejoin the club he had left before the First World War – when it was still Woolwich Arsenal – over a dispute about a mere eleven shillings expenses. Chapman also persuaded Sunderland to sell Buchan, by then a veteran but a very serviceable one, promising the player an extra payment of £100, real money then, for every goal he scored.

Was it Chapman or Buchan who then invented the 'Third Back Game', which was to transform English football for over thirty years? The Third Back Game, fruit of the change that year in the offside rule, which meant that only two, rather than three opponents, were needed goalside of an attacker to put him onside. Generally the credit was given to Chapman, who supposedly refined Buchan's original plans. But when in later years I asked Buchan about it, he claimed the credit for himself.

On the field he may well have been a player of unusual intelligence, but, as we know, a football brain is *sui generis*. It does not preclude intellect outside the field of play, any more than an intellectual need necessarily be an unintelligent footballer. But the football brain is essentially a thing of instinct, the *reductio ad absurdum* being a player such as Paul Gascoigne, who is wonderfully inventive, aware and original on the field, but displays few of these qualities off the pitch.

Meeting Buchan in his later years, I found a large, prosaic and amiably banal man; his words, on or off the radio, were delivered ponderously in his South London accent, though his father had been a Scottish policeman. One had to take the football brain on trust. He became an honest, dull, successful journalist, and a well-known broadcaster; no John Arlott, surely, but effective in the sheer pedestrianism of his delivery and the plodding of his prose.

Point, counterpoint. In the early 1950s, when I had gone to live in a cheap and cheerful *pensione* on the Florence Lungarno, I yearned to hear his five-minute Saturday-evening broadcasts, summing up the day's English football, but my battered American radio needed to be repaired.

So I would go, for those five precious minutes, to the room occupied by Jay, a melancholy young American painter who dressed gloomily in long, khaki, Moroccan robes that brushed the floor. She was an abstract painter, and her abstracts filled the Stygian room, their funereal colours making it seem darker still. One Saturday, when I arrived, she was kneeling just beneath the table where her radio stood, evidently in the middle of a *crise de nerfs*, tearing up her paintings. I should have seen as much and left, but those minutes, the information they conveyed, however plodding, were too important to me. Over the radio came Buchan's dreary voice. 'Sheffield Wednesday . . . and although Derek Dooley didn't score . . .' RIP! 'I think you're most insensitive!' 'He did help his team to get a point in a two-two draw at Highbury.'

Earlier that year, in Florence again, it had been Buchan, in his kindness, who had helped the hopelessly inebriated Stanley, a fellow journalist, on to the coach that would take us to the Italy versus England match, after a generous lunch provided by the Tuscan sports journalists, in the Via Tornabuoni. Throughout the game, Stanley slept in the sun, while Buchan complained about being left with a casualty.

One more Italian memory, from some two years later, comes to mind. The city, this time Bologna, where the England under-23 team, including the precocious, ill-fated seventeen-year-old Duncan Edwards, was due to play its Italian equivalent, in the first game of its kind. At the bar of the hotel where both teams were staying, I found myself speaking to the Italians' manager, Silvio Piola, once a crack centre forward, famous, or infamous, for punching a goal against England in Milan, which was given by the German referee.

Both of us were trying to be modest. 'They're young,' said Piola, genially sly, with a shrug of his shoulders, 'you can't tell what they're going to do,' and he shrugged again. Buchan, standing by, unable to understand Italian, finally began to shrug, himself. 'Well, everybody's doing it; I might as well do it, too.'

Another journalist arrived. 'That young fellow,' said Buchan, indicating a Tuscan youth coach, 'he speaks English. But Piola, he don't speak at all!'

He wrote an autobiography, A *Lifetime in Football*: every paragraph a sentence, every sentence a paragraph. Not an ounce of humour, but the anecdotes were marvellous, and some of those fustian radio phrases still linger in the mind. 'So I'm taking them to win.' 'And now it's cheerio and good luck.' Once, in a barber's shop in Sunderland, the city where he flourished, I heard his voice emerging from the radio while the clients waiting to have their hair cut listened in a state of apparent stupor. Was this his ideal audience? I remember wondering at the time, yet what he had to say was always relevant.

In Bognor, we were caught, you could say, in Kyota Court, a kind of middle-class estate of flats, before the word 'estate', once grandiose in its implications, came to mean nothing better than a high-rise slum. Trespassers were discouraged, which came in useful when I was being pursued by fellow pupils from the council school – a culture shock – which I first attended. Graham, whom I thought my friend and whom I had invited to my eighth birthday party, had betrayed me: 'Those boys want to talk to you,' he said, but I was wary.

Subsequently, I would go to a local prep school, Holyrood, where I found my closest friend from University College junior school already there. The intention had been that I would go from UCS juniors to UCS seniors, but the war changed that entirely. At UCS junior, I had shown no interest in football. Indeed, all I can remember of it was slinking into the opposing penalty area and, to the scorn of its defenders, telling them that I was 'spying'. It was my father, and his tales of Arsenal, which would change that.

He came down to us at weekends, and wrote to me during the week: 'My dear son Brian' – affectionate letters that rolled across the commas, and occasionally included verse.

I kicked a ball, I scored a goal,
My goodness, how the ball did roll.
The goalie jumped but was too slow.

He was a marvellous teller of children's tales, inventing a young hero he called Johnny, and, to some extent, his Arsenal stories were simply an extension of these. He took pleasure in Dickens and often quoted Sean O'Casey: 'Sure, the whole world is in a terrible state of chassis.' Or: 'And I looked at that chiseller playing in the gutter, and I said to myself, something will come of that there chiseller.'

Not till the beginning of 1942 did he take me to a professional football match. During that time, we had moved to a rented house in Aldwick Bay, gone back to London, then moved out again after a bomb destroyed a house at the corner of our unadopted road in Finchley. I was sent to a fearsome school in Brackley, Northampton-shire, where I caught measles, was neglected, contracted mastoid trouble, and had a painful operation at University College Hospital in central London, where the fire-bombs were coming down.

Then, with a black patch over one ear, I found myself at Thenford House, the eighteenth-century mansion, also in Northants, now occupied in such expansive style by Michael Heseltine. This came about because my sister had been billeted with the family of the school's headmaster. Newlands had been evacuated from Seaford, on the Sussex coast.

Thenford House had sweeping grounds, a ha-ha, a stunted oak where maybugs flew in summer, and a Siamese cat crouched, waiting for its prey. There were woods, a lake – Heseltine has dug a second one – and ample fields for games. Were I to see the place today, I would doubtless be impressed by its sweep and scope, its meadows, trees and water. But boarding school is boarding school, not least when, like my sister and myself, you are obliged to spend the Easter holiday there. Then, the place becomes a kind of open prison; nor, with its high ceilings and its cold dormitories, was it ever comfortable. We all had chilblains every winter.

It was in January 1942, that my father took me to that first match, and it could hardly have been a more exciting beginning: England against Scotland at Wembley, each team glittering with stars. England were captained by Eddie Hapgood, Arsenal's left back, an elegant, Corinthian figure, a Bristolian, who played the game impeccably. The centre half was Stanley 'Flipper' Cullis, so nicknamed for the way he extended his arms when on the ball, a stopper centre half capable of great feats of skill. The forward line was exceptional. On the right wing, Stanley Matthews, with his amazing, irresistible swerve, partnered by the little blond Middlesbrough inside forward, Wilf Mannion.

At centre forward was the powerful and majestic Tommy Lawton, the perfect successor at Everton to another legendary header of the ball, Dixie Dean. It was said of Lawton that he could actually hang in the air, and he was just as dangerous on the ground. The inside left was Jimmy Hagan, adroit, skilful and inventive. On the left wing was another Arsenal hero, Denis Compton, the Brylcreem Boy with his picture plastered all over London; a supremely gifted ball player, whether it be a football or a cricket ball, he was a footballing juggler with immense confidence and a devastating left foot. Adventurous, unorthodox and gloriously unpredictable whether he was playing on the left wing or dancing down the wicket to make a good length ball into a bad one, Compton excelled. Over the years, I would go anywhere to watch him play either sport.

As for Scotland, who were comprehensively beaten that day, 3–0, their wing halves were Bill Shankly and Matt Busby who, in the years to come, would be the outstanding club managers of their time at Liverpool and Manchester United respectively. Yet what I still remember best is the preliminaries. The Scottish soldier, tartan scarf flying, and the sailor cheerfully joining the pre-match kick-in with the unprotesting Scottish players. Before she inspected the teams, Mrs Churchill announced somewhat tremulously over the loudspeakers that she must quickly leave, as she had to meet her husband, Winston, who had just come back from meeting Stalin, in Moscow.

I remember Wilf Mannion skipping across the frosty pitch, while a man behind us shouted, 'Come on, Mannion, boy!' Hagan scored almost immediately, England won 3–0 and I went home, vastly excited, to draw inept pictures of what I thought had happened. One, I remember, was 'Hapgood gets knocked out', a dreadful moment. Another – and here, again, I have a picture in my mind infinitely better than the picture I drew – showed Cullis, crouched over the ball, stoutly holding off the Scottish forwards in what was, then, never known as the midfield.

I wrote to Hapgood for his autograph and, back at Newlands, it arrived. A boy called Baker snatched it from me and ran around the school's bay-windowed main room, shouting, in a parody of my enthusiasm. Each week, I wrote, or tried to send, a letter to Hapgood. I even resorted to verse:

When Hapgood takes the field each match,
Then Arsenal have no fear.

'Bags' Lawrie, a master nicknamed for his plus fours and deputed to preside over Sunday-evening letter-writing, was ruddy-faced, a heavy smoker and prematurely bald. He would have none of it. Given to occasional, sudden outbursts of violent rage, mysteriously un-motivated, though a good teacher of maths and algebra, he told me, 'I'm not sending that.' So the letters came to an end, but my passion for football grew.

My father was interested in rugby, too, and would talk often of a famous Guy's Hospital team of the 1920s, containing a South African star called Albertine. He took me to a few matches, one at Wembley, which I quite enjoyed, but as time went by my interest waned and, when ultimately I came to play the game, I detested it. I was inept. At the end of a term in which I had been scoring goals for the second eleven, I was banished from the rugby game, and played soccer instead with a bunch of juniors.

'Can't you tackle, Glanville?' sneered Cappy, the headmaster, during one rugby game. I was very thin and slight, qualities that were of secondary importance in soccer, where skill and some intelligence could prevail.

'Cappy' was Captain Hugh Faithful Chittenden, MC, and rugger was his game. He was a good and fair headmaster, ruddier than 'Bags', moustached and formidable when he raised his voice in class to boom at an offender, 'Tense, boy!' He, too, taught well, especially Latin, and if he was somewhat unimaginative, a stereotyped prep school headmaster of his time, there was nothing cruel or sadistic about him, as there was about so many headmasters of that epoch. There was an honesty, a decency, a latent kindness in him, which elicited not only respect but some affection.

Many years later, when an arts magazine, in an article about burgeoning novelists, mentioned both myself and Frank Tuohy, who I knew had been at Newlands, I sent it to him, and met him again at a tea-time reunion in Brown's hotel where he lamented that the school, now back in Seaford, was no longer what it once cosily was.

Captain Adamson, known always as 'Fruity', a nickname he detested, was a soccer man. He had even played for Oxford University, late in the previous century, but had not gained a blue. He was very old, very gnarled and wore green plus fours, essentially a Victorian figure with a Victorian's extraordinary versatility and ingenuity. He, too, taught Latin, as well as geography, and he was the only one who has ever interested me in science, with his clever models of the combustion engine, with its piston as a movable object.

'You're back to your old sloppy ways,' he would tell a miscreant. He lectured occasionally on football, and told us to kick corners with our toes, by way of contrast with professionals: 'Look at their legs:

same thickness all the way down.' Told by me on a Sunday morning that Arsenal had won the day before, his answer was always, 'Who were they playing? The blind school?'

The nickname 'Fruity' was conferred on him by an enormously tall master called 'Andy' Anderson, a far, far younger man of humorous mien who delighted in quiz questions, and was extremely popular. 'Fruity' had an old man's insensitivity and a certain selfishness. If a clever, vulnerable boy cried in class, he would contemptuously send him out of the room.

When the school moved to the more confortable and compact Wardington House, his quarters were quite literally a stable stall. One day, by chance, he left the door open and, peering in, we saw the model he was making with infinite care: a ship, superb in every detail. The kind of thing to fascinate prep school boys but, working secretively on, he would never show it to us.

Later that year, 1942, my father at long last took me to an Arsenal match. They were playing at Tottenham Hotspur's ground then, at White Hart Lane, ironic indeed when you recall the bitterness that ensued when Arsenal, then Woolwich Arsenal, moved across the river from Plumstead in southeast London to build a home at Highbury. Spurs felt their domain had been invaded, and there was bad blood between the clubs for years. Needs must, however, and at that time Arsenal had no home. Their stadium, with its two art deco grandstands, had been taken over by Air Raid Precautions and, besides, a bomb had landed on the north terraces. It would be over four years before I ever set foot in Arsenal Stadium.

My father and I would enter the stand at Tottenham; then he would give half a crown to the man on the wooden gate, and we would go up the steps to the better seats. That afternoon, Arsenal were playing Brighton and Hove Albion. It was a wartime league match; clubs were matched together on a regional basis, and guest players were allowed. For the moment, Arsenal didn't need them. With the exception of the famous England international forward, Cliff Bastin, whose deafness obliged him to be an air raid warden, Arsenal's players were mostly in the Royal Air Force or the Army; particularly the Air Force.

None of the players was involved as part of air crew, tank crew or infantry. They were drafted largely into the Physical Training Corps, a practice which made little Aldershot, no more in peacetime than a lowly Third Division (South) club, a glittering array of stars, all employed at the PT base of 'Soldier Town'.

Brighton, in their blue-and-white stripes, were no match for an

Arsenal team full of internationals, who scored six goals against them. I remember just one Brighton player clearly. His name was Wilson; he had red hair, though he was largely bald, and I believe he was playing outside left.

Arsenal had Denis Compton on the left wing, the sleek-haired, powerfully acrobatic George Marks in goal, the muscular Norfolk man Alf Kirchen thundering down the right wing, the elegant Jack Crayston at right half and my new ego ideal, Bernard Joy, at centre half.

Ah! An amateur centre half, playing for the Arsenal! Named on the programme as Flight Lieutenant B Joy, with the initial before the surname, as was the custom, then, in denoting amateurs. If Joy, so tall, so blond, so dominating in the air and resilient on the ground, could play for Arsenal as an amateur, then maybe I too could do so, one day. To play as a professional was, for a prep school boy, in those days, quite taboo.

So Joy, in a different way from Eddie Hapgood and Denis Compton, more accomplished players both, became a new hero. He was, I learned, a schoolmaster in peacetime, though in years to come he would become a journalist and a colleague, and we would go round the world together.

In the red shirts with white sleeves that would become so dear to me, in their white shorts, their blue- and white-hooped stockings, Arsenal, then, were still a power in the land, living on the momentum of their triumphant pre-war years in which they had won so many honours and incurred so much jealousy and hatred, not just at Tottenham, but all over England.

In those days, the programme was not the shiny, advertisement-filled, expensive thing it is today, but a single buff sheet costing a penny with the teams printed on one side – each player with his military rank alongside his name – and some club notes on the back. A message on the front gave instructions on what to do in the event of an air raid, though I was lucky enough never to experience one at White Hart Lane.

Once a game was over, or almost over, we followed the same ritual. My father and I would cross the High Road, take a trolley-bus back a couple of stops, cross the road again, and take another trolley-bus going westwards, where there would always be empty seats.

The authorities' decision to draft footballers into physical training units distressed some people, notably the relatives of those who were on active service. Frank Butler, the sports columnist who wrote, then, for the truncated versions of both the *Daily Express* and the *Sunday*

Express, put it well when he said that, once the war began, the pimply young men waited to see their sporting heroes jumping out of planes and leaping on to beaches. After a time, the pimply young men, to their surprise, found that they were doing these things by themselves. Their heroes were safely based at home.

It was a resentment that would reach some kind of a crescendo, late in the war, when the very powerful British Army representative team, including such stars as Tommy Lawton, and the complete England half-back line of Cliff Britton, Stan Cullis and Joe Mercer, toured Italy, playing against teams of combat soldiers, who were known to exhort them: 'Come on, the stay-at-home soldiers!' But civilian morale was surely helped by their presence there: a distraction from the bombs, the sirens, the shortages of food and the often distressing news.

At the end of the season, that is the end of the Easter holidays, there was disappointment. Arsenal had reached the semi-final of the London War Cup, in which they were drawn to play Brentford, at Chelsea's ground, Stamford Bridge. Brentford were another London team, from down the Great West Road. They wore red-and-white stripes, had been in the First Division just four years when the war began, and were known, for all their modest status, as Arsenal's bogey team.

Rhyme, reason and logic, I would learn, did not come into it. Some teams simply had the Indian sign on others, and Brentford had it over Arsenal. The match at Stamford Bridge, on the Fulham Road, was drawn 0–0, necessitating a replay. I have just two memories of the game. One involved Jack Crayston. While engaged in a heading duel with a Brentford player in midfield, he finally let the ball loop over his head, only to catch it with his heel and send it flying over the head of his opponent.

The other image concerns Laurie Scott, a quick, compact little full back from Sheffield, serving in the RAF, who had not long since won a place at left back in the Arsenal side while Hapgood, its distinguished incumbent, was serving somewhere far away. I can see Scott winning one tackle, winning another, and emerging with the ball as both Brentford players fell to the ground.

Brentford beat Arsenal in the replay but, by then, I was back at Newlands. In the Final, at Wembley, they would meet Portsmouth who, three years earlier in the FA Cup Final itself, had astonished Wolves, the favourites, by thrashing them 4–1.

It so happened that I had to come up to London for an appointment with the dentist who was trying, none too successfully, to regulate my teeth; this made it possible for my father to take me to the Final. After some cogitation over which team I should support – Portsmouth, because Brentford had beaten Arsenal, or Brentford, for the same reason – I decided on Brentford. I apologised to John Maybury, a Portsmouth boy and the head of our small dormitory, who said he didn't care.

Portsmouth had half their 1939 Cup Final team and were the favourites, but this time the boot, almost literally, was on the other foot, and Brentford won 2–0, both goals scored by the English international outside left, the sleek-haired Leslie Smith. I went home and enthusiastically wrote doggerel about it, forgivable perhaps in a ten-year-old:

Smith's foot and the ball have met,
One goes crashing through the net

which my father, with equal enthusiasm, read to unfortunate friends, over the phone.

Arsenal, now, had become an obsession, and would remain so for years to come. Freudians, or Kleinians, might find some sort of explanation for it; displacement, compensation, sublimation of some kind or another? Who knows? What I am sure of is that it was a solace and a comfort in the loneliest days of boarding school. False drama it may have been, but there was always something happening, something to look forward to or be disappointed by. In the four-page daily newspapers of the time, a minuscule portion of the back page would be devoted to football. How eagerly, compulsively, one scoured those spaces for news of the Gunners! No transfer tales then; transfers were put on ice until the end of the war. But there was team news, news of unexpected guest players: like Berry Nieuwenhuys.

Nieuwenhuys was a South African outside right, one of several South Africans who played for Liverpool, and one who would make one appearance at Tottenham as a guest for Arsenal. I remember this only because of the way the programme change was announced. The fashion, then, was not to broadcast such facts over the tannoy, but to entrust them to a little old man whose job it was to spell them out with a series of yellow letters painted on black squares, studiously aligned along the bottom of the grandstand. In this case, the poor old fellow struggled pitifully with so exotic a name. Slowly, slowly, through trial and error, one saw the word emerging from its various versions, until there it was. NIEUWENHUYS. I think he played well.

At Newlands, one of my greatest consolations was the Estherby household. My mother had found it. During the war, she cut a dashing and romantic figure in the khaki uniform of something called the 'Women's Legion'. It drove canteens down to the docks and, in my mother's case, drove officers of the Dutch Army – comfortably quartered in Hereford and Arlington House, in Mayfair – round London.

Ever resourceful, she virtually billeted herself on the Estherby household in the nearby village of Middleton Cheney when, at weekends, she came down to see me. What choice could have been more perfect? Eddie Estherby, who was away for most of the week on war work in Liverpool, was a middle-aged tennis coach, who had once had the incomparable Fred Perry as his pupil. Much more important to me was that he was an Arsenal fan who had seen more than a thousand of their matches, and had the programmes to prove it. With characteristic kindness, he gave me several of them, including one that still seemed to emit fire from its black and white pages – the programme of an early 1920s match against Spurs that followed a bitter encounter at Tottenham, a week earlier.

Arsenal, then no more than a mediocre team, had had the temerity to go to White Hart Lane, and win. The fashion then, potentially so explosive, of playing home and away games in successive weeks, between the same clubs, meant that Arsenal and Spurs confronted each other again, immediately.

The programme notes, confrontational and combative to a degree, were written under the *nom de guerre* of 'Gunner's Mate', a pseudonym for George Allison who, in 1934, would become Arsenal's manager. During the war, one would see him in propaganda films: a squat, plump, rumbling figure, who had eliminated all trace of his original north-east accent. He came, in fact, from Middlesbrough, and had attached himself to Arsenal in their Woolwich days, when he was making his way as a young journalist, eventually representing the USA's Hearst newspapers. His accent, now, aped the received English of the period, the A's carefully if perversely pronounced as E's, as per the Prime Minister, Neville Chamberlain, himself, when war was declared: 'I am speaking to you from the kebinet room in 10 Downing Street.'

How Gunner's Mate, in that treasured programme, excoriated all Arsenal's critics of that victory! One of them had been a referee, 'But those who remember his efforts in that respect,' wrote Gunner's Mate, ferociously, 'would be suitably sceptical.' He had hard words for the Tottenham supporters, recalling a recent game in which Smelt, the Burnley full back, clapped his hand to his face, having been hit by a missile. Bad blood boiled.

By the time of the death of the incomparable Herbert Chapman in March 1934, when a bad cold turned into irresistible pneumonia, George Allison had become a director of the club. As a publicist and journalist, he was unquestionably effective. To make him the new manager seemed an extraordinary choice. His knowledge of the game was scant; his relations with his players uneasy. Where he and Arsenal were so fortunate was in the presence 'below stairs' of Tom Whittaker, an extraordinary trainer.

Extraordinary for two reasons. First because of his famous healing hands. This was long before the days of deep diathermy heat and ultrasound. Most trainers were bucket and sponge – the so-called 'magic' sponge – men little-schooled in physiotherapy. When Whittaker returned from an FA tour of Australia with a broken leg, his career finished, in Chapman's first summer at Arsenal, Chapman, with typical inspiration, decided he would turn him into a trainer. Did he, in some way, divine Whittaker's undoubted healing powers? For that was what they surely were. Whittaker, and those hands, played an absolutely crucial part in Arsenal's increasing success, precisely because he could put injured players quickly back on the field who, at other clubs, might be *hors de combat* for weeks.

Secondly, Whittaker, under Allison's regime, became the players' father figure, the man to whom they could turn when the somewhat tactless and uncertain Allison had unsettled them.

If this was lucky for Allison, it was also a fortunate situation for Whittaker, for in professional football it is the manager, good or bad, who is the lightning conductor. However great a contribution the coach or trainer makes, he is in some sense protected, as Whittaker himself would discover when he became the Arsenal manager, after the war. 'What you need,' said a sympathetic Harry Homer, the Oxonian who by then edited the Arsenal programme, 'is a Tom Whittaker.'

Eddie Estherby was full of good stories of Arsenal's golden era. He was a cheerful, humorous, generous man, at this time in his career, with an equally kind and genial wife in the resilient Della. John, their only son, would, sadly, die young, and thus wreck the marriage and the lives of both of them. Without Della, Eddie became a sad, confused fantasist, while she went off to work in Austria with the British Army, hiding her grief behind synthetic jollity.

In those days, however, Eddie made light of the turn his life had taken, and regaled me, when I visited him, with fascinating anecdotes of Arsenal's *wunderjahren*. Of Eddie Hapgood, for instance, who came to Arsenal from non-league football at Kettering so frail that when he headed the ball he was knocked out. Then Chapman put him on a diet of beefsteak, and he could then head with impunity.

One story concerned Alex James, the little Scottish inside left who became the hub and inspiration of the Arsenal team with his legendary long shorts and his devastating passes. Clashing with Chapman over pay – exiguous in those days – he was told he would be sent on a sea cruise. Tom Whittaker accompanied him down to the docks, where the ship turned out to be a tramp steamer. 'I'm not going on that!' insisted James. 'Boss's orders,' said Whittaker, and James duly embarked.

I was able to visit the Estherbys, in their little house, on Sunday mornings, while the rest of the school attended church nearby. One Sunday, I had the temerity to stay for the kind of lunch never dreamed of at Newlands, and was beaten for my sins by Cappy, who administered the customary three strokes for going absent without leave.

The 1942–43 season would turn out to be a watershed for Arsenal; one in which a team still largely that of 1939 would win both Southern Cup and League, but which would prove the last in which the club flourished. It could hardly have begun better. In August, Arsenal's first League South match was at The Valley, south-east London, against Charlton Athletic, and Bryn Jones would play! Bryn Jones, who was the most expensive player in the history of British football, signed by Arsenal and Allison from Wolves for £14,000, in 1938. The little, wiry-haired, Welsh international was expected to inherit the role of Alex James, who had retired in 1937, but it was a little bit like understudying Gielgud or Olivier. Jones had undoubted qualities, but he was not the same kind of player as James, and in his one pre-war season, he had found it difficult to fit in.

There, nevertheless, he was, at Charlton, having for some time been posted out of London with, I believe, the Royal Artillery; and I, still ten years old, was anxious to see him. When my father and I arrived by tram, the customary means of transport to The Valley, and on whose post-war disappearance many blamed a decline in Charlton's crowds, it was to find an odd Arsenal team.

George Swindin, who was meant to play in goal, had not got leave from the Army, so Arsenal replaced him with another hero of the time, Leslie Compton. Elder brother of Denis, Leslie had joined Arsenal as a full back as long ago as 1932, when he was expected to take over from the retiring captain and right back, Tom Parker. Chapman, however, decided that he was too slow and, instead, worked his Svengali ways on a young wing half, George Male.

Leslie played in a couple of international trials for England before the war, without winning a regular first-team place with Arsenal; but when war came, he flourished, even as a centre forward for a time, once scoring ten goals in a match against Clapton Orient and their amateur goalkeeper. Cheerful and *dégagé*, a larger, less flamboyant figure than his illustrious younger brother, Denis, he, too, was a cricketer, a wicket-keeper for Middlesex, and, as such, perhaps fitted to appear in goal.

Indeed, that summer I had been to Lord's for the first time, to see the brothers play for a Middlesex and Essex side against Kent and Surrey. Denis made a spectacular running catch on the boundary off Godfrey Evans of Kent, later to become a renowned England wicket-keeper.

Bryn Jones was everything one might have hoped him to be. In the white shirt and black shorts, which Arsenal donned for the day, he danced his way time and again through the red shirts of the Charlton defence, scoring no fewer than three goals. The grandstand, I remember, was sparsely peopled. I remember, too, a little group of laughing men sitting some rows behind us, calling out, with ironic enthusiasm, 'Come on, Treacle!' This, I found out long afterwards, was the nickname of the Charlton outside left, Harold Hobbis, who had played for England in Vienna in 1936 when he was kicked in the stomach, and Austria beat England for the first time.

I did not see all the game or all the goals. Small the crowd may have been but my father was cautious and insistent; we must leave before the end to make sure we got the tram. So at 5–0 to Arsenal, with Leslie Compton till then unbeaten in goal, leave we did. Next day I discovered that the final score was 6–2. Charlie Revell, then the Charlton outside right, later their captain and left half, had cut in twice to score late, irrelevant goals. From that moment, Bryn Jones was added to my pantheon.

Nemesis caught up with me at Christmas. Christmas Day, 1942. In those times, and till well after the war, there was a full football programme on both Christmas Day and Boxing Day. Arsenal were to play Chelsea away and at home. In these times, teams complain about having to play twice in a week; the prospect of playing twice in 48 hours was then simply taken for granted.

To Stamford Bridge, on Christmas morning – these were traditionally morning games – I would go with my father; and with Uncle Willy Warshaw. He was a Chelsea supporter and, in fact, an honorary uncle, with a platoon of honorary nephews whom he generously took to games at Stamford Bridge and at Lord's, where he was a member of the MCC. He and his pretty, red-haired, tense wife, Auntie Muriel, had no children of their own.

Uncle Willy was in schmatters, the rag trade. He was fat and bald and jolly. During the First World War, it was somewhat surprising to learn that he had been an air gunner in the Royal Flying Corps. Once, he told me, they had taken a German as prisoner, whom he had overheard bemoaning his lot in Yiddish: 'So I used to slip him bars of chocolate.'

He became famous in our family for a particular phrase, though he didn't enunciate it till some six years later. Then, he and Auntie Muriel were on holiday on the Italian coast, at Alassio. My parents and I were on holiday down the coast in the Ligurian resort of Spotorno. Italian holidays were something new and rare in 1948. My parents and I travelled up to Alassio and had dinner with the Warshaws on the terrace of their hotel.

'Shirts!' cried Uncle Willy. 'Look at this shirt!' and he plucked it for emphasis. 'You know how much it cost me? Down the drain – that's what we call this long road through town. Three thousand lire. How much is that? It isn't even two pounds. How much would it cost in London? At least a tenner.' And then, the unforgettable phrase: 'I don't call that spending! I call it saving!'

In London, Uncle Willy and Auntie Muriel lived in a comfortable flat in Dorset House, just behind Baker Street. I was often there for tea, especially after he had taken me to a match. Once, from outside the sitting-room door, I suddenly and shockingly heard her tell him, 'I'll kill myself.' Then the moment had gone, and the tea party resumed. Perhaps he wasn't easy to live with; he loved to flirt with pretty women and once, I heard, an Italian woman, taking him too seriously, had slapped him. But for me and the other honorary nephews, he was the jolliest uncle imaginable.

At Stamford Bridge Stadium, I sat down and wept. Never had I seen Arsenal lose, but I should have been warned. On Boxing Day, the Royal Air Force was to play the Army in Cardiff, which meant that half a dozen Arsenal players were forced to sit in the stand and watch in impotent despair.

Both the Compton brothers were there and sleek George Marks, who would keep the legendary Frank Swift out of the England goal, until he injured an eye playing at Wembley against Wales, early the following year. Then there was the tall, commanding Bernard Joy, whose fair head reached almost every high ball that came into the box, and Alf Kirchen who, like Marks and Joy, would be playing for the RAF.

'We've got no full backs,' Uncle Willy wailed, when the programme changes were made known, and I felt secretly smug about it. One of those full backs was called W Winterbottom, none other than Walter Winterbottom, then a Manchester United player, based in the Air Ministry. In 1946 he would become England's first team manager, and stay in office sixteen years. Chelsea had other guests that day in Billy Liddell, the Scottish international outside left of Liverpool, who ran like an express train, and the equally muscular Scot, Peter McKennan of Partick Thistle, at inside right.

But there was no Joe Payne. Secretly, again I had been glad he was injured. Payne it was who had once scored ten goals in a game from centre forward, for Luton Town. In his place played somebody of whom I had never heard, B Bryant, otherwise Bernard Bryant, of the East London amateur team, Walthamstow Avenue. But Bryant was someone I would painfully remember.

And Arsenal? They had Noel Watson-Smith. Another amateur, from the club Yorkshire Amateurs, a goalkeeper of sorts, and like an amateur he played – another name that I shall never forget. The outside right, replacing the explosive Kirchen, was somebody called Colley, whom my father termed 'The Invisible Man'. Arsenal were overwhelmed. Bernard Bryant scored four. Suddenly, irresistibly, I burst into tears. A sympathetic man in the row in front turned round and told me, 'If all Arsenal's fans were like you!' 5–2 was the final score.

The following day, my father and I did not travel to Tottenham. We stayed at home and listened to a commentary by the incomparable Raymond Glendenning, of the moustache and the mellifluous voice, of that very game in Cardiff that had robbed Arsenal of their players: the Army versus the RAF. Uncle Willy turned up for tea. 'Five–one,' he gloated. Life would never be the same.

Prep school was bearable, despite a lurking strain of anti-Semitism – all the more insidious because it seldom quite showed itself as such – until my poor sister was brought out of the headmaster's family and put into the school. For some reason, this seemed to canalise and aggravate hostility towards me. Both of us were ruthlessly baited, even by boys who, previously, had been friendly and helpful. It was at times like these that Arsenal were a very present help in trouble, a soothing distraction. Though in the autumn of 1943, I had briefly turned my back on them.

It was petulant behaviour, wholly conditioned by the fact that I had been so used to success: their success. In the Southern Cup Final at Wembley, they had annihilated Charlton Athletic, 7–1. My father, sitting at the opposite end of a long row of adults, would lean forward and beam at me after every Arsenal goal. Four of them went to their centre forward, Reg Lewis who, eight years later, would score both Arsenal's winning goals in the FA Cup Final, itself.

'Charlton,' wrote Frank Butler, my favourite journalist at the time, 'were like a fat man collapsing into a deckchair.' The goalkeeper who was beaten seven times was not Sam Bartram, Charlton's red-headed and flamboyant symbol, but one Sid Hobbins, of whom more will be heard later in a curiously different context.

With the new season, Arsenal's triumphant team began to disintegrate. Players were posted here and there. They lost an early game at home to Portsmouth, a centre forward called Wilkes, a Navy man, scoring two, and although I had not been there, I flew into a sulk. On my return to Newlands, addressed, as I often was in football games, as 'Arsenal', I would respond, 'I don't support Arsenal; I support Golders Green', this being the amateur club that played in green shirts in Cricklewood. In their previous incarnation, as Hampstead FC, they had nurtured the Comptons.

Meanwhile, we were in Wardington now, with a complement of just 40-odd pupils. The country house was so much smaller, snugger, warmer. We would march to a games field where cow-pats abounded. I was in the second eleven now, at outside left, and scoring goals. Our games – first and second elevens suitably mixed – were often watched by a likeable farm-hand, complete with cap and gum boots, who knew the game well. We would chat with him as he stood on the touchline.

One day, Commander Lanning was asked to 'take', which meant referee, the senior game. Commander Lanning was in the Royal Naval Volunteer Reserve, though in plump, grey-haired middle age, he was now a chair-bound sailor, working in the Admiralty. Before the war, he had been joint headmaster of the school. On the occasions that he came down from London to stay weekends at Wardington, he would slip into our dormitory early in the morning, clad in a red dressing-gown, and tickle selected boys. I was never one of them.

Commander Lanning, it was fairly plain, disapproved of me. Nothing else could account for his Freudian error when, at the school assembly, he read out the names of the teams for the first game. Mine was not among them. I piped up, 'Sir, you've left me out!'

'What?' he responded gruffly. 'What do you mean?'

'I'm the second eleven outside left, sir.'

He consulted his list. 'You can play outside right.'

'But I'm left-footed, sir.'

'You'll play outside right.'

Which I did, the fat commander trotting along beside me, puffing, and calling from time to time, 'Where's that left foot?'

Eventually, I showed him. Little Timothy Inglis, the second eleven's inside right, rolled the ball to me on the edge of the penalty area. I hit it with my left foot and the ball rose sweetly, past the goalkeeper, Jeneid, and into the far top corner. 'Good pass,' said Commander Lanning, to Timothy Inglis, and turned his back on me. 'I saw you put in a nice one down there,' said my friend, the farm labourer.

Before our second eleven game away to Beechborough, another school evacuated to the Midlands, Commander Lanning took a team photograph of us. Fruity Adamson ran forward carefully to mark the words SECOND XI on the ball held by our captain. Beechborough had some emotional masters. 'Fight, fight, I implore you to fight!' cried one of them, when their first eleven was losing. Another, the following year, when their clever outside right was twisting our defenders into knots, stood nearby on the touchline gloating. 'What's he going to do now? What'll he do, now?'

I scored twice that afternoon against Beechborough seconds, and Commander Lanning was generous enough to say, 'I saw you put in a nice one, down there.' My father was told that I had been considered too frail for the first eleven, and when I was chosen, the following year, it was an anticlimax. I was in and out of bed and hospital with suspected appendicitis until brusque, big Mrs Chittenden, the headmaster's wife, decided enough was enough, and sent me to a private hospital in Oxford to have the damn thing out. It was an anticlimactic end to my last term at the school. Cappy came to see me. 'You've done well at Newlands,' he said, 'I'm proud of you.' And I remain grateful to him.

I had passed into Charterhouse, one down from the top entry form, the Special Remove. My parents, fortunately, had allowed me to choose my own public school, and I was determined it should be one that played soccer. The choice was between Charterhouse and Malvern which did, in fact, play rugger in the Easter term. We had a holiday governess who was pretty and bright, called Flick, otherwise Olga Felicia Newton. Like so many English girls of that period, she mourned a fiancé killed while flying for the RAF. In my own family, we clung to the fragile hope that my favourite cousin, Norman, missing after he had flown as a bomber's navigator over

Düsseldorf, would one day come back. I kept his photograph by my bed in the dormitory at Newlands, but hope went unrewarded.

Flick told me that there was no comparison between the schools; Charterhouse, where Newlands frequently sent pupils, was much superior. So Charterhouse it would be. Meanwhile, to my self-pitying dismay, I was told I could not play football again for months, which meant I could not turn out for Finchley Hornets. I pleaded tiresomely with my parents, but they were properly adamant.

Finchley Hornets was a club I had formed with two neighbourhood friends, Edward and Ian Kessly. They were Mancunians, Edward a supporter of Manchester United, bombed out of Old Trafford and playing at Maine Road, Ian, the younger brother, a supporter of Blackpool. Ian was tall for his age, thin and precocious. 'He looks like Swiss boy,' said our Swiss cook. Edward was sturdier and deliberate, a centre forward who plastered down his hair in the accepted style. Finchley Hornets had played just one game, which I had missed, as I had gone back to Newlands. We advertised in the local paper for players and had some success.

The match had been away to a team called Edgwarebury and, to my great glee, the Hornets won it, 11–0. I celebrated by drawing one of my inept cartoons: 'Stung eleven times!' Edward wrote me an enthusiastic letter, greatly taken with the Meadows brothers. Horace had played in goal, Jimmy, irresistibly, at outside right. 'He is a miniature Matthews. He wriggles and wriggles all over the place.'

Later in life, Jimmy Meadows would play for Watford. He would even captain Watford, and was involved in the fix whereby, in the 1950s, they allowed Brighton to beat them, and go up.

On the morning of our predicated match, some kind of a return, a telegram came to the door: MATCH IMPOSSIBLE. PLEASE CANCEL. EDGWAREBURY. So all my agonising had been for nothing.

In January, I began at Charterhouse. I was still, frustratingly, 'off' games; in those days, an appendectomy entailed months of convalescence. After the relative tranquillity of a small prep school in a compact country house, the dimensions of a public school were overwhelming. At Charterhouse there were more than 600 boys of all shapes and sizes, most of them much larger than myself, who at that time was small and thin. There was no lurking anti-Semitism this time, only what EM Forster had called 'Jew consciousness', but quite frightening to a thirteen-year-old, unaware that much of it was superficial. Interviewed, once, for a magazine article, I told the journalist that Charterhouse on my arrival was like Auschwitz without the chimneys. He wrote that it was like Auschwitz without the Schindlers. The horrific news of the death camps was only just beginning to percolate, but it made no difference.

Instead of Cappy who, for all his brusque orthodoxy, was, in the last analysis, a sympathetic and supportive figure, I had to contend with my forbidding housemaster, Patrick Hollowell. He had been a notable footballer, in the great Carthusian tradition, a left back, virtually contemporary with the resplendent AG 'Baiche' Bower, the last amateur to have captained England. A left back himself, Bower, unusually, had not won his school colours; he had left to join the Army before he could claim them but he, like Hollowell, had survived the war.

Hollowell was a tall, powerfully built, brown-skinned, balding man, whose Carthusian career had been interrupted only by the rigours of the war in which he, like Cappy and so many schoolmasters who survived, had won the Military Cross. On the wall of his study, which one dreaded visiting, hung a group photograph of the immediate post-war Cambridge University team. With him were two people I would later come to know well, each of whom, as an amateur, gained full England caps.

One was the centre forward, AG (Graham) Doggart who, in time, would become a much put-upon Chairman of the Football Association, with a strong wife and an FA Secretary who bullied him. The other, then an inside right, was FNS (Norman) Creek, who himself would, after schoolmastering, come to work for the FA. Both were grammar school boys though Doggart's son went to Winchester and became an England batsman as well as a competent inside left.

Hollowell, though feared, was widely imitated. He had a curious, slightly nasal, singsong voice. 'Stimulus, plural stimuli,' he would say, brandishing a pair of dividers menacingly. His nickname was 'Compost', this because he worked long hours in the vegetable garden, which ran down the side of the hill to the main road to Godalming from his boarding house, Bodeites, the use of compost being what he advocated and practised.

Sometimes he would talk about his football career. 'I was playing for the university against Chelsea at Stamford Bridge, and one of their forwards fouled me deliberately. I looked at the referee; and the referee winked at me. Then a few minutes later I knocked the man over; and I weighed fourteen stone! And I looked at the referee; and the referee winked at me.'

I, like many others, found him utterly unsympathetic in every sense, and totally without insight. 'For some reason best known to himself,' he wrote, on my third term's report, 'he has decided to do

no work at all this quarter . . . a criminal waste of a good intellect.'
The fact that I was still trying to settle down after persistent bullying
was something he neither knew nor wished to discover. Psychology
was a closed book to him; tact an unknown quantity.

His obsession was with brown wholemeal bread which, to the
general disgust of the house, he insisted on our eating. Once, when
rebellion burgeoned, he addressed us all in the writing room, where
the junior boys had their carrels – desks behind partitions. 'There
was one boy,' he told us, 'whose boast it was that he had never eaten
a piece of brown bread. That boy was the most unhealthy boy I ever
knew. He was permanently constipated!' The brown bread remained.
When I left school, he wrote to my father, 'I think he has a flair for
something, but I am not quite sure what.'

An early solace was to watch the first eleven football, on Big
Ground. It played in uniform shirts but socks with multicoloured
tops, denoting the boarding house that each player belonged to.
Hedley Le Bas, the goalkeeper, would always put a toy elephant in
his goal. Later, when head of Caxton Press, he fell prey to a vicious
campaign of misinformation by Robert Maxwell, who was pursuing
the company. The Rimell brothers played at left half and left back
respectively. Michael Rimell, a tall, handsome figure, was the left
half and the captain. Behind him played his younger brother, Tony,
a left back with a formidable sliding tackle, who would eventually
win a Cambridge blue for cricket.

The blond centre forward, a notable opportunist, was GED Spratt,
wearing the white stocking tops of Duckites, or Girdlestoneites; he
would in due course become Lord Mayor of London. On the quick,
sandy surface of Big Ground, the team won most of its games, often
through the unorthodox gyrations of its long-legged outside right,
Wilson, nicknamed 'Sticks'.

I would also watch Peter May playing for Saunderites
under-sixteen team at inside forward, towering above his contemporaries, expert in the air, subsequently to delight us with his masterly
batting. What innings he compiled on the Green, against the major
rivals! How elegant that sweeping shot to the leg boundary! At
Cambridge, curiously enough, he would captain the university at
soccer, but not at cricket, in time becoming one of the finest England
batsmen of all time.

Oliver Popplewell was the third Carthusian to play in that
Cambridge team, as wicket-keeper. Later he would become a leading
judge. So did John Alliott, who was in the top history form with me
at the time I left, and who, himself, went on to Cambridge. He and

I had played directly against one another for Newlands and Falconbury, respectively, at both first- and second-eleven levels, he at right half, I at outside left. Indeed, the last game I played for Newlands, on that pitch at Wardington, had been against Falconbury and Alliott. Much criticised for past performances, I made tremendous efforts that day, and was praised for them by Fruity Adamson; I had done very well 'until it came to putting the ball across'. But at least I had avoided his classic criticism, 'You're back to your old, sloppy ways.'

My own footballing career at Charterhouse was a bleak disappointment. It began quite well, at inside left for Bodeites' colts and yearling teams, but by the end I had been relegated to centre forward for the job-lot team of so-called Et ceteras. A game in December 1948, for the house team against Old Bodeites, in which I scored a goal and made one from outside left, was some small consolation. Slowly my puerile ambitions eroded. When I told my father, with callow defiance, that I still hoped to succeed, to play perhaps one day for Arsenal, he replied reasonably and mildly that it was surely enough to be interested in soccer, and play an adequate game. I would have none of it; but time convinced me.

Never, in my years at Charterhouse, did I play on Big Ground. It would have seemed chimerical that nearly three decades later, much taller and heavier, I would captain a Chelsea Casuals team against the school first eleven several times.

I did, however, write football reports for the school magazine, the *Carthusian*, which in their somewhat adolescent way created something of a stir. Colin Harris, the editor of the magazine, always an enthusiast, was delighted with them. So, surprisingly, was RL (Bob) Arrowsmith, another dyed-in-the-wool Carthusian, who hobbled around on a stick; a large man, ruddy-faced, of arcane locution, given to caps and yellow pullovers, who would eventually succeed Hollowell as housemaster of Bodeites.

The Arrow was a classical public school eccentric. 'You wrote to me, did not you?' one heard him, once, enquiring of an alumnus on Old Carthusian Day. Asked whether, when he played cricket for Charterhouse, he was a batsman or a bowler, he replied, 'My dear Sir, neither; I was a social asset.'

He once addressed a boy in his Latin class, 'Samuel, Samuel, why sleepest thou?' To which Samuel instantly replied, 'Speak, Lord, for thy servant heareth.' At which the Arrow put him in detention.

He was also known to say of a cricketer, 'My dear sir, a fielder like the Ancient Mariner; stoppeth one of three.' He it was who presided over the *Carthusian*, telling Colin Harris that my reports were 'the best for twenty years, the best I've ever seen.'

This was vastly encouraging but, thinking back, I find it hard to defend much of what I wrote. Michael Whinney, the captain and right winger of the team, no great footballer but a young man of substantial charm, was heard to say 'I'd like to scrag Glanville' after I had said his 'performance was rather that of an all-in wrestler than a footballer.' An Old Carthusian properly wrote in to admonish me for saying of Ritchie, a centre forward who had missed badly, 'he is however to be congratulated on this achievement. Great skill was called for, to avoid putting the ball into the net.' A Duckite, Pickersgill, approached me after the magazine had been published and asked me whether it was fair of me to say, 'Pickersgill evidently fancies himself as a dribbler. Time will disillusion him.' But Perkins, the blond centre half, who eventually joined the Army, was more genial.

I had written, after he gave away a penalty, 'Perkins stretched out his hand to see whether it was raining. It was not.' Approaching me as we both walked down the road to our respective houses, he said, 'Now I'll know when it's raining.'

Diligently, through those years, I kept my Arsenal almanacs, the beginning of journalism, written often, alas, in journalese. 'Ian McPherson; call him Mac the Magnificent!' They were compiled in notebooks, or in compact loose-leaf bindings. Every Arsenal match, whether I had seen it or not, was detailed. When they played away from home, I would write off to the local paper for their Saturday evening football edition, which in those days came in a rainbow of hues; pink, buff, blue and green. I collected what action photographs I could. Things were easing up now, after the war; at last you could buy football magazines with photos.

My obsession with Arsenal continued, though, strangely enough, whatever the dreaded housemaster might think, it was not interfering with my studies. These early terms at Charterhouse were strange ones. Fit and able-bodied masters had gone off to the war, some, alas, to die. At Newlands, where very young old boys came down from their public schools to teach us – inspiringly – before being called up, we had a hero in Maity. Otherwise LA Maitland, an Old Carthusian, who sometimes joined in football games, his shirt flapping outside his shorts, and taught French with flair.

He told us funny stories, such as the supposed scene on a battleship at the end of the last war, when a dozen American sailors carried a huge banner round the deck inscribed: USA WE WON THE WAR, followed by a little British seaman with a postcard inscribed: WE HELPED THEM. Maity joined the Fleet Air Arm, became a pilot, crashed, and died, before he could even see action.

Not till the 'Oration Quarter', the autumn term, did the young soldiers, sailors and airmen who had survived the war come back to teach at Charterhouse.

In the meantime, their deputies, a mixed and motley bunch, did what they could. 'Bushy' Lake, nicknamed for his abundant white moustache, was in his eighties, and, a Wykehamist, had taught at Charterhouse for sixty years. He wore a tweed cap and once, up on the stage at calling over, I heard him, in an old man's appropriate stage whisper, tell the formidable headmaster, 'Glanville and Packham: the two worst beginners in Greek I've ever had', which I was sure was true. Long, long afterwards, two of my children, the eldest and the youngest, would read classics at Oxford, though they began to learn Greek only at sixteen. Mark duly got his degree. Jo, at Worcester, obtained a first in Mods, the second-year exam; a college scholarship; and a distinction . . . in Greek.

Mr Nicholas Philpot arrived midway through the summer term of 1945, in steel-rimmed glasses, heavily creamed black hair, and what his pupils called his IRA jacket. He was from Dublin. Another master, Gerry Facer, introduced him and went out. Philpot mounted the podium, opened a battered brown case, said nothing, and sniffed. Taking out books, he continued to sniff, until the whole class was sniffing with him. These would be days of anarchy.

'In fifty-five years' time,' he was once heard to say, 'the world will be destroyed by fire.' Also, 'A man's only half-educated what don't know Latin and Greek.' Again, 'Byron said, writing maketh an exact man.'

Uselessly, he wielded a metal ruler to try to keep order. Once, when he found a boy drawing pictures in his class, he swept the paper to the floor crying, 'If I asked you to do that, you'd be doing something else!'

Needless to say, he was abominably treated and left before the end of term. Left in such anarchy that no form order could be established so that, *faute de mieux*, the whole form was elevated to the under fifths, where School Certificate was taken. I was widely expected to fail it. The French master, mysterious Mr Glasgow, with his indoor pallor, his pin-stripe suits, his air of saloon-bar sophistication, admitted on my report that my French had improved: 'But this has been something of a deathbed repentance, and may prove to be too late.'

It wasn't. I even got matric, even got a credit in maths, in which I had been bumping along at the bottom of the bottom division. Jotson, DD of Daviesites always came top, but we all knew it was because his prep, or banco, was done by a rangy, red-haired Cambridge scholar called Farquharson. In the event, Jotson, a sturdy blond right half for his house team, failed School Cert. maths.

Though Charterhouse was a soccer school, passionate interest in professional football was disdained. I had to find fellow fans where I could. One was David Griffiths, of Pageites, who talked invariably, as a Newcastle United supporter, of Albert Stubbins. But that red-haired centre forward was transferred to Liverpool, and Griffiths spoke of him no more. In time to come, both his sons would capably keep goal for Chelsea Casuals.

In Bodeites, my two friends with football enthusiasm were Gordon Watson and Charlie Hole. Charlie, a farmer's son from Sussex, had bright-red hair, was as thin as a lathe, stood well over six feet – he would eventually reach six foot nine – played in goal, and idolised Sam Bartram. 'Flame-haired Sam Bartram,' he would read, admiringly, from a photo caption. Unlike Gordon, precociously well-informed about almost everything, Charlie was no intellectual. He Brylcreemed his hair, admired himself endlessly in the washroom mirror, chanting, 'Am I beautiful? Yes I am!' and had an antic sense of humour.

Once, when I had laboriously been composing a set of limericks about Arsenal players, to enter some competition, he appeared in the doorway of the study I then shared with Gordon, produced a piece of paper, and read this tribute to the Charlton centre half:

Whenever I think of drips,
This one gives me the pips.
I'm referring of course
To that shitting great horse,
Six-foot curly-haired Kipps.

From time to time, jointly or severally, the three of us, and a boy from the next house down the road, Jones, of Hodsonites, would make daring and illicit trips to London, to watch games. Why three of us, on the first occasion, should choose to risk a beating by going to see a mere, dull, rain-sodden friendly at Craven Cottage between Fulham and Arsenal, I cannot say. We would go not from Godalming, where we might well be spotted, but from the next village station of Farncombe. I have memories of that occasion.

For one thing, it was the first appearance Arthur Milton ever made for Arsenal. He was a blond, fresh-faced seventeen, he played inside right in the deluge and hardly touched the ball, yet in retrospect it was a significant occasion, for he would become a double international, even if hardly of the refulgence of Denis Compton who, I seem to remember, was also playing that day, back from Army service in India and carrying excessive weight.

Milton would turn into a thrilling outside right of tremendous pace, fine control and a devastating finish. He had just one game for England, which I saw, at Wembley in 1951, against the then exceptional Austrian side, its inspiration the attacking centre half, Ernst Ocwirk. Milton, I seem to recall, came in at the last moment, an adventurous choice. Twice, in the early stages, he raced past his man to put over searching crosses. Each time Ivan Broadis, the beneficiary, missed his chance. Milton faded from the game and never got another England cap.

As a cricketer, he made many runs for Gloucestershire and played Tests. When his sporting career was done, he became, quite cheerfully, a postman. Nowadays, footballers without a tenth of his talent make millions.

I remember, too, from that game, an episode involving Ronnie Rooke and Alf Fields. Rooke was the veteran Fulham centre forward, a man whose face might have come off the side of a cathedral, possessed of a ferocious left-foot shot. Though I could not have guessed at the time, he would, within the year, become the surprising saviour of Arsenal. Alf Fields, whom I would later come to know quite well, was a tall centre half, a typical third back, a kindly, modest man who for years selflessly coached the Arsenal juniors and had won the British Empire Medal in Italy. On this occasion, I recall his unflinching courage when Fulham were awarded a free kick on the edge of the box. Ronnie Rooke blasted it at the defensive wall with his unforgiving left foot. Fields coolly and casually headed the ball away.

Rooke – it is one of the Cinderella stories of football – was 33 years old and wallowing one morning in the Fulham bath when he was summoned to the club's office. This was located in the old cottage where Edward Bulwer-Lytton had allegedly written *The Last Days of Pompeii* and was a small, unpretentious room, usually occupied by Fulham's long-time chief administrator, Frank Osborne, at his desk with a brown hat pushed back on his head.

Waiting there that day were George Allison and Tom Whittaker of Arsenal, who were then in parlous straits, in real danger of dropping down from the First Division, where they had been so controversially promoted in 1919, thanks to the lobbying and finagling of their overbearing chairman, Sir Henry Norris. To his amazement, Rooke found that they were there to sign him. Still incredulous, he agreed, and Arsenal had made the bargain of their lives. Not only did they sign their saviour, but they signed him for peanuts; a fee of £1,000 or so, plus a couple of reserve players, Dave Nelson and Cyril Grant.

As it happened, Arsenal's home game that Saturday was against Charlton Athletic; tense times for Charlie Hole and me. I had the result, in Bodeites, before Charlie returned to the house. 'What happened?' he asked me, urgently. I indulged myself by giving him the full result. 'Arsenal one, Charlton Athletic nil.' And who had scored the goal? Why, Ronnie Rooke, rising out of the mist to head the ball home from a corner. I still can see the heartening photograph, in my mind's eye.

Rooke's goals, that season, helped Arsenal to stay up; but the following season he was rampant; astounding. At the age of 34, he scored no fewer than 33 goals from inside left, and helped Arsenal to win the Championship. One of those goals I still remember. It came in an August game against Manchester United, already a mighty force, playing football largely superior to Arsenal's. Then, Rooke got the ball, advanced towards goal, and suddenly, from a good 35 yards, let loose one of his left-footed shots. It screamed past Crompton, United's keeper, into the top corner of the net. Arsenal won, 2–1.

'You never talked about Ronnie Rooke like that when he was playing for Fulham,' Tommy Trinder would reproach me, in his dressing-room at the Palladium. At that time, he was regularly top of the bill, a Londoner with the brim of his white hat turned up, and an astonishing gift for the impromptu. The most notable, perhaps, occurred when he got up on a stage and delivered his usual line, 'Trinder's the name.'

'Why don't you change it?' called Orson Welles, from the audience.

'Is that a proposal?' asked Tommy.

I was in the dressing-room, with my parents and sister, because Tommy was a patient of my father's. He would give us tickets for the front row stalls and make jokes about us. Once, notably, dressed as Carmen Miranda ('Oh no no no no, Columbus. You've discovered too much tonight!') he approached the leader of a Latin American combo and asked the poor bewildered fellow, 'Is your name Brian Glanville?'

He gave brief mock radio commentaries on games between

'Preston Dead End and Sheffield Tuesday', and obediently put on all his make-up, before my little sister would agree to kiss him.

And Alf Fields? He was playing in that Manchester United match, and playing well, standing in for Leslie Compton on whom – oh distant days! – Middlesex Cricket Club had first call, as their wicket-keeper. Arsenal set a new club record by winning their first six games, but in the last of them, at Highbury, George Swindin came rushing out of goal to dive on a ball which Fields was preparing to play, smashed into the centre-half's knee, and did it, however inadvertently, such damage that Fields was out of the game for months, and was never quite the same player again. Leslie Compton was released by Middlesex to resume his place the following Saturday at Preston, and there he ineluctably stayed, winning his first full England cap (he had played during the war) at the age of 38.

He succeeded my idol, Bernard Joy, by then writing for the *Evening Star*. How distressed I always felt when Joy – to me incomparable – was criticised. He had actually been the last amateur to win a full England cap when chosen against Belgium in Brussels in 1936. But while Stanley Cullis was still with the Army at Aldershot, there was no way Joy was going to get a second chance.

Cullis, at last, was posted abroad in 1944, and wonder of wonders, Joy was chosen! In the *Daily Sketch* LV Manning, the most respected football writer of his time, father of the future sports columnist Jim Manning, wrote, 'Joy deserves this belated honour.' But, for the first half of the game at Wembley, Scotland ran rings round England, their centre forward, Milne, putting them ahead. England recovered to score six goals, but, on the Monday morning, the shameless LV Manning wrote, so callously, 'Joy has had his match.' How could he so metamorphose in a single weekend?

Worse was to come when Arsenal, at last returning to Highbury, played their public trial match there in August 1946. Paul Irwin, a South African then writing the sports column for the *Sunday Express*, wrote, to my alarm, that Arsenal needed, inter alia, a new centre half. I wrote to him, to ask what he could mean. The reply was trenchant, if inelegant.

'Joy is clumsy, heavy-footed . . . He can dominate in the air, where the Arsenal amateur's height helps, but he isn't my centre half, and, these days, I don't think he is Arsenal's, either.'

In parenthesis, it should be said that hope remained alive, since Irwin, the previous year, had committed one of the most famous gaffes in the history of sporting journalism. This occurred when the Moscow Dynamo team arrived late in 1945 to play a series of friendly games. It happened at a time when feelings towards the Russians, who had shown such colossal and decisive bravery in the war, were still very positive in Britain, while an aura of mystery still tended to surround things Russian.

Irwin went to watch the Dynamo players in training at the White City in west London and reported scathingly that they were 'just a bunch of earnest amateurs', incapable of competing with our professional clubs, 'so slow that you can almost hear them think'.

In fact, as soon as they began their first game against Chelsea at Stamford Bridge, in a stadium packed to the touchlines with eager fans, the Dynamos were so quick that it was hard to catch them. Bobrov, Beskov, Kartsev and the rest played beautiful, rhythmic football, and if the referee, Lieutenant Commander Clark, did award them a blatantly offside goal, it was all in the good cause of Anglo-Soviet friendship, and nobody begrudged it to them. The result was 3–3.

The Dynamos then went to Cardiff where they annihilated Cardiff City 10–1. 'They are a machine,' marvelled Cyril Spiers, the Cardiff manager, once an international goalkeeper, 'and not an ordinary football team.' Would Arsenal, next on the list, be able to withstand them?

The Dynamos, who had scornfully moved out of the barracks accommodation first given them, into the Russian Embassy, were a cynosure. How did they do it? Was it because so many of them also played ice hockey? How they had emerged so fit and fast from the brutal privations of the war was another conundrum. George Allison reinforced his Arsenal team. He brought Bernard Joy back from serving on the Continent, enlisted Ronnie Rooke, and, above all, included the most magical English player of his generation, Stanley Matthews, the outside right with the amazing swerve who had left so many full backs for dead when he lurched to their right and glided up the touchline.

I did not see that, or any of the Dynamos' games; I was back at school. Indeed, on the day of the Arsenal match, at Tottenham, Charlie Hole and I were busy going absent without leave from F Company, on a Charterhouse field day. F Company was a kind of depository for boys not yet old enough for the junior army corps, and not quite good enough for the Boy Scouts.

My own exclusion had disappointed me. Newlands was run on a Boy Scout basis. I myself had been a second in the Otter patrol, with second-class badge, including knots, and a book reader's badge to boot. The Reverend George Snow, the Charterhouse priest, who ran the Scouts, immense at six foot seven in his scouting shorts, asked me over to his little house on the hill, below Bodeites, to put me through a test. In the time that I had been a Scout, he said, had I always kept the Scouts' Law. 'Oh, yes,' I said; what else could I say? He pondered for a moment. 'I don't know whether I could really say that myself,' he replied at last. And he eventually rejected me, after putting me through other tests, which was no doubt quite illegal, but inappellable.

So it was F Coy: on bicycles with packed lunches, cycling about the Surrey countryside, led by a tall, gawky, senior Bodeite with a high-pitched voice, renowned for his slightly effete ways and obsessive punctilio. Once Charlie and I had managed to slip off on our bicycles, the rest of the day was our oyster. It was a risk, we knew. It could entail a beating, we knew. But the thought of spending the rest of the day cycling with F Coy was intolerable. So we swanned about, at one point receiving from a newspaper seller the copies he had not disposed of, and reading in them of the challenge between Arsenal and the Dynamos.

On our way back to Bodeites, passing through Godalming, we met, horror of horrors, the housemaster. What could we be doing there? Charlie, ever inventive, had a quick explanation, though he would have to do much more, and more elaborate, talking on our behalf when we were reported to the head of house.

Arriving at Bodeites, we were told by the butler, 'Harry' Haines, of bizarre goings-on at Tottenham. The pitch had been virtually eclipsed by fog, but the Russian referee had allowed the game to go on, and had tried to control it from one side of the ground, with the linesmen placed on the other! Arsenal had lost 4–3, or so it appeared. Mr Haines, whose job was to look after the kitchen and wait on tables ('This fish wasn't caught; it gave itself up'), concluded, 'Oh well, we'll see what LVM says about it in the morning.' This of course being LV Manning.

In the event, he wrote of a 'fog farce', with one slightly strained image that I still remember. 'A thousand men lighted a thousand cigarettes, and it looked like a thousand bonfires.'

It had been a fiasco. At one point, Dynamo had had twelve men on the field; but the referee, Nicolai Latychev, had refused to stop the game. Nearly seventeen years later, he would control the World Cup Final in Santiago, Chile. LVM said that one thing did become clear: Stanley Matthews could run rings around the Dynamo left back, Stankevich. It was a poor consolation.

Drawing at Ibrox 2–2 with Glasgow Rangers – TIME SAVES DYNAMO

FROM A KNOCK OUT said the headline in the *Daily Sketch* – Dynamo refused to play a representative team at Wembley; they had said specifically they wouldn't in their original demands, and they flew off home, unbeaten, leaving a chastened British game behind them. In due course, a journalist called Vladimir Sinyavsky wrote scurrilous things about the visit, especially the Arsenal match, in which George Allison became the fat capitalist villain, insisting the game go ahead 'because bets had been placed'.

In the school holidays, I would sometimes cycle down to Claremont Road, the home of Golders Green FC where the Arsenal third team trained. 'I can't see what the fascination is of all these men with hairy legs,' said my sister, scathingly, when she once accompanied me. But it was fascinating for me to talk freely with none other than George Male, who was in charge of the team.

Modest, deliberate and meliorating, Male was very patient with me, even when I once remarked that he had 'only' won nineteen England caps. David Jack, he pointed out – an inside right of vast renown – had won still fewer. In a caustic moment, Jimmy Logie would later tell me that George Male would have made a perfect nanny. That was cruel. He was essentially a decent if pedestrian man, and the club looked after him as it never did his more illustrious partner at full back for England and Arsenal, Eddie Hapgood. Male lived on into his nineties, and died in 1998.

We spoke, at subsequent times, of the black eye he received from Silvio Piola, playing for England against Italy in Milan in 1939. Insult was added to injury since the German referee, the intransigent Dr Pecos Bauwens, gave a goal when Piola fisted the ball into the net, over his shoulder, following through to catch George Male in the eye. 'He didn't mean it,' Male would solemnly reiterate, 'it was just an accident.'

Once, when I was living in Florence, Piola and numerous others, there to attend a coaching course, were sitting at tables near me in the Piazza della Repubblica. I called over to him, mentioning that goal. '*Era un bel colpo di testa*,' he said, grinning, 'a fine header', but then, mimicking a punch over his shoulder, he added, 'No, no; I went like that.'

After matric, I read history. I did not want to read history. In these fraught days, when parents, middle-class parents at least, agonise over their children's academic choices, determined to see they get into this school and that university, it is strange to look back on the insouciance, the public-school arrogance, of those times. Ideally, I should have liked to study modern languages, which meant French and elementary Spanish. The latter was taught by a tiny, grey-haired, almost parodic Spaniard called Del Rio. He wore a beret and cycled everywhere, a faithful Alsatian dog at his heels. But the dog died and the word was that Del Rio, heartbroken, therefore left the school.

Whatever the truth, there was no one to teach elementary Spanish. Given the realities of the war, I had not wanted to learn German, hence the utterly wasted terms failing to master Ancient Greek. Had there been an English department, that would have been my choice, but there wasn't. No one from Charterhouse approached me to tell me what had happened or to ask me what I preferred. Still fourteen years old, I went back for the Oration Quarter of 1946, looked at the notice-board and found, almost as some sergeant-major might have decreed it, 'You and you and you – 'istory!'

So a history specialist I became and did quite well at first, largely because I wrote decent English. Though in time I became obsessional about my history studies, forcing myself through fifty pages of some history book each day, I had no real gift for it. 'He has considerable ability of a sort,' wrote acidulous little Mr White, who had served as an Army officer in the Middle East, 'but his approach is not that of a scholar.'

'Then you should find out what that is,' said my father, with innocent optimism. The truth, I suspect, is that I was simply too immature to master the material. When eventually I took, and passed, Higher Certificate, largely in my own time – the history specialists did not sit it – Mr White took great glee in reading out the report of the examiner, Professor Jack Simmons, in front of a class that included a wholly new intake, John Alliott among them. 'Glanville must be taught to think. Glanville has a disorderly mind.' But at least, at sixteen, I had passed in all three subjects.

In the event, I need not have bothered. I had sat the exam only because I thought I would leave school at the end of the summer and go straight into journalism, apprenticed to some local newspaper until my call-up came, at seventeen, for National Service.

The careers officer came down to the school to give us the boon and benefit of his advice. I seem to remember he was called Captain Pullein Thompson. The careers master at the school could not have been more curiously cast. His name was EA Malaher, renowned for his paralysing shyness, his tortured handwriting and his alleged meanness. A satirical house magazine called the *Red Rag* lampooned him in an answer to correspondents: 'We recognised the handwriting, but couldn't pay the postage due.'

Mr Malaher taught me Latin, and I did, once, hear him laugh.

That was when a large Duckite called Davis, whom I used to help – whispering in class – with his Latin, was due to play that afternoon for the first eleven against another school. 'Remember,' said Malaher, with a hitherto unsuspected smile, 'they shall not pass,' and burst out laughing.

Another of the Old Carthusian persuasion, middle-aged, morose, given to grey Homburg hats, he lived alone in a boarding-house across the way from Bodeites, his single room festooned with horse brasses. He did not hold with Zionism: 'How many of them want to scratch out a living with their bare hands?' Not for him the generosity of Sir Ronald Storrs, once the chief administrator in Palestine, who came down to address the school, and said that 'the Jews have made the desert bloom', and added that anyone who contradicted that was 'sinning against God and sinning against the Light'.

Grim, repressed Mr Malaher introduced me, in his room, to the careers officer, who bluffly told me, 'I'm going to give you a thick ear on journalism, tonight.'

In the lecture theatre that evening, he did his best, his idea of the craft seemingly confined to doorstepping and intrusion. 'You have to be insensitive,' he said. My father, on being told this, said he didn't like the sound of that very much, 'being insensitive'. It was eventually decided that I would stay on at Charterhouse and take a scholarship for Oxford.

My obsession grew – as my obsession with Arsenal, though not my allegiance, gradually diminished. I must have a history scholarship; if not, I wouldn't go to Oxford. At that period, it should be said, boys from the top forms of a school like Charterhouse had little difficulty getting into Oxford or Cambridge, scholarship or no. Academics were my new heroes, professors of history now – with footballers, of course – the stars in my firmament.

My devotion to Arsenal had been rewarded at Christmas 1947, when Marksman himself, Harry Homer, Oxonian editor of the club programme, which he peppered with literary allusions, invited my father and myself to watch a game with him from the west stand enclosure on Boxing Day. I had been corresponding eagerly with Harry Homer for some time, and the invitation was a glorious surprise.

Arsenal, that day, were playing Liverpool, having met them up at Anfield, on Christmas Day. Harry Homer was a tall, high-complexioned, sandy-haired man of middle age, with a healthy moustache. He had spent the war in the RAF. He was cheerful, breezy and extrovert. He told me, with great feeling, of Arsenal's misfortunes at Anfield, the day before. A Liverpool player had blatantly handled in his penalty area, unpunished by the referee. Joe Mercer, Arsenal's respected left half and captain, restored to health by Tom Whittaker's magic hands after Everton had humiliated and discarded him, approached the referee, saying: 'Please, I beg of you, consult your linesman.' But the referee was impervious.

For the return game, Liverpool had switched Billy Liddell, Arsenal's nemesis almost exactly five years ago, in that ill-omened game at Stamford Bridge, from left to right wing, so that he could face Arsenal's reserve left back, Joe Wade. The stratagem worked. Liddell was too fast and strong for Wade. Once, in my anxiety, I called out to Joe Mercer to clear the ball. Harry Homer turned to me, sternly. 'He's got his orders. It's no use you shouting at him.'

Twice, alas, Liddell whizzed by Wade; twice he crossed the ball, and twice the red-haired Albert Stubbins, once adored by David Griffiths, swept the ball into the net. Arsenal lost, 2–1. Decades later, the genial Stubbins would apologise for 'spoiling your Boxing Day'.

It was some consolation to be taken down, by Harry, to the dressing-rooms. There, I saw Reg Lewis, Arsenal's prolific centre forward, who would get both their goals in the 1950 Cup Final against Liverpool themselves, gently rubbing the welts and bruises on his shins. 'Did Liverpool do that?' I asked, aghast. 'Just a few little taps,' he laconically replied.

He spoke to me of the forthcoming FA Third Round Cup tie at Highbury against Bradford Park Avenue, then a Second Division team. It was nonsense, he said, to think that when a team was in for the Championship, as Arsenal now were, they did not do their best in the Cup. Words that would soon come back to haunt me.

As I left the dressing-room, who should be standing outside but another idol, Denis Compton, whose winters then were largely given to England's cricket tours. Reverently, I shook his hand. 'Hallo, Mr Compton.' 'Hallo, boy,' he said.

Then Bradford – who no longer now exist as a pro club – came to Highbury at the turn of the New Year and inconceivably, incredibly, knocked Arsenal out. Knocked them out with a single goal scored by Billy Elliott, an outside left who would later play for England. In the west stand, where I sat, scores of big Yorkshiremen stood, bellowing 'Ilkley Moor baht aht'. So much for the Cup, last won in 1936. But there was quick consolation in the League, Arsenal going up to Maine Road, Manchester, where United were still playing, to draw 1–1 before a crowd of 82,000, against their closest competitors.

In December 1948, having temporarily turned my back on

journalism, I went up to Magdalen College, Oxford, to sit a scholarship. With me went 'Bertie' Robertson, a tall, amiable, competitive boy whose father was at that time commanding the British Forces on the Rhine, and whose grandfather had been the first field marshal ever to rise from the ranks, famous for his unreconstructed accent: 'Fetch 'Aig!'

I had been to Oxford often enough in my Newlands days, but now, to be in its historic heart was overwhelming and disorienting, the more so when I sat at the long, polished tables in the examination hall in Keble College, that Victorian eyesore among the architectural glories, and struggled with the papers. 'By 1914, European liberalism was bankrupt. Discuss.' At just seventeen? Boom, boom, boom, went the bells, tolling my knell.

Yet even here, in Oxford, football wasn't far away. Placards advertised a match, PEGASUS V. ARSENAL. Little did I know that this, too, in its minor way would prove a piece of history. The birth of that marvellous Pegasus team, made up of alumni of both Oxford and Cambridge, which would twice go on to win the FA Amateur Cup in front of colossal crowds at Wembley. They beat an Arsenal eleven that day, 1–0, but I did not notice the result.

Hardly had I entered my room in Magdalen than the door burst open and in came a figure who seemed to embody the proletarian principle. He was thin, sharp-nosed, of urban pallor, with hair heavily greased down. 'I know you,' he cried, in a strong London accent. 'I'm sure I know you. Name's Frank Stirling, Kilburn Grammar.'

Robertson and I grew very friendly with him. He would say things such as, 'I've been doing a lot of amateur dramatics this term, thereby gravely jeopardising my prospects of a scholarship.' In the event, he didn't get one, but he did get a viva, which was more than we did.

George Orwell described life at Eton as 'five years in a lukewarm bath of snobbery', and public-school prejudice had changed little since those days. One dusky evening, outside an Oxford cinema, fellow Carthusians, involved with other colleges, surrounded us. 'Who's that shocking fellow?' they enquired.

'He's not a shocking fellow,' we replied. 'He's very nice. He's Stirling.'

Nearly four years later, in the summer of 1952, I went up to Oxford to stay with Gordon Watson, who found me a bed at University College. The following day, after lunch, we were drinking coffee in the junior common room. Looking across it, I saw, to my surprise, a figure who was indisputably Stirling. 'Is that man's name Frank Stirling?' I asked. 'I'm sure I know him.'

'I say, Stirling,' drawled a blond Etonian, standing with us. 'There's someone here who thinks he knows you.'

Stirling turned round. 'Oh, is there?' he enquired, in the most impeccable of Oxford accents.

Tail between my legs, I went back to Charterhouse, consoled only by scoring, next day, against Old Bodeite house team. No one had tried to help me fill in my application form, which was a complicated grid involving several colleges. When I sent it off, the housemaster limited himself to rebuking me for putting 'Oxfordshire' on the address, instead of 'Oxon'. The following term when, with obsessional desperation, I tried to sit a scholarship to London University, the housemaster came past me at lunchtime and said, 'I hear for your scholarship you have to take French as well as history.'

'Yes, sir.'

'You're mad,' he said.

A Magdalen don wrote to Freddie Ives, our history master, who was famous for his virtuoso one-man performances of Shakespeare's tragedies. It said: 'His level is that of a good, sound commoner.' I could have gone to Oxford, then, had I wanted, but refused, out of pure perversity. No wisdom in the choice then, even though, in the last analysis, I am sure it worked out for the best. I had been bending myself into shapes, trying to make myself a historian. Now overcompensation came to an end, and at least I was left with a very good knowledge of British and European history. Those fifty pages a day had not been read in vain.

And now, God help me, it would be the law.

2

JEWISH FAMILIES PLAYED SAFE. If I was not going to follow my father as a dentist, and a very good one, if I had at least for the moment put journalism aside, then being a solicitor would always ensure a good living. I would not, immediately, have to be conscripted. It could be postponed for the five years it took to serve my articles and pass the exams. Since National Service seemed to most of us in Bodeites an irritating waste of time, and since I had been a notably recalcitrant member of the school corps, this was a substantial consolation. I knew that one of my JTC persecutors, who became head of the school, had read with amusement a limerick I had contributed to the house magazine, *Bode in the Hole*, to which, at fifteen, I had been appointed by the junior section.

Not everyone here finds the Corps
A waste of good time and a bore.
For there's many a lout
Finds it pleasant to shout
And to matter a little bit more.

Yet, though I resigned myself to articles and legal studies, I had not repressed my journalistic ambitions. Not only did they coexist; they were, if anything, stronger than ever. I wanted to be a football journalist. I wanted to be a novelist. If I had to be a lawyer, so be it.

On Golders Green tube station, I picked up a small, shiny publication dedicated to helping freelances, and found a reference to a magazine called *Sport*, a weekly based in the magical canyon of Fleet Street. Basing my article on a match I had seen at Tottenham the year before in the Olympic tournament, when the gifted Swedish team thrashed Austria, I wrote an article about England's coming tour, and what awaited them in Stockholm. I sent the piece off, and waited anxiously to hear.

Not hearing, I eventually mustered courage, and visited *Sport*'s offices. Like so many such small publications then, they were to be found up endless, winding, dingy stairs, high above the 'Street of Adventure', a curious contrast to the mighty palaces occupied by the *Daily Telegraph* and the *Express*, with its black glass façade.

The editor received me amiably. His name was Alex Lee, a lean, languid man in early middle age, never enthused by anything. In press-boxes, where he sometimes came to sit beside me, he displayed a dry, sardonic humour. If two players clashed and fell together, he would invariably say, 'He'll have to marry him, now.' Arsenal's right winger, so often on the scene after some injury, he categorised as 'a great big girl'. When I asked him about my former hero, Frank Butler, he replied, 'A little man who wears good suits with dirty collars.'

Yes, he told me, to my unconfined joy, there was a chance my piece would be published. *Sport* was planning to start a monthly magazine. And published it eventually was, in a short-lived magazine called the *Sporting Herald*. I remember visiting the office, being handed the new magazine by the secretary – a tiny cockney lady with bright-red hair, seldom without a cigarette – and being overcome by a feeling of sheer delight, never experienced before, or since. 'At last,' said my father, when I brought it home and showed it to him, adding, 'but you're only a baby!' I had a photo taken of myself that re-emerges from time to time, snapped in the garden of our house in North Finchley, holding up the double spread, wearing a grin of toothy delight.

From the *Sporting Herald*, which lasted but a few glossy issues, I moved on to *Sport* proper. This was exceedingly fortunate for me. ABC circulation certificates pinned to the editorial walls alleged that the magazine was selling 50,000 copies a week, though Sid Silver, the bespectacled, sceptical businessman behind it, would later suggest this wasn't so. There was no doubt, however, that it was very widely read, especially by soccer fans and, above all, within the game itself. I was paid thirty shillings a time for a full-page article and was only too glad to get it. In no time at all, it would be my passport to Rome and the *Corriere dello Sport*.

The offices of *Sport*, once I was chained to my articles in the City, became my solace and my refuge, my escape from the misery of contemplating those internal, white-tiled walls, and the complexities of the National Conditions of Sale.

After touting me round various solicitors' offices in the West End and in the City, my parents finally fixed me up with Oppenheimer, Nathan and Vandyk, in Copthall Avenue, behind London Wall.

My father took me along to be grilled by Lord Nathan of Churt and, to a lesser degree, by Arthur Vandyk, two of the senior partners. The third, and most senior partner, the revered and redoubtable Herbert Oppenheimer himself, I never met during the unhappy year I was there. 'Cock up something he's interested in,' said a managing clerk, 'and *you'll* meet him.'

Lord Nathan was a squat, bulky, orotund man who boomed at me formidably for over an hour, at the end of it conceding that I seemed 'rather a nice lad'. He had been Minister of Aviation in the Labour Government but eventually resigned after some minor embarrassment over taking members of his family on a flight. Staggering out of his office and into that of his secretaries, I remarked, bemused, 'Lord Nathan's pretty overpowering, isn't he?'

'Do you find him so?' asked one of the girls, coolly.

I was accepted, a substantial fee was paid, and I was put to work in the office of Mr Cockett, a strong socialist, and a decent man, who wore glasses, a moustache and a cycling medal. 'Go on!' he would often say. Only twice did he grow angry with me. Once because I was reading a preface by Bernard Shaw, rather than the Conditions of Sale; and again because, getting hopelessly lost, I had been wandering around Bloomsbury with a big banker's draft in my pocket. Under Mr Cockett's able tutelage, I learnt gradually how to draw up conveyances, and was privy to endless, stupendously boring discussions between him and the punctilious young Mr Gestetner, of the duplicating firm, setting up some kind of a staff fund. The dictaphone was often in use; it was then a *sine qua non* in such offices.

Arthur Vandyk, genially benign, played little part in the main business; he had suffered a head wound in the First World War and, by all accounts, had never quite been the same. His remit was to look after the staff. Once, after my débâcle over the Conditions of Sale, he took me out to lunch at the Great Eastern Hotel, and asked whether I might not be happier in sports journalism. I mumbled something silly about professions for 'gentlemen'; after all, public school was not far behind, and I was not yet ready to take the obvious plunge.

My first day at lunch, at Oppenheimer's, was much less salubrious. The Honourable Roger Nathan, a huge, dark-haired young man, kindly took me along to the sort of restaurant that he clearly thought appropriate for one of my lowly status. It stood close to Liverpool Street Station, and I never saw the Honourable Roger in it again. It consisted of a large room with many tables, patronised chiefly by clerks, where watery soup was purveyed, along with wretchedly thin cuts off a tasteless joint. At the end of the meal the Honourable Roger asked for two bills, and solemnly handed me mine. It came to six shillings.

I hardly saw Lord Nathan again for a decade or so, and then it was in Copenhagen; it proved my undoing. I was covering the European Maccabiah Games for the *Jewish Chronicle*, had spent the day on the beach and had arrived at the evening's final banquet terribly hungry, carrying a half-bottle of whiskey. Alas, the meal was endlessly postponed while Lord Nathan, the guest of honour, rumbled his banalities. I drank too much whiskey on an empty stomach, and got drunk as a consequence. Not the thing to do in any Jewish gathering, least of all when the return flight to London is delayed eleven hours. Black sheep at the airport. Yet, all in all, it was a useful dress rehearsal for covering the Olympic Games in Rome the following year, for the *Sunday Times*, where I imbibed a great deal of wine, but didn't get drunk at all.

'We're always interested,' said Alex Lee, when I visited *Sport*'s office to propose some feature. But there were other times when, if I complained of anything, he would retort, 'You came to us. We didn't come to you.'

At the offices of *Sport*, I would meet Ralph Finn, a real novelist, a real writer, who contributed a column to the magazine, and a match report every week, to the *People*. He had written a novel called *All is Mist*, published by Hutchinson during the war, in which he stayed a civilian. I was fascinated by it, so much so that, once, reading it on the tube, I was carried past my stop at Golders Green. During the war, Ralph told me, he had been a star feature writer on the *People*, a paper with a huge Sunday circulation, specialising in stories of human interest. After the war, they had elbowed him out. Somehow, somewhere, things that should have happened hadn't happened.

With him, I could talk about Gerald Kersh, who was my favourite author of the time, though, when I had mentioned him at Charterhouse to Freddie Ives, there was the sneering response, 'He'll be forgotten in ten years.' At that time, though, I was fascinated by Kersh's tales of being a Jew in the Coldstream Guards, and of trudging Soho before the war. His writing was vivid, and funny, and uneven. 'A writer of power and fury,' said the novelist John Brophy, father of the formidable Brigid, but time would prove Freddie Ives right, and time would erode my admiration. His memoirs, *I Got References*, were gloriously comic; there were comic scenes in *The Thousand Deaths of Mr Small*, a novel about Jewish life in London, which induced hilarity, but the parts were usually greater than the whole; talent unmediated by artistic conscience. At that time, Kersh was still writing his 'Man of the People' column in that newspaper.

Nothing, over the years, reduced Ralph's high opinion of his destiny. After the 1954 World Cup, he produced a paperback on the back of which he had clearly written the biographical notes. 'Ralph Finn has lived sport . . . at home he has a cabinet of trophies which would be the envy of many a professional athlete . . . thousands read his column in *Sport Express* every week . . . millions read his match reports in the *People* . . . so often has he been proved right that he has come to be known as "The Sporting Prophet in Our Midst".'

Sport Express was what *Sport* came to be called. Silver and Lee discovered that the *Daily Express* was planning to bring out a sports weekly. They seized the potential chance, and changed the title of their magazine, in the hope that the *Daily Express* would have to buy them out. But the predicted sports weekly never appeared.

How good a novel was *All is Mist*? I've no idea; I never read it again, and do not intend to do so. I merely live with the memory of it at the time, when it seemed immensely compelling, this story of a frustrated schoolmaster and his bigger, more down to earth, Philistine brother. There was a long episode in which the unhappy narrator, prey to obsessional neurosis, consulted a leading psychiatrist. Ralph told me that to prepare this episode, he had been allowed to sit for hours behind a screen, listening to consultations.

Frustrated in sports journalism, he turned to advertising, but always kept a toe in the waters of football. Chutzpah was the essence of him. In time to come, he would found a sports news agency known as Rafinn, which claimed to send material all over the world, though whether anybody used it was a moot point. Bullshit baffles brains; especially in the football world of that era.

I remember, at West Ham United, seeing two tall, dark young men I had never set eyes on before, and never would again, making their way into the press-box. 'Who are they?' I asked the press steward, who replied, with reverent tones, 'They're from the Rafinn agency.' Chutzpah indeed, for they had not one but two seats in that press-box.

In later years, Ralph would have two seats in the Tottenham press-box, where initially he brought Mr Bernstein. Bernstein was a tall, thin, morose man with an uncertain moustache, a penchant for shapeless hats and a belted raincoat that seemed to hold him together. He wrote for nobody that one could identify, never took any notes at games but the attendance figure and, initially, at least, he idolised Ralph Finn.

'Morrie Woolf,' he would say, at Arsenal or at Tottenham, in the press room, referring to the tiny, young Jewish editor of an ephemeral sports magazine. 'Ten-guinea shirts, fifty-guinea suits, and telling Ralph what to do. Ralph!'

He would often talk about his two nephews; one was 'a brilliant boy', on his way to Oxford. The other was a promising footballer; Bill Nicholson of Spurs had taken a look at him. Often I tended to get them mixed up. 'What, the brilliant one?'

'No, the footballer.'

'What, the footballer?'

'No, the brilliant boy.'

Who knows why he and Ralph finally fell out and refused to speak to one another; though Bernstein, in his now morose silence, a hero lost, continued to get press passes, and continued to write down the attendances.

Ralph was an expert corner cutter. In later years, he would, though no longer a working journalist, continue to occupy his seat at Tottenham; and to bring there his nephew, who looked older than himself and had no visible connection with football. In time, the authorities at Spurs got rid of the nephew, but had an infinitely harder job in getting rid of Ralph, who would protest with such epistolary vehemence that one regime, at least, would, with a sigh, let him stay. Another was adamant; there was no place for him. The protests continued, bitter and self-righteous. Had he not written books about the Spurs? You wondered whether he might have claimed a squatter's title. But credit where it's due; even when, in the 1980s, Chelsea had slung the press out of the east stand and stuck them in a little TV gantry on the other side of the field, Rafinn somehow contrived to keep a seat, usually occupied by a plump little dark man who may have been Ralph's greengrocer. He was certainly no journalist.

Then there was Soccerette. This, in the very early 1950s, was a table game invented by Ralph, and played with magnets. He demonstrated it at football grounds; at Leyton Orient, even at Arsenal Stadium, surrounded by a curious entourage. There was Charlie Boy, a tall, heavy-boned cockney with a long red nose and a mournful delivery. There was Major Bill Wade, so-called, whose abundant grey air sprouted unfashionably from beneath a black trilby. And there was Mr Kenzie, of the booming voice, whose calling card informed you that he was secretary of the London Transport water polo club. Major Bill was, it was said, having an affair with Charlie Boy's daughter. One of them, presumably, had put money into the scheme, though none of them ever seemed to have much.

At Highbury, Mr Kenzie used a small, transparent plastic container with a soccer figurine inside it to show, with a magnet from beneath, exactly how the players should be manoeuvred, while Don Roper, the Arsenal winger, after being boomed at relentlessly, politely paid attention. 'They'll smash it,' said Ralph, sadly.

In the end, the game got on the market, but things somehow went wrong. 'Never take a percentage,' Ralph told me.

In his latter years, he once informed me – in the Tottenham press-box, of course – that there were now 'three doctors in my family. My son, who's a Ph.D., my son-in-law, who's a medical doctor, and me.' He seemed to have acquired his doctorate by correspondence from some American college.

In the weeks after I had left Charterhouse for good, I played out the last of my games of table football. This, perhaps another obsession, was something that had been taught me by Peter Kay, a boy in Bodeites. It was a game played on any flat surface – in this case, on the desks of our carrels – with drawing pins marking out the goals, and coins as the players. There were specific rules. If you intended to shoot, you had to say, 'Shooting!' so the goalkeeper could position himself. A team that was awarded a corner had two bites at the cherry: the corner itself, and another free move. There were no offsides. Wise Gordon Watson pointed out that the defining factor was not the distance of the ball from the goal, but the man from the ball.

At home, I elaborated the game on the shiny dining-room table; and later, when we got one, on the ping-pong table upstairs in our games room. The Kessly brothers took to it with glee, as did another friend, Geoffrey Davis, who lived in my street, with its gravelly, unadopted road. Given the war, it would still be unadopted when we sold the house, in 1951.

Poker chips, suitably numbered, were used as players. Mine, mauve on one side, blue on the other, were quite large; the Kesslys', fairly small. Friends like these were invaluable in the holidays, for after so many years away at school one's home acquaintance was inevitably limited.

All four of us played in the final fling of Finchley Hornets. We met a team, whose name I don't remember, on a farcical pitch, which had a deep trench dug across it at one point. The goals were just bamboo sticks, with no crossbar. We won quite easily. Edward, who scored a true centre forward's goal, and Geoffrey, at centre half, played very well indeed. A low centre of mine was turned between the sticks by one of their defenders, but Edward generously said that I should count it as my goal.

When the Kesslys left for South Africa, and I fell out with Geoffrey over an unreturned pair of shinpads, holidays grew lonely. It was then that I started playing table football against myself, working out an elaborate league, with games of ten minutes each way, which took two years of the holidays to complete. After that, as an envoi, I played out a cup competition, in which I included Glasgow Rangers and Hibernian, drawn against one another in the first round. Arsenal were not included in either competition; I was afraid I would cheat for them.

Ludicrously, I can still remember results and matches in those tournaments. How Wolves, setting the early pace in my league, thrashed Chelsea 6–2 at Stamford Bridge, and Newcastle 7–1 at Gallowgate with a hat trick by their right half, honest Tom Galley. And how Chelsea, even when they transferred the prolific Tommy Lawton and pushed Ken Armstrong up, as the real Chelsea did, still set the pace, winning the title from a resurgent Manchester United and an unlucky Blackpool with a win at Stoke on the last day of all.

Stoke City themselves surprised everyone – or me, at least – by winning the Cup Final 3–1 in a replay with Liverpool, having won a remarkable semi-final against Blackpool when their goalkeeper, Denis Herod, made two astounding saves.

My mother despised such activities. 'Joe, Joe,' she would incite my father, 'he's playing that soppy game again.' But play it I did.

Now I went to games without my father, but he had been Virgil to my Dante. I recall another game at Charlton, a week before the FA Cup Final of 1947, in which Charlton were due to play Burnley. There was nothing at stake for either Charlton or Arsenal; both were safe in the League, and Charlton brought in several reserves, including the newly signed Benny Fenton, later a notably idiosyncratic manager of Millwall.

My father and I arrived early, and took up our position on a mud bank that stood behind one of the goals. There were, so far, few others there. 'Have twopence,' said my father cheerfully, offering a man a cigarette; their price had just gone up. By the time the game began, he and I could hardly move. There were 60,000 in the ground. I can still visualise the goal Arsenal scored, bang in front of us, through Jimmy Logie, the ball hitting the stanchion and bouncing out again.

At Millwall, my father told me, when, once, he came down to Charterhouse to take me out, he and a friend had been jammed on the terraces, hardly able to see. 'Who are you pushing?' a huge docker demanded of the friend, and gave him a fierce push in return. Moments later, said my father, his friend was waving to him from far down in the crowd: 'It's great here! I can see perfectly!'

'So I went up to the man,' said my father, 'and I asked, "Will you give *me* a push?" and he did, so there we were, watching together.'

Not only did I slog my way through the dismal days at Oppenheimer's; not only did I have to grind my way through law books when I went home, afterwards; but I had also enrolled as an internal, evening law student at King's College. This meant attending lectures and tutorials there, and at other colleges, several times a week. 'You're the kind of student we want here,' said the amiable tutor at King's.

'Yes, but you're not the kind of student they get,' said Maxwell Telling, sardonically. Maxwell was an internal student, too, of a very different stripe: a properous publisher of codes, who drove a powerful Allard car. The trio was made up by Louis Blom-Cooper, today a QC of renown, but, then, making his way doggedly as a student and barrister. Both he and Maxwell had been captains in the war, Louis serving in Burma. Louis had curly black hair, spectacles, and a squat, strong frame. He was partly of Dutch descent, and would, eventually, take his Ph.D. in Holland. He shared my love of football, and, when Gordon Watson and I came to run *Sport Express*, he had his first journalistic assignment as Lew Cullis – named after Wolves' famous manager – our amateur football correspondent. From there, he would graduate to writing football reports for the *Observer*; he came to me for help in rewriting the first major piece he ever contributed to them. We argued fiercely over every comma, but afterwards he would tell me, gratefully, 'They'd never have taken it if it wasn't for you.' He did not need me for long.

It was in the summer of 1949 that my parents took me on holiday to Italy, again, with unlooked-for consequences. Meanwhile, I had begun writing *Cliff Bastin Remembers*. Bastin had been another of my Arsenal idols, the 'Boy Wonder' who had begun playing for Arsenal at the age of seventeen, won an FA Cup medal at eighteen, and secured every honour available to him at the age of nineteen.

He had, I knew, been a remarkable outside left, once scoring 33 goals in a single league season, but by the time I began watching him, in the war, his pace had diminished, and he mostly played at inside left, with occasional sorties at wing half. Driving from time to time with my parents along the North Circular Road, I had sometimes glimpsed a sign which read THE CLIFF BASTIN CAFÉ. Thus germinated the idea: his autobiography.

Various examples of the kind had been published, since another of my heroes, Eddie Hapgood, had produced his, under the title *Football Ambassador*, in January 1945. This, which I read with avidity, was followed by Tommy Lawton's *Football is my Business* and Frank Swift, the spectacular England goalkeeper, with *Football from the Goalmouth*, all published by Sporting Handbooks of Bedford Square. All were great fun for a young schoolboy, packed as they were with cheerful anecdotes, and ghosted by a sportswriter called Roy Peskett. In time, when I wrote a novel about a broken-down goalkeeper called *The Dying of the Light*, I had great fun in parodying such books, juxtaposing what had actually happened with the jaunty euphemisms of that genre.

But if Hapgood, Lawton and Swift, I suddenly reflected, then why not Bastin? Bastin, who had been such a star of his time; Bastin, such a Titan of the Arsenal teams that had bestrode England between the wars. It was conceived from the first as an act of homage, a labour of love. Had I thought about it rationally, or been sufficiently informed, I would have told myself that Bastin, now, was a back number; that he had retired more than two years ago, after a sad last season in the Arsenal league team. Indeed, some whim of George Allison's had induced him to use the older, slower Bastin in his former position of outside left when the First Division was revived in August 1946. At Wolverhampton, Arsenal were thrashed 6–1. But acts of piety are not based on reality.

I telephoned directory enquiries and asked for Bastin's address and number. 'Cliff Bastin?' said the operator. 'That sounds like Arsenal.' I wrote to Bastin, proposing such a book, and got a reply. 'Thank you for your letter and glowing tribute to my career,' it said. He had already received an offer, he wrote, from a publisher called Findon's, to bring the book out priced at one shilling, 'Which I thought a bit of an insult.'

So I went to see him, in his flat above the café, on a Sunday evening – the exigencies of work would always make it Sunday evening – and, in due course, we agreed to do the book. In retrospect, it seems surprising that he wanted to: I had no publisher lined up, and no reputation. We would split the earnings 60–40, in his favour. So I began. It entailed Sunday visits to the café, and Saturday-morning labours in the British Newspaper Library, in Colindale.

Bastin, by then, was still only 37 years old, and heavier, inevitably, than in those earlier, youthful days when, light-brown hair parted fashionably – for footballers – down the middle, he had formed his famous partnership with Alex James. To some extent, his deafness defined him, cocooned and isolated him. He was very defensive about it, never wanting it mentioned. It had, certainly, blighted the final, diminuendo, years of his career. But then, by his own confession, he had been unusually detached, even in his teens. He told me how, when the formidable Herbert Chapman came to his Exeter house to try to persuade him, a seventeen-year-old, to sign for Arsenal, he was thinking largely of the tennis match he was due to play that evening.

He had no humour to speak of. When the book came out, he was accused of being conceited. Willy Meisl, the Austrian journalist long domiciled in London, brother of the celebrated Hugo – father of the Austrian *Wunderteam* – wrote, 'It is obvious that Bastin likes Bastin a lot, and considers him an outstanding footballer.' But Bastin's assessment of himself was all of a piece with his whole *Weltanschauung*. There was what might be termed an innocent candour about him. Once I mentioned to him that some critic had written that Eric Brook, the powerful Manchester City winger, had been as good a player as himself. He paused for a moment, thought about it, then shook his head gravely and said, 'No.'

On those Sunday evenings, his wife made us mugs of strong tea, and thick cheese sandwiches. Sometimes, in the background, one could hear her shouting at the children. She was hospitable and friendly, far more outgoing than he. But those evenings were fascinating to me. Arsenal's halcyon years were brought vividly alive. Famous matches were recreated. Downright judgements were delivered; these, as I later found, to the distress of some of those who were judged. It would prove a highly controversial book, though this was never my intention at the time, nor his. I indeed had no idea it would stir up so much controversy; I had entered into his mind-set, even though, in retrospect, the way I wrote the book was not as authentic as it should have been. Too much of me – or, rather, of the way I might think or express myself – rather than he. Could one really imagine Bastin, advising young players to shoot as often as possible, adducing, ' 'Tis better to have loved and lost than never to have loved at all'?

We gave a full chapter to his partnership with Alex James, the tough little Scottish inside left who was the motor of Arsenal's success, and could scarcely have been a more sharply contrasted character: Bastin's West Country calm, complemented by James's volatile, abrasive persona, product as he was of a harsh mining background in Bellshill. Like Hugh Gallacher, he had escaped the tyranny of the mines, their ever present dangers, thanks to his supreme footballing talents. But though less prone to provocation than Gallacher – James's own legs were discoloured by years of ill-treatment – he was a rebellious figure. This was not without reason, for even star footballers were limited to a parsimonious eight pounds a week, reduced in the summer.

In the book, Bastin said, somewhat euphemistically, that James might have made more of his chances in life. On the only occasion I met James, in a press room, he said, huffily, 'You're the one that wrote that Bastin book! He wasn't such a great player!'

Bryn Jones, James's purported successor, was also, I discovered years later, distressed by the book. Bastin had not been kind to him, declaring that Jones could never have been the inside left to take over from James, since at Wolves, the club that sold him, much of his work had been done by the players who buzzed around him. The conventional wisdom was that the intervention of the war had prevented Jones from fully adapting his style. Besides, James himself, when he arrived at Arsenal from Preston in 1929, had not found it easy, at first, to play as Chapman wanted.

Bastin, in conversation, dismissed the tales that James had told him: 'Stay out on the wing, and I'll give you the ball.' He had always, he said, preferred to play ten or fifteen yards in from the touchline. Indeed, he really thought himself not to be an outside left but an inside left, the position he played for Exeter City before he joined Arsenal. On England's 1933 tour, when the exasperated Italian fans in Rome cried, 'Basta, Bastin!' (enough of Bastin), he played both inside left and outside left, with tremendous success. That was the tour on which Eric Brook, an unreconstructed Yorkshireman, faced with the beauties of St Peter's, could only remark, 'Someone's pinched my fucking boots!'

It was also the tour on which the England players were presented to Mussolini. Bastin recalled that the Duce's personality was such that it totally overshadowed even that of Herbert Chapman, who was present. He also remarked that everyone in Rome seemed to be in some kind of uniform.

Bastin, like James, made peanuts out of football. It is sad and sobering to think what two such refulgent stars would have earnt today; how, with any kind of providence, they would have lived, on retirement, at great ease for the rest of their lives. No question of running a North Circular café, and travelling by tube, as Bastin did – unrecognised, even on his way to Highbury – to report matches for the old *Sunday Pictorial*.

We called the book *Cliff Bastin Remembers*, having toyed with the title *Boy Bastin Remembers*. With characteristic effrontery, I got in the habit of going, in those priceless lunch hours, down to Bedford Square, where Robin Owen, the chief editor at Sporting Handbooks, tolerantly received me. He was very interested, he said, in the idea of the book, which could follow Hapgood, Lawton and the rest. Once, reclining happily in his armchair, he reflected on what a fine job he had, one in which he could keep playing with ideas.

Then there was Michael Ivens. Now, the name has long been well known; he was the combative moving spirit of 'Aims of Industry'. Never, in the months I knew him, could I have envisaged such a future, never could I have seen him as a future tribune of the Establishment, the scourge of the embattled Left. At that time, when he was in his early twenties, editing one of those glossy little weeklies called the *Sports Reporter*, he seemed a genial, lively rascal, humorous and anarchic, writing most of the magazine himself. 'So don't let Irish readers be getting worried,' he authentically wrote, when contributing a column under an Irish pseudonym. He told me once, on the telephone, that he and I were the only people in sports journalism who knew what we were doing. I was hoping to join the *Sports Reporter* for the princely fee of two guineas an article, as opposed to the thirty bob I was getting from *Sport*.

The *Sports Reporter*, like other magazines, had its headquarters in Soho and was owned by a Mr Kaplan. I wrote, with brash arrogance, to Michael, 'Tell Kaplan it's two guineas or nothing.' Mr Kaplan opened the letter, and it was nothing. 'That damned little phrase of yours nettled Kaplan,' Michael wrote to me. His eventual letter of farewell concluded, 'Judge not my irritating character too harshly.' It was the last thing I was likely to do. We did not speak again for some 25 years, by which time he had undergone his metamorphosis.

I saw Eddie Estherby once more when my father sent me down to the tennis club he was now running at Leigh-on-Sea. It would be the last time I would see the Estherbys together as a happy family. Eddie had a couple of hard green courts, promoted small exhibition games, and had grandiose ambitions which, perhaps inevitably, tended to be ridiculed by the local pundits. He had hopes of his son, John, as a tennis player, but since even I, mediocre as I was, contrived to beat him, I wondered whether they could ever be realised. Eddie was as bright, humorous and optimistic as ever; Della as cheerfully hospitable. He coached me patiently on the green courts, trying to make me see the stroke through: 'This is BIF week,' he said, 'British Industrial Fair, but we don't want to biff the ball.' I tried not to.

Before very long, John died suddenly, and the marriage sprang apart. In her profound grief, it was perhaps too much for Della to go on being such a diligent support to Eddie. As for Eddie himself, I did see him again just once, years later, by which time I was living in Holland Park. Suddenly, out of the blue, he telephoned, and I at once invited him over. Just as Della, when she had come to dinner at my parents' flat, not far away in Oakwood Court, had seemed transformed, giggly and uneasy, so Eddie, too, had suffered a sea change. The cheerful humour had gone. He was curiously embarrassed, almost bombastic, never relaxing for a moment. In time to come I heard that things had gone badly wrong for him, his bright ambitions – 'The Eddie Estherby Sportique' was written on his calling card – in tatters. Had John not died, things would surely have been better. As it was, I never saw or heard from him again, but I shall always remember his kindness.

That August, my parents took my sister Marilyn and me on holiday to Forte dei Marmi on the Tuscan coast. We swam and sunbathed, and I played tennis with a local family who had a court. We visited Florence on a boiling hot day, and went down to Rome, while my stomach fought unavailingly with the richer diet. I had with me, more in vanity than in ambition, my file of *Sport* magazine, containing my articles. At full-page length, they looked rather better than their thirty bob's worth. Certainly they would now serve me well in Rome.

Brashly ambitious, I decided to present myself at the offices of the Roman daily paper, *Corriere dello Sport*, to see if I could find work. My first attempt was unsuccessful; it was still early in the afternoon – siesta time. In the evening, I went back, and there they all were. With what in retrospect seems surprising tolerance, they received me most politely, looked at the file of magazines, and produced a fluent English speaker. His name was Vittorio Finizio. He was, I imagine, in his latter twenties, a pale, slight, sensitive man with glasses and receding hairline; scholarly and precise, he was a contrast with his rollicking, noisy, boyish companions, though he could join in their fun. Although he had long lived in Rome, he was by origin a Neapolitan, had great love for his native city, and had written a monograph about it.

He deplored any kind of vulgarity – which made him a natural anti-Fascist – not least that of those who came to Rome from other cities, then aped all the worst, bombastic qualities of the *romanaccio*. He had been brought up in Rome by an aunt, and once told me that, reflecting, 'I realised that everything I knew had been taught me by her.'

At times, when he might thrust his hands forward to emphasise a statement, he might be taken to task by Ennio Cencelli, the effective editor who, like Alberto Marchesi and Rino Molinari, was known to have Fascist leanings. Cencelli would mimic Finizio. 'Do Englishmen do that, Glanville? Do they do that in England?'

Finizio, when I came to live in Rome and we could converse in Italian, told me of a friend who had been travelling in Europe and extolling the virtues of other nations. 'Ah, the English! Such democracy! Such a sense of fair play! Such civility! And the Germans! Such discipline and organisation! I took a train, and eventually crossed the border. As I went to enter a compartment, an Italian wrenched the door open and asked, "Are you for Lazio or Roma? If you're *laziale*, you can't come in." *Ero tornato in Italia.* [I was back in Italy.]'

Finizio spoke good English, had worked as an interpreter in the war, and had a cogent way of seeing things. He once said to me of the Roma and Italy goalkeeper, Giuseppe Moro, '*Si lamenta sempre, e così facendo, cerca di farsi simpatico.*' (He's always complaining, and that's how he tries to make people like him.) He would expertly translate my articles for many years. When, eventually, I was able to write them in Italian myself, he told me, 'Very well, if you want to amuse yourself, but to me, it's no problem.'

He had, beyond doubt, a refinement which distinguished him from most of the Roman sports journalists. He wrote elegantly and understood football well. The misery and horror of it was that he would succumb in middle age to a mysterious illness which, having almost been fatal, reduced him to a strange, sad, giggling parody of himself. He might approach you in the press gallery of the Olympic Stadium and ask you the significance of two addresses. One would be that of the SS when the Nazis occupied Rome, the other of the Gestapo.

In the event, *Corriere* told me I could write for them, and gave me a typewritten card to say as much. It would prove a marvellously fecund and productive relationship across the years, even if it did end so sadly, and even if I did twice leave them before that, to write briefly for other newspapers.

On the train which took us across Europe, and back home, I had another piece of luck. Our family travelled on a sleeper carriage and there, in the depths of the night, standing in the corridor, my father and I fell into conversation with a middle-aged man who turned out to be Captain Agius, a director of Allied Malta Newspapers. During the conversation, he happened to mention, with a smile, that his paper, the *Times of Malta*, bought features from Reuters for a minuscule fee.

Back in London, I found that my 'damned little phrase' had lost me my chance with the *Sports Reporter*. This was a blow; but then I thought of Reuters. If they syndicated features, why not mine? Nothing ventured; nothing gained. With the blithe, brash optimism, or chutzpah, of a seventeen-year-old, I proceeded to ring up Reuters and talk to the sports editor. It turned out to be Vernon Morgan, another Old Carthusian, as it happened, though I had no idea of that at the time. Far from dismissing me, he told me, genially, that he believed Reuter features were looking for a football column at that moment, and invited me to come to the office.

So I presented myself at 85 Fleet Street, that impressive pile which, over the years, has resisted the intrusions of Japanese banks, and was shown into a large, light-filled office where Vernon Morgan told me, 'I've given your billet-doux to Stanley Clarke.'

Vernon, once an accomplished runner, was a portly, avuncular figure who treated me with a generosity I scarcely deserved. Stanley Clarke, the Reuters features editor, was a large, brisk man who received me with equal amiability. Yes, they were indeed looking for a columnist; I was engaged. Once a week, at four guineas a time. A sub-editor asked me cheerfully what he might put in my biography: 'Have you ever made a century at billiards?' I would go on contributing the column to PA Reuters features, as they were, or PA features, as they became, for the next forty-odd years.

Poring through papers at Colindale – there were times when I told people the book might better have been called *The British Museum Remembers* – and slogging out to Edgware on Sunday nights, I managed to finish the book. Now and again, Cliff would ask me to tone down his pungent comments. I could not, for example, quote him as saying of England's 1934 touring team, which had lost both its games in Europe, 'There were two many lazy players in the side.' But, by and large, he was ready to stand up and be counted. For the moment.

At Oppenheimer's, I was increasingly unhappy with the work, but happy enough with the people around me, whether it be honest Mr Cockett, blue suit, cycling medal and left-wing predilections, young Bill Taylor, an aspiring Fabian whose grandfather still worked in the basement offices, or Fred, the messenger, who had been a boxer and wanted to get back in the ring.

He came to me once and asked if I would write a letter for him, to the *Weekly Sporting Review*, another of the periodicals that mushroomed in those post-war days. I was to ask what had happened to that promising fighter, Fred. 'Then I'll write in and say, here I am, and I'm ready to make a comeback.' The arrangement was that my own name would not appear on the original letter, but it did. He signed it himself. I was angry. I don't think he ever fought again.

But now, there were the pains. Violent pains in the chest, which would suddenly assail me of an evening, usually on my way back from work. My father eventually started taking me to doctors, and to specialists, and none of them could find anything wrong. One of them, with consulting rooms in Harley Street, was physician-in-chief to the Royal Navy. He, too, found nothing. Many years later, chance had it that I had to see him to be checked over for an insurance policy, not least because I had had tuberculosis and, thanks to a still more flagrant misdiagnosis, three operations on a TB spine.

The doctor smiled and said, self-deprecatingly, that one could not always be right.

Sporting Handbooks turned *Cliff Bastin Remembers* down. It was a fearful blow. All those *têtes-à-têtes* with Robin Owen. All that apparent enthusiasm for the book. But it had disappointed him. He referred me to the latest of his firm's football autobiographies, that of the celebrated Raich Carter, to see how it should be done. It was hard to bear, and harder still to tell Bastin.

What next? I was a tyro. I knew nothing about publishers, still less about agents. It was my father who, characteristically, came to my aid. He had a patient called David Low, a sophisticated, somewhat eccentric, publisher and *littérateur*. David Low suggested his friend Mr Finlayson, a Scottish publisher who had had great success with a football book. I say Mr Finlayson, because in those more formal times, when Christian names were not employed at the drop of a hat – oh for the formalities of Italian, French and German, where the second person singular and 'polite' forms are differentiated! – I would never call him anything else.

The book with which he and his firm, Art and Educational, prospered, was one I had myself bought in Foyles, that chaotic nirvana in the Charing Cross Road, and hugely enjoyed. It was called *Spotlight on Football*, the autobiography of Peter Doherty, a red-headed maverick and greatly gifted Irish inside left. Where Hapgood, Lawton, Swift et al. had happily accepted the status quo where even Bastin said, in our book, that in his view all footballers should be paid the same, Doherty was an embittered rebel. If the game depended on footballers' sons, he wrote, it would die away. He was the first star to kick against the pricks, to decry the authoritarian, oppressive system, which was so utterly loaded in favour of the clubs, which had pegged the maximum wage to £8 ever since 1919, and which could tie a player to his club for ever. The book sold 30,000 copies.

Mr Finlayson's other great success, published under the imprint of the Ettrick Press, was a little book called *Teatime Tips*, which had also sold in its many thousands. His offices were in Bloomsbury Street, the very heart of the publishing world, and there I was cordially received by him, and by his one assistant, Harry. They were a complete contrast to each other. Mr Finlayson was a very small, dark-haired, bespectacled Scot, pleasantly relaxed, with an engaging sense of humour. Harry was tall and lean, his long, fairish hair dangling each side of his face, itself enriched by an abundant, undisciplined moustache. He was volatile, sublimely tactless and self-absorbed; or rather, absorbed in opera. This was his consuming and controlling passion. He was the founder and inspiration of a body called the Verdi Society. Above the long table where he worked hung a poster of a massive and renowned soprano. His phone calls, frequent and intense, were almost invariably to do with the Society. Mr Finlayson, a tolerant fellow, did not seem to mind.

Yes, they were interested in the Bastin book. Yes, the book was being read. And read. And read. Weeks went by, with no decision. I made infinite visits to the office. Harry kept me and the book at bay. Then at last my illness caught up with me. Tuberculosis of the chest was diagnosed.

I was distraught. My father came upstairs, where I lay in bed, to visit me. 'It's not a year out of your life,' he said, consolingly, 'it's a year *in* your life.' A *year*!

But the book would come out. Thanks to my father. Perturbed by my health, he had divined what it was that was holding up Mr Finlayson and Ettrick Press. He had gone to him and asked if it would make a difference if he himself were to put £400 into the book. Mr Finlayson said it would. And so, through my father's generosity, *Cliff Bastin Remembers* would appear. I was immensely grateful to him, yet at the same time, I felt guilty, a feeling that would persist across the years, a feeling that, whatever its eventual reception, the book had not been published on its own merits. But then, what did I or my father know of publishers, or of whom to turn to when Mr Finlayson and the Ettrick Press stalled?

In the event, a book that I had conceived as an act of piety, a labour of love, would put me on the map. More than 45 years after its publication, it would change hands at £40 a time, and Arsenal fans would approach me in the streets around Highbury and on the tube to talk to me about it. Not least when, in 1997, Arsenal's centre forward, Ian Wright, was supposedly about to beat Cliff Bastin's scoring record. The figures, in fact, had been cooked. Bastin was still far ahead on league goals, and ahead on cup goals, too. Wright had scored freely in competitions – the League Cup and European cups – which did not exist when Bastin was playing. As I later found out, Bastin himself had somehow developed cold feet; he hadn't wanted the book to be published, so again my father had to intervene, promising him his money.

Now I was confined to bed, at home, in Finchley. A huge nurse was engaged to look after me. I read a lot, and tried to write short stories. A bland, silver-haired Welsh specialist, Dr Lloyd, whose sons had been my contemporaries at Charterhouse, and who visited me periodically, crooned, 'What a boy, what a boy', suggested I read poetry, and prescribed no treatment whatsoever. I told myself I wasn't really ill.

In the end, my mother, in despair, drew a sharp and arbitrary line on my temperature chart and I was admitted to the private wing of University College Hospital, where another, more decisive, specialist, the white-haired Dr Andrew Moreland, put me on streptomyacin injections.

TB does curious things to the mind. While in hospital, there were times when I knew my behaviour could be spoilt, irrational and perverse. There were dramas with the nurses, young girls who were sometimes as unreasonable as I. I used the telephone beside my bed to try to drum up more work and, to a surprising extent, succeeded. *Corriere dello Sport* was sent to me every day. I tried to learn Italian, had the Hugo's 'Teach Yourself' books, three of them, and twice succeeded in losing the largest and most crucial one. So I ploughed my way through *Corriere dello Sport*, first reading through Vittorio Finizio's translations of my own articles, before gradually moving on to the rest of the paper.

Through *Corriere dello Sport* and whatever name I now had in Italy, I was able to get work from *Il Calcio Illustrato*, the green and brown weekly football magazine which, then, was the best of its kind in Italy. I began writing for an Indian magazine called *Sport and Pastime*, published in Madras by its parent newspaper, the *Hindu*. Today, I am still writing for *Sportstar*, *Sport and Pastime*'s successor.

Above all, I started writing a novel. For some time, I had been trying to write short stories. Harry, Mr Finlayson's amanuensis, one of whose roles was that of an aspiring agent, was especially keen on *The Kidnapping of Gaffer Dodkins*, but he could not find a home for it. Poring through the *Writers' and Artists' Yearbook*, I found, in the publishing section, that T Werner Laurie were especially interested in fiction 'by young and promising authors'.

I wrote to them; I suppose I must have enclosed some of the short stories that had regularly been coming back to me, so much so that I called one period 'The Week of the Long Envelopes'. But, in return, I had a letter from an editor, Douglas Baber, which said that, if I ever wrote a novel, 'We would be very glad to give it a careful reading.'

Accordingly, I began my novel. Predictably, perhaps, it had football as its subject. The idea for it came to me in reading about the Bogotá saga. Neil Franklin, then the England and Stoke City centre half, an elegant performer and a proper successor to Stanley Cullis, had suddenly decamped with his club colleague, the outside right George Mountford, to play for a club called Santa Fe, in Bogotá, the capital of Colombia. The Colombians could do this, without let, hindrance or benefit of transfer fee, because Colombia at that time had fallen out with the official international body, FIFA, and were thus free to do what they wished.

Franklin and Mountford had reportedly been offered the fabulous sum of £50 a week, as against the meagre £8, which was all they got in England. The *Daily Express*, still the newspaper I most avidly read, published a piece headed, NOT EVERY SHOT IS AT GOAL IN COLOMBIA. There were, it reported, revolutionaries in the hills trying to overthrow what appeared to be a dictatorship. Hence my *donnée*, an ingenious one, whether or not I was equipped to do it justice.

My idea was that an English centre forward – whom I named Morton – was lured, as Franklin had been, to Colombia, or its equivalent, at the behest of the General who was its dictator, the idea being to distract the thoughts of the football-obsessed people from revolution. But the revolutionaries in the hills knew a trick worth two of that. They planned to invade the capital, take Morton prisoner and instal him as puppet President of their country, Pandemonia.

At the height of summer, I was taken off streptomyacin and moved to the convalescent home at Mundesley, on the Norfolk coast. Would that I had stayed on streptomyacin. While in University College Hospital, I developed severe pains in the back. Eventually, I was visited by the acknowledged expert in such matters, Professor

Rosenheim. The professor examined my X-rays, examined my back, and pronounced, 'A chill in the back from early childhood.' Nothing to worry about. Go and sin no more.

I went. The following winter, in Norfolk, with snow on the ground, the agony in my back returned. It was hard to walk. When I would rise with difficulty from a chair, a pleasant, piano-playing patient called Soden would joke, 'The oldest member.' Respectful of the diagnosis of so eminent a figure as Professor Rosenheim, Dr Day, the chief physician at Mundesley, slapped a belladonna plaster on my back, which seemed to work. When, subsequently, my father spoke to him at Mundesley, he told him how pleased he had been with my quick recovery.

This was early in 1951. Each winter thereafter, I suffered those pains. Three years later, as I shall recount, I was obliged to leave Florence overnight and travel across Europe, stopping in Zurich and ending in London, and University College Hospital, again. There, I was to undergo two minor operations and a major one, a bone-graft, after which I spent two months on a plaster bed, immobile.

More than forty years later, on the way to visit a tiny grandson then in the UCH, I drove past one of the hospital's newer buildings. It was dedicated to Professor Rosenheim.

Mundesley was another world. My father accompanied me from London, looked out of the window of my room on the top floor at sunlit cornfields, shook his head, smiled, and extolled the view. 'If you can't write here ...' Tuberculosis has lately made a sinister return in Britain, after a long, happy hiatus, but in 1950 it was still rife. Mundesley Sanatorium was packed with people, both in the main building, where I was domiciled, and in the so-called Brick Block, where the more serious cases, such as those who had undergone thoracaplasty operations, with ribs removed, were housed.

Our Hofrat Behrens was Dr Day, a man with literary leanings, a desire to widen his patients' horizons, and a Draconian attitude to discipline. Early in my stay, my old studymate and friend from Charterhouse, Gordon Watson, now commissioned in the Air Force, serving his conscription, motorcycled over from his base to see me, and committed the crime of remaining during the rest hour. The rebuke was severe.

I had my typewriter with me, and was able to go on writing articles destined for Italy, India and Reuters, while finishing my novel, *The Reluctant Dictator*. This I eventually sent off, with tremulous hope, to T Werner Laurie, waiting meanwhile for the publication of *Cliff Bastin Remembers*, which would not come until December. The sanatorium had an excellent library, which helped one to pass the hours. For the moment, and for the weeks to come, I was still confined to bed. But the fashion there was to get a patient up in due course, then subject him to longer and longer walks – in the flat countryside, or on the stony beach.

Concurrently, one would be moved out of the main building into a glass-doored chalet on the hillside opposite. The ultimate stage, which I myself experienced, was to be placed in a three-sided white-painted hut at the top of the hill, near the ablutions, its third side covered only by a tarpaulin. This I survived without excessive trouble, but the recovery was illusory.

The population of the sanatorium was highly varied. Colonel Garrity, a Liverpudlian, used to bring one newspapers and the like. He spoke of Berry Nieuwenhuys: 'Now ther's [sic] a player.' John Stevens, an Irishman, had fought behind the lines in Yugoslavia with the Royal Marine Commandos and once traversed a whole line of latrines, carrying a machine gun, as unwary German soldiers relieved themselves early in the morning. He had survived the war, survived adventures in India, but then succumbed to TB.

So had Jim Gladwell, who had commanded little ships as a Royal Navy Officer. Tall, dark-haired and well-built, a former oarsman at Oxford, an Old Salopian, he combined slightly old-fashioned courtesy and diction with a marvellously obscene cornucopia of verse and song.

Take it in your hand, Mrs Murphy.
Sure, 'tis the finest piece of mutton in the town.
It has hairs on its neck like a turkey,
And it spits when you rub it up and down.

'Come in, my dear fellow,' he would say, when one entered his room, on the hill. 'Make yourself at school.' A practising barrister before TB afflicted him, he would lament, 'I'm nigh on thirty, now.' His use of language was a delight, but on one sad evening when, by general request, he was to make the keynote speech on behalf of the patients at the annual Mundesley dinner, he stumbled strangely through his words, while a *Daily Mail* reporter from Ulster sucked a cigar and muttered that a man of his attainments shouldn't be subjected to such tedium.

We had a footballer, too; or rather, a famous footballer who had become a well-known manager. I heard about him early in the New

Year; though I hadn't known of him, before. His name was Charlie Spencer, and he had played for Newcastle United and England. I looked up his record; of his caps, most had been won on a tour of Australia. But he had played for Newcastle in the FA Cup Final of 1924 and, I discovered, had given the pass whereby Stan Seymour, the man who later dominated the club as chairman, had scored the first goal in a win against Aston Villa. 'I know who they gave the blame,' he would tell me.

I got off, one might say, on the wrong foot with him. At a film show in the sanatorium, I did not recognise the bulky, grey-haired figure in a red dressing-gown who was sitting right in front of me. When someone mentioned his name, I responded, 'Yes, I've heard about him; big fellow with a bullet head.'

And that was the greeting I had from him when I first had occasion to go to the room on the first floor that he reluctantly shared with the little Scots headmaster of a school for retarded boys, who had frequent recourse to his sputum cup. 'Big fellow with a bullet head!' cried Charlie, from his bed, but relations improved after that. He was a splendidly unreconstructed Geordie from Washington, County Durham, then a mining village, famous for its footballers. There was, for example, 'Little Alfie Hagan', father of the subsequently more famous Jimmy, who had played for Newcastle with Charlie. 'He was eccentric: he always wanted his meat and his vegetables on different plates.'

After retiring from the game, Charlie had done great things with Grimsby, keeping them in the First Division till after the war on minuscule average crowds of 11,000. Another ex-Newcastle player, the famous but notorious Scottish centre forward Hughie Gallacher, one of the Wembley Wizards who had crushed England 5–1 in 1928, had a spell there. 'Fought with Connor (another international), had a bloody fight with Connor, then when I got back they'd gone to Connor's house for dinner.'

There was Harry Betmead, an elegant centre half who had been capped by England, but whom Spencer, himself a centre half of a different breed, remembered for his maddening lapses: 'Dribbled the ball into his own goal!' And Fred Westgarth, another dyed-in-the-wool Geordie, who kept pigeons in the roof of the stand at Hartlepool United.

'Fred Westgarth: rough diamond; *rough diamond*! I phoned him once, and he said, "When'll we plee?" I said, "New Year's Dee." He said, "New Year's Dee? New Year's Dee? When's that?" He did!'

He was a married man with children, but he had a striking

girlfriend, a redhead in her thirties, who would come to visit him from time to time. One afternoon, his roommate related, she was sitting on his bed, chatting, when there was a patter of light feet, and his little daughter ran into the room, signifying a surprise visit from his wife. Charlie simply looked up and said, 'Hallo! Clash of fixtures, here!'

'Here he is, the boy wonder!' he would greet me. 'Glanville's the name; no need to buy a programme.' Typical of his pre-war kind, untouched by the middle-class morality that would afflict future generations of footballers, he was a mine of anecdote and reminiscence. His *bête noire* was the notoriously tricky manager of Millwall, Charlie Hewitt, invariably referred to as 'Bluidy 'Ewitt'. He had apparently tried to sell to Charlie, at Grimsby, an Irish goalkeeper called Hinton, pretending the fee he had paid was far larger than it was. Charlie Spencer found out: 'He's a rogue! A rogue!' Later, when I wrote a short story about him called 'The Dying Footballer', which Willis Hall turned into a television play, I fantasised about a meeting between them when Norwich City, near to Mundesley, played Millwall in the Cup.

In fact, it was mighty Liverpool whom Norwich played in the third round of the FA Cup in January 1951, and I was given permission to go. I was able, too, to sit in the press-box. It was a memorable game. Norwich then were just a Third Division side, but a good one, a young one, with an impressive half-back line of Pickwick, Foulkes and Ashman, and a lively attack, inspired by a Welsh inside right called Noel Kinsey. Liverpool, however, were a very big deal, having been beaten in the Cup Final only the previous season by Arsenal, and still with Billy Liddell running powerfully on the wing and Albert Stubbins scoring goals from centre forward; those old nemeses of Arsenal.

And Norwich won the game, 3–1; a remarkable occasion. They were encouraged by the lusty choruses of, 'On the ball, the City, never mind the danger!' On that brisk winter day, Norwich themselves were altogether too brisk and bright for Liverpool. I hoped they would come up that season from the Third Division South to the Second, as their burgeoning team surely deserved, but in those distant days just one club came up from each section of the Third Division, two in all, and it was the more experienced Nottingham Forest team that won promotion, ahead of Norwich. One could hardly foresee then that Norwich would in time become a First Division team. As it was, their engaging side, lacking the incentive that promotion might have given it, gradually tailed off.

By then, I was walking great distances. It was, after all, part of the cure. Overcoatless – that was part of the discipline, too – I would set myself longer and longer distances at faster and faster rates. Sometimes I would go down to the seashore and walk along that desolate, stony beach where one could collect strange objects. Once, striding through the country, probably on my way to one of the pretty churches I liked to visit at Knapton, Bacton, Gimingham or Trunch, I met a tiny old man with a cap and an earring. 'How old do you think I am?' he asked me, in broad Norfolk parlance. 'I'm eighty-two! And I've loved every minute of it!'

In December, the Bastin book duly appeared, and created a small furore. It was abundantly reviewed in the national press, which picked up on its apparent controversy. Later, George Allison, Arsenal's former manager, in a magazine called *All Football*, wrote an article under the headline, 'Cliff Bastin Remembers and Forgets', Bastin having scorned his knowledge of football. Telling me, indeed – though we did not put this in the book – that Allison had once recommended a player he had seen with another team, only for the scout who went to watch him the following week to find that the player had been dropped. Willy Meisl had his knowing say in *World Sports*. *Tit Bits*, then a very different publication from what it ultimately became, devoted half a page to it, the editor Trevor Henley later telling me they had thought Bastin to be 'a conceited person'. This, as we have seen, was not quite the case.

For me, it was enormously exciting, and perhaps the most pleasing aspect of all was when I received the gift of a Parker pen and pencil set from anonymous Arsenal supporters, 'For bringing back the life of Cliff Bastin'. I have long since lost both pen and pencil, but strangely, I have kept the note.

Early in the year, too, I heard from Werner Laurie. I had guarded myself against rejection by devising a clerihew, Werner Laurie having been the original publisher of EC Bentley's idiosyncratic verses.

T Werner Laurie are sorry
They cannot publish
Your rublish.

Instead, I received a heartening letter, enclosing an enthusiastic reader's report. The managing director of the firm, George Greenfield, it said, would like to talk to me about the book. I got permission to go down and lunch with him in London.

We met at the Authors' Club, in Whitehall Court, where George

Bernard Shaw had once lived. Later that year, in his dour novel *The End of the Affair*, Graham Greene ridiculed the club, giving it another name, as a place where the novelist narrator went in the certainty that he would never meet another author.

Yet to me the place seemed magical enough. I was met by George Greenfield, who was 36 at the time, a handsome figure, in the Ronald Colman style, with neatly brushed dark hair and a trim black moustache. His voice was elegantly modulated. After lunch, he introduced me to the editor of *John O'London's Weekly*, that endearing literary magazine that I had read ever since my days at Newlands, and where John Betjeman wrote some of his most charming verse.

> Let us not speak, for the love we bear one another.
> Let us hold hands and look.
> She, such an ordinary little woman,
> He, such a thumping crook.

I have never forgotten it. The editor asked me where I came from, and was disappointed to hear that it was London. 'Graham Greene was in here!' he proclaimed. 'Picture of successful author.'

George Greenfield made kind and helpful comments about the book, and I agreed to go away to revise it. Later, he would become my irreplaceable and invaluable literary agent; it was a sad day for me when he retired. A brave infantry officer in the Middle East during the war, eventually promoted to the staff, he would tell an astonishing story of an Army truck guided through an abandoned British minefield, by what turned out to be the ghost of a young subaltern, lying dead beside him. He was a shrewd critic, unblemished by his studies at Downing College under the Draconian FR Leavis.

In March 1951, after seven months in Mundesley, a great deal of reading, an immense amount of walking, and after living with a heterogeneous collection of fellow patients of every kind and class – from the patrician to the proletarian – I was at last allowed home, supposedly cured. The gamble I had taken when, falling ill, I had told my father that I would not go back to the law, seemed to be paying. The Bastin book had done more for me than I had ever thought, let alone hoped, as this had never been the object of the exercise. *The Reluctant Dictator* was due to be published. I was still writing for the Italian press, and the door to magazines had been opened. Among them *Everybody's*, long since defunct, but, then, a very popular weekly illustrated magazine, its benign sports editor a former Army officer and boxing champion called Dudley Lister. 'You'll make a fortune one day,' he said. I mumbled something palliative about it being better to reach a decent standard. But at nineteen, I felt I could at least make a living.

Charlie Spencer was eventually discharged, and became the manager of a non-league club, Hastings. Alas, his TB was not conquered, and he did not have very long to live. Jim Gladwell went back to the bar; I met him now and then. Over thirty now, he lost all his hair, which seemed cruel to me. John Stevens I ran into once when we both had appointments with Dr Andrew Moreland in Harley Street. Each time I saw him, Moreland gave me a clean bill of health on my chest, but said nothing about my back. After all, Professor Rosenheim had spoken.

I continued to go out without an overcoat, and to walk great distances across London; often to the offices of the Ettrick Press, where Mr Finlayson's short legs still dangled from the table, and Harry continued his primary involvement with the Verdi Society. The Bastin book was going well. Solosy's, a newsagent on the corner of Charing Cross Road and Cranbourne Street – where my father and his younger brother, Gerry, had their surgery – had it on view in the rack and sold over a hundred copies. In the event, it sold a few thousand. Bastin, remembering, had by no means been forgotten, but, after all, his playing career was part of the past.

Tom Whittaker, Arsenal's manager since 1947, had written the foreword to the book. I went to see him at Highbury, for an article that I was writing. A heavily built northeasterner, still the avuncular figure he had always been, but under far more pressure, now, he sat behind his desk and told me he had never seen the book.

I was perturbed by this, and reported it to Mr Finlayson. 'I believe he brought some copies along to the ground,' Tom Whittaker had said. Mr Finlayson, untypically, was still more put out. He had, he said, supplied Bastin with early copies, precisely so that Whittaker should have them. He wrote sharply to Bastin and received a sharp letter in return, accusing me of fabrication. I wrote to Bastin to say that I in turn had accused him of nothing, but had merely reported what Tom Whittaker had said, which brought a more measured response. He realised I was the innocent party. Whittaker, he said, after the controversy caused by the book, had actually told someone, concerning the introduction, 'I wish I'd never written it.' 'In future,' Cliff wrote, 'watch your step at Highbury.'

It was my first intimation that Whittaker, so idolised for so long, might have feet of clay. As Harry Homer said, he needed – a Tom Whittaker.

I had a new venture now with the Ettrick Press; a *Footballers' Who's Who*. Mr Finlayson was enthusiastic; Harry was indifferent, or rather, absorbed elsewhere. My father generously, again, waived the return of his money, so that it might be invested in the new book. It entailed a huge amount of work, writing to every league club to chase up information, and resulted, finally, in a tiny, square book, with a head and shoulders photo of Jackie Milburn, 'Whor' Jackie, the talismanic Newcastle United centre forward – scorer of both goals in the 1951 Cup Final – on the cover.

The Ettrick Press was not doing quite as well as it had been. The successor to its bestseller, *Teatime Tips*, a little book called *With Ring and Grill*, was a disappointing anticlimax. Some interesting books continued to emerge, such as Fred Urquhart's short stories, 'The Last GI Bride Wore Tartan'. But publishing was no longer as easy a ride as it had been in the wartime and immediate post-war years, when books sold in their tens of thousands. A small publisher had to fight to survive.

Meanwhile, I continued to write for *Sport* magazine, whose offices now had moved from the dingy premises in Fleet Street to Stamford Street, EC4 to SE1. Reg Drury had joined the magazine as their assistant editor; he would for years to come be a motif in my life.

A quintessential cockney, with the wit and speed of response that went with the territory, Reg had grown up in Hackney, the son of a humble municipal worker. He was tall and very thin, the evident product of an impoverished childhood, but his energy was immense. He even still played football on a Sunday, something that made me laugh at him, little knowing that in years to come he would be captaining me, and inspiring Chelsea Casuals.

In Hackney, he had played for a Jewish Maccabi team, though he wasn't Jewish himself, and had picked up some of the patter. 'You were *gornisch* today, Reg,' one tactless supporter had told him, when he came off the field after a less successful game; *gornisch* being a corruption of the Yiddish words for 'nothing'. He might have been an amateur footballer of some renown. Playing at the age of sixteen in the public trial for Enfield FC, always a prominent club of its kind, he had scored a hat trick from centre forward for the reserves against the first team, and Enfield had offered him terms. But so had a local paper in Tottenham, who had given him the opportunity of covering the Spurs games. It was no contest for a realist such as Reg; he chose journalism, and continued to play on Sundays.

Outstandingly honest, remarkably well informed, greatly respected in the game, he wrote an absorbing lead article for *Sport* – or *Sport Express*, as it became – every week. His knowledge of English football, footballers and clubs was encyclopedic. My favourite memory of it concerned a match which Chelsea Casuals played on a mud heap at Chadwell Heath, against a team called Tavistock. We were very heavily beaten; it was the only time in its now forty-year history that Casuals had entered a competitive tournament: the *Jewish Chronicle* Invitation Trophy, Gentiles admitted.

After the rout, we changed in an adjacent Nissen hut. A centre half with massive thighs, one of several former and present professionals in their team, stood on a chair and said, 'I played league football.'

Reg, through his spectacles, transfixed him with a gimlet glare. 'What's your name, son?'

'Strain,' was the reply.

'Ah, yes,' said Reg, 'Watford and Millwall!'

'He was pleased, Brian, he was pleased,' he told me subsequently. 'It was like, one game in two seasons in the Third South with Millwall, a couple of games with Watford. I said, "Who are you with now, then?" He said, "Gravesend and Northfleet. We won seven–one, yesterday." Well, I knew that couldn't be the *first* team, because they'd gone down 2–0 at Bath.'

I lived in Oakwood Court, near Holland Park – still closed, then, to the public – with my parents, for the next eighteen months. It was a frustrating period. Medically, I was still part-convalescent. I had to keep early hours, keep out of smoke-filled rooms, the lurking fear being that TB could always strike again; though had I but known it, it was already busy in my back.

Having been out of London so much and for so long, I had only a few friends, notably Gordon Watson, with whom I would happily stay in Redhill, where his father practised as a GP and his mother kept a cool, detached eye on him, and another Charterhouse friend, Clive, a gifted pianist turning into an accountant. I began another novel, named, at my father's suggestion, *Heavy Waters*, an attempt at a political satire. I went to an infinity of theatre matinées, many of the plays commercial and ephemeral, though Jean Anouilh, then greatly in vogue, was better than that.

I badly wanted to write plays myself and had read a book from Mundesley's excellent library called, *So You're Writing A Play!* by Clayton Hamilton. The title was coy; the advice seemed good; but I couldn't get off the ground, quickly blocking on the single idea I had. Even in 1965, when I published *A Second Home*, a novel about a neurotic Jewish actress, and was approached by well-known directors, I was convinced I couldn't write plays. In 1981, I found, at last, I could, with a play called *A Visit to the Villa*, put on at Chichester and eventually broadcast, with John Gielgud in the lead, on BBC World Service. But it would be a very long haul.

My father was as encouraging as ever; I had read him chunks of *Heavy Waters* as he lay in the bath, each morning. In the event, George Greenfield devastated me by turning the book down. My world turned upside down. Was I a novelist at all? Was *The Reluctant Dictator* just a flash in the pan?

It came out early in 1952, and was totally ignored by all the 'quality' papers and the literary weeklies. Probably I had no right to expect anything else, but it was demoralising at the time.

In due course, reviews came in from the provinces, largely positive, while *Reynolds News*, a Sunday paper for which Reg Drury would eventually work and I would write literary profiles, said 'It is full of fun and worldly wisdom. He should go far.' Stephen Graham, the author of a celebrated book about Russia, sent me a handwritten note: 'Bravo! The Reluctant Dictator is great fun. You ought to get it filmed.' How the book got to him, I've no idea, but there were transient possibilities. Tommy Trinder, quickest of comedians, showed interest. So for a time did George Cole. And, when I went to work in Italy, the book apparently appealed to the director and novelist Mario Soldati. That was as far as it went.

Heavy Waters was turned down by several other publishers, before I decided to retire it, but the consolation was that it was generously received by Secker and Warburg, the publisher to whom I would most willingly have gone. When I sent the manuscript to them after Werner Laurie's rejection, it was, I felt, an impossibly long shot, but they published so many of the writers whom I most admired, such as George Orwell, Thomas Mann and Alberto Moravia.

David Farrer, their literary director, who in time would become my mentor, wrote me a very pleasant letter about the book, which helped to deaden the pain. With my next novel, I would be more successful.

Needless to say, I spent much of my time in Fleet Street, frequently with Stanley Halsey, of the *Sunday Pictorial*, to whom I became a kind of amanuensis. Stanley was a rare, slightly exotic, bird among the sports journalists of the time. Middle-aged, of ruddy countenance, and well spoken, he had been a naval officer in the war, and was said to have spent at least one term at Eton. He was gloriously vague, perpetually troubled and a notable drinker with a penchant for puns. William Thackeray was his favourite author. Sensitive and well read, he seemed strangely unfitted to his job, which he defined as being 'in pursuit of the paragraph. Whether Fred Fickleprick will go from Rochdale to Crewe Alexandra.' In a word, he dealt in transfer tales and football gossip, haunted by the rivalry of a saturnine colleague, Jack Peart, son of a former manager of Fulham.

Stanley had a well-known line of stock responses and familiar questions. 'How am I looking, old boy?' was one of them. If you asked him how he was, he would answer, 'Fit as a cello!' When a non-league club called Gorleston, from Norfolk, surprised several league clubs in the FA Cup, he wrote, 'Boxing managers have their ulcers, but soccer managers have their Gorlestons.'

He moved in an aura of conspiracy. Now and again he would ask me to telephone a manager or a player from whom he hoped to get a story. Often we would lunch at the bar of some Fleet Street pub, or sit in the Kardomah café, where once his eye was taken by a little woman, with hair that was prematurely grey: 'Ships that pass in the night.'

He was famous for his drinking binges. Once, in Vienna, he had left his passport in a bar when unable to pay, and there had been frantic activities before he could leave with the rest of the England football party. There had been a similar, still more hectic, adventure in Russia, after which it looked as if he might even be dismissed, only for his sports editor George Casey, a robust Londoner, to tell him at the end, 'All right, you can have your bloody job back!'

Did I fail him in Florence? I asked myself that at the time, but, in retrospect, it would have been hard to help him. The occasion was the lunch given by the Tuscan journalists at the Ristorante Doney in Via Tornabuoni, before the match at the Stadio Comunale between England and Italy.

Stanley arrived there pretty well plastered, speech notably slurred. 'What you want, old boy,' he told a patiently attentive Vittorio Finizio, 'is *Italian* players in *Italian* teams.'

When the lunch began, I was sitting on his right. Attentive waiters kept coming round and refilling his glass. You're his friend, I kept telling myself. Why don't you do something? But the wine kept coming; Stanley kept drinking, and he became less and less coherent. Eventually Clifford Webb, a big, brash, red-faced Bristolian, who wrote for the *Daily Herald*, shouted at him across the table, 'Halsey, you're drunk. Halsey, you're a disgrace to the English Football Association!'

'Now then, Webb,' said Stanley, as best he could.

After a little while, Harold Mayes, a thin, acerbic northerner, from the old *Empire News*, broke off a piece of bread and, almost meditatively, threw it at Halsey. Other journalists on that side of the table copied him, till Stanley became the subject of a small bombardment. Eventually, loyal Charlie Buchan got him on to the coach. He slept throughout the match in the hot sunshine, but it was a Sunday game, and his column had already appeared.

Some years later, he disappeared. The word went round that he had died in hospital. Many of us mourned. There was always something deeply endearing about him, a curious dichotomy between what he was and what he did. There was, I believe, even a memorial service for him, to which George Casey sent a wreath.

Years passed. Then a journalist who had left his car in the Scotland Yard car park was driving it out when he recognised, with a shock and a start, the car-park attendant. It was Stanley Halsey.

'And I spent all that money sending flowers for the bastard!' George Casey was reported to have said.

Strange indeed how things transpired for me. I had decided I must leave London and live on the Continent, taking to heart the words of EM Forster, that all young English novelists needed a spell in Europe. In London, I was blocked. Going frequently to read in Kensington Gardens – Holland Park was still closed; far, far off was the Thursday pick-up game I would initiate in the future – I avidly devoured Cyril Connolly's *Enemies of Promise*, and planned a future which might liberate me from frustration. It would be Italy, I had decided, rather than France. My two holidays there with my parents had endeared the country to me, and besides, I had my connections with *Corriere dello Sport* in Rome and with *Calcio Illustrato*, in Milan. But would it be Rome or Florence? I had been to both cities; both had fascinated me. But luck and Fate had it that in May 1952, for the first time ever, England would play against Italy in Florence.

I travelled, by train, across Europe, and stayed at the Pensione Bartolini, on the Lungarno Guicciardini, recommended to me by Professor Lawrence Lacey, a teacher with the British Council. The Bartolini was not, it would eventually turn out, the Pensione Bertolini of which Forster had written so fetchingly in *A Room with a View*. It was located on the top floor of an old palazzo. At night, a huge key would let you through the formidable front door, and then there was a multitude of stairs to climb. For a twenty-year-old former public school boy – we were far younger then than our later equivalents – the Bartolini was a revelation and a joy. It was full, at the time, of engaging young Americans, seeing out what remained of their GI Bill of Rights, which enabled them to live a kind of Shangri-La life abroad, a year for every year of their military service.

Thus, there was the New Yorker Frank McManus, a tough little man who had won medals in the infantry and become a radio broadcaster. 'You get up in the morning around ten,' he reflected, 'you go into the town for a coffee, you have lunch, a siesta, then around six o'clock you go down to the Excelsior Hotel for a cocktail; yes, you can get into a pretty civilised routine.'

But alas, those GI Bills would run out, plunging their holders into the cold climate of the Eisenhower years, when grey conformity was the norm. From New York, McManus wrote to me, two years later, 'I pound the sidewalks, unloving and unloved.' Carter, a journalist on the *Toledo Blade*, and Carl, who had worked in Germany in a motor pool, but was a humorous intellectual, lasted longer, even found themselves an apartment, up on the steep Costa San Giorgio, behind the pensione, but they, too, had to go back, in the end.

But these Americans were fascinating to me, an utter contrast with the stereotypes to which I had subscribed. This was a new world in which one need no longer be lonely or isolated. There was company each day in the big, bare dining room, redolent of past pasta, with its massive stove for winter, and its huge windows looking out over the Arno and the makeshift Ponte Santa Trinità: still a Bailey bridge then. Besides, there were the infinite glories of the city, with its palaces and alleys, its museums and its towers, its *campanili* and its statues. Simply to be there, to walk around there, seemed a joy.

How different things were, then! The Florentine men would walk two or three abreast, arm in arm, many of them wearing those ghastly, multi-striped, tight suits which are never seen today. People often spat in the street. There were no coins, so that the smaller denomination notes, some of them from the American occupation, grew dirtier by the day; one's wallet bulged with them.

I went to the Fiorentina offices in the Stadio Comunale, which looked up to the hill and villas of Fiesole, and tried to find my press pass. An elegant middle-aged man kindly drove me back to the city; none other than Mario Pizziolo, who had played right half for Italy, in Florence itself, in the 1934 World Cup.

The England team, and the journalists, were invited to a match of *calcio in costume* (football in livery), played as it traditionally was between two of the *quartieri*. Played, this time, not in the Piazza Santa Croce, where it would later resume, but in the picturesque little amphitheatre of the Boboli Gardens, behind the immense stone bulk of the Palazzo Pitti. Later, when I lived in an apartment in the Via Romana, near the palace itself, I used to go to the amphitheatre on sunny days and read there.

It has been claimed, especially in self-aggrandising Fascist times, that *calcio in costume* was the true begetter of Association Football, though in fact there was a huge hiatus before it was practised again, this century. It had supposedly been played when the Emperor Charles V was besieging the city in the sixteenth century. Though the ball used was round, the game had more to do with rugby than football. The goals, at either end, ran the breadth of the field. Almost any kind of tackling was legitimate. 'Is that what they're going to do to us?' asked one of the English players.

Among them were Tom Finney, that peerless outside right, who, in the words of one of his keenest admirers, Bill Shankly (who had played with him at Preston), 'had two people marking him at the kick in', Jack Froggatt, a left winger turned tough centre half, and the prolific centre forward, Nat Lofthouse. He it was who, in England's next game, would earn the soubriquet of 'The Lion of Vienna', for the memorable goal he would score against Austria in Vienna, running half the length of the field, defying bodily harm, to be felled at last only when he had scored the winner. Lofthouse was sitting right behind me in the Boboli, beside Jack Froggatt, whom I told the news that he would be marking Silvio Piola, recalled to the *azzurri* at the age of 39. 'You always get the old 'uns,' Lofthouse said.

Towards the end of the game, Froggatt, tired of being elbowed by the now static Piola, simply kicked him. The referee did not see it. The spectators did.

So, at a remove of thirteen years, the saga of Piola's games against England ended. In 1939, he had punched George Male – however inadvertently. In 1952, he had been kicked by Jack Froggatt; quite deliberately. It was his last match for Italy. The result was an undistinguished draw, in which the elegant, beautifully balanced, elusive Finney had rough treatment from the Italian left back, Manente, and complained he had scant protection from the referee. Ivan Broadis scored for England, Amadei for Italy.

Ivan was, in fact, Broadis's real name, though he was always known as Ivor. This came about because, when he first signed as an amateur for Spurs, his signature was almost illegible. His career was an unusual one. A Londoner, born on the Isle of Dogs, he became an RAF pilot in the war, and afterwards turned professional with little Carlisle United in the Third Division North, as player-manager.

There, his performances were so impressive that larger clubs pursued him, and he eventually transferred himself to Sunderland, forming a celebrated inside forward partnership with that maverick star Len Shackleton. Curiously, Shackleton himself had once been on amateur forms with a north London club, Arsenal. Foolishly indeed, they had let him go, only for him to become one of the most entertaining and skilful inside forwards of his day.

During the war, in the exiguous programme notes that he wrote on the back of Arsenal's team sheet, George Allison alluded to the fact that 'Shack', by then a Bevin Boy, working down the mines, was now turning out for Bradford Park Avenue, recalling 'when this then frail boy was playing in our Enfield nursery'.

I wrote to Shackleton requesting his autograph, and asking whether he was, in fact, still an Arsenal player. The reply on the postcard was short and pungent. 'I have no connection with Arsenal. My own club is Bradford.'

George Allison, it transpired, when 'Shack' published his controversial autobiography, *Clown Prince of Soccer*, had called him into his office to tell him that Arsenal were not keeping him; then, by way of somewhat crude consolation, he had shown him the new television set he had had installed. Far from being consoled or impressed, Shackleton was incensed; it was, he felt, a patronising gesture to the country bumpkin.

Surrounded by such genial Americans, and seduced by the beauty of the city, I had no doubt, now, that it was Florence, not Rome, that I would choose. I went home, deciding I would leave again for Italy soon after my 21st birthday. When I went, I told myself, I would stay there. I was fed up with life in London. I would continue to write novels but they would not, I told myself in my arrogance, be novels about expatriates, the kind that Aldous Huxley and the rest had written. I would penetrate Italian life, and write about Italians themselves. Fond illusion.

At home, I had begun another novel called *Henry Sows the Wind*, about a struggling gossip writer on a Sunday paper. *Footballers' Who's Who* had been well received, and my invitation, in the introduction, to readers to write to me with comments elicited a wave of interesting, constructive, largely appreciative, letters. But the grey little book wasn't easy to sell, and newsagents found it, in Mr Finlayson's words, 'too easily whippable'.

Occasionally, I tried to function as a sales representative, going, on one occasion, to a leading wholesaler in South London. In their huge warehouse, I was told by one of their managers, at machine-gun speed, 'Three things we look for. Colour-bulk-and-price-right.' It seemed to me we may have failed on all fronts.

So a week after my 21st birthday, which had passed in total anticlimax, I took the train from Victoria, where I was seen off by my mother and my Auntie Jenny; the boat across the Channel; and the train across Europe, stopping in Milan. On that train, as I brushed past an elderly Italian traveller, he kicked me. But, fortunately, he was no Froggatt.

3

O N THE WAY DOWN to Florence, I stopped briefly in Milan, and went to see the MB Dimt agency, which had been handling my articles for *Il Calcio Illustrato*. It was run by a Hungarian refugee and his dark and earnest daughter. She feared that the magazine was trying to depress the price of the articles and I, having met its editor in London the previous year, was afraid that it was true. He was not an easy man to withstand, especially for a nineteen-year-old journalist unused to overwhelming onslaught.

Leone Boccali was a short, plump, bespectacled, shaggy-haired Milanese, who shouted whether in normal converse, or on the radio, when he broadcast. I had met him first at Wembley in May 1951, when England played Argentina in a friendly. He regarded me from his seat in the upper row of the press-box and observed, not altogether amiably, '*Ah: jeune journaliste.*' My spoken Italian, then, was negligible and we had to converse in French. I saw something of him in the ensuing days, first when he and other Italian journalists were dining in a functional Italian restaurant in Bloomsbury. I could not follow most of what he said, but gathered, on mentioning Vittorio Finizio, that Finizio had picked up his umbrella.

Later, in a taxi on the way to a railway station, he assailed me over the fee for the articles, which the Dimt agency, to their credit, faithfully translated. He wanted to economise. At one point, in some despair and confusion, I found myself asking him if someone might translate them for nothing, provoking the scornful if logical reply, 'Who does anything for nothing?' Under subsequent pressure, I would reluctantly part with the Dimt agency, and Boccali had the pieces translated in his office. Uncouth, insensitive and humourless he may have been, but as I got to know him I realised he was also an honest, dedicated man, and an excellent editor. When he ultimately retired and the editorship passed into the hands of two bright, volatile Neapolitans in Rome, *Calcio Illustrato* was doomed.

Years after our first meeting, when I happened to be in Milan again, Boccali and his wife took me out to dinner. We must hurry, he said. *Lascia O Radoppia*, the Italian equivalent of the television quiz *Double Your Money*, was on that evening, and he had set the questions on football.

So, after we had dined, the three of us repaired to a rather gloomy café, and went behind a curtain to join a small audience ensconced before the television set. The show duly came on, compered by a brash, brisk, crew-cut interlocutor called, improbably, Mike Bongiorno. The first contestant was a large, lugubrious *professore* who was due to answer questions about hunting.

There was a substantial preamble. 'Professore,' asked Mike Bongiorno, 'is there any real difference between, say, hunting a lion and hunting a bird?'

'No,' answered the *professore*, heavily sententious, 'because for the real hunter no difference exists, whether you are hunting big game or something small.'

After this had gone on for some time, it came to the first question; clearly a very simple one. The *professore* stood silent. There was a pregnant hiatus. 'Professore,' said Bongiorno, and asked the question again. Still the *professore* remained silent, head bowed, and another dreadful silence followed. 'Professore,' said Bongiorno, at last. 'I'm going to ask you this question for the third and last time.' Again he asked it. Again the *professore* was silent, till at last, as though the words had been squeezed out of him, he replied, '*Non so.*' (I don't know.)

At this, I burst into irresistible laughter. No one else even smiled. Boccali and the rest looked at me as if I were mad.

Moving slowly along the Wembley press-box that afternoon when I first met Boccali I saw another, unmistakable figure. He was sturdy, short and old, with a turban of white hair. It could only be Vittorio Pozzo, the man who, as Italy's *commissario unico*, their mentor and manager, had won them the World Cup, in both 1934 and 1938. I introduced myself, was graciously received, and spent a glorious, memorable time with him, the day after the match.

We travelled across London, now by tube, now by single-decker bus, on our way to Hendon Hall, where the Argentine team had been staying – once a famous actor's house – while Pozzo talked about the past: the Ancient Mariner talking, but this time to a fascinated

Wedding Guest. He told me how, when he managed Italy, he had been referred to by a French journalist as 'the poor captain of a company of millionaires'. Perhaps, he said, that was his secret. So much for those who, in present times, have cast doubt on the potential of a manager who earned less than his players. 'Kind, but with a strong hand,' said Pozzo, as we sat on the tube and I scribbled notes. 'If I let them make mistakes, I lose my authority.'

The Argentines received him reverently. They had lost 2–1 to England after taking the lead and putting England's then unbeaten home record against foreign teams in the balance. Rugilo, their big goalkeeper, had flung himself about heroically, to earn the nickname 'The Lion of Wembley'. Pozzo and I were invited on to the coach that took them into town. I remember they had with them a young English interpreter, a genial figure in a brown hat. 'They're superstitious,' he told me, 'they like to know God's on their side.' Though on the previous afternoon, God had evidently been an Englishman.

There was so much more I wanted to ask Pozzo. About this so-called Battle of Highbury in 1934 for instance, when England had deployed no fewer than seven Arsenal men against Italy, who had recently become World Champions. Eddie Hapgood's book had described how an Italian broke his nose with an elbow, then laughed in his face at the official banquet: 'If I hadn't been a pretty even-tempered fellow, I'd have gone over the table at him.' Italy had been down to ten men for most of the game, and had reacted ferociously, going three behind, and ultimately losing only by 3–2. But Cliff Bastin, who played inside left that day, had told me, when we wrote the book, that he had played in much harder games. I wanted to know about Pozzo's early years, in England, before the First World War, but these were questions I would ask him later, in Turin.

It was a joy to come to Florence. In the Bartolini, I had a tiny room in a corner of the top floor, from which you could see a woman on a terrace call her cats, 'MOS-china! MOS-chi!' and look out over the brown-tiled roofs. There was a small four-legged *porcellino* (a four-legged stove) in the corner, but, whatever the weather, I never used it; I had been toughened by Mundesley. There was no running water in my room. One of the tiny, singing, hard-working maids would bring hot water in a jug each morning. They brought up Continental breakfast, too; lunch and dinner one ate in the big dining room.

Some of the Americans were still there; others had been obliged to go home. Transient young Americans would appear. There were two elderly English spinsters, teachers of English, who had been living in

Florence since before the war. Miss Clay was blonde and unpredictable: 'Not so bad, you know,' she would reply to those who asked how she was, the voice curiously singsong, the mouth slightly twisted as if in lingering despair. Once, surprisingly, she was visited by an elderly Italian admirer. 'Some old Fascist dug out of a gaol,' said a middle-aged American, cruelly. She bitterly disapproved of Carlo, a small, neat southerner in his forties, who was doted on by Jenni, the little, dark, vivacious *padrona* of the Bartolini. 'Do you know what she was doing? She was down on her knees, cleaning his shoes!'

'*Che lingua parla?*' (What language are you speaking?) Carlo would taunt me, when I tried to speak Italian, but some months later I would have the ultimate accolade: 'You've stolen our language!'

I spoke it, then, fluently but ungrammatically; I had never found the missing Hugo volume of grammar. But I had brought with me a *Teach Yourself Italian*, and, when I had been there some six months, would climb the splintery wooden stairs to the platform on top of the *pensione*, and study, alarmed by the mistakes I had been making.

I lived in two worlds. There was football, and there was the more intimate and personal one of my friends, most of whom cared nothing for football at all, not least because so many of them were American. There were poets and painters and scholars, some on the GI Bill, some on Fulbright scholarships – which would be so much harder to come by in the conformist, Eisenhower, years – and some on what we used to call 'fatherships'. We met at the *pensione*, in cafés and, when I could no longer face the Bartolini kitchen twice a day, in restaurants. My daily refuge was the British Council Reading Room, located in the exquisite, ochre-stone, Palazzo Antinori, under the eye of the snobbish, buck-toothed, Signora Salvadio. '*Scheiss freundlich*', Willi Mallmann called her. He was a big, dark, heavily built Austrian whom I had met, with the Parenti family – his in-laws – in Forte dei Marmi three years earlier, playing tennis. Willi, a substantial intellectual, didn't play tennis, but he swam. Shit-friendly, one might translate his German expression. He was, in fact, bilingual, his mother being a huge, imposingly regal, American lady from the formidable Otis (elevator) family, with a villa up in the hills of San Domenico. The reading room was warm and comfortable, full of deep-cushioned sofas and armchairs, newspapers, though they came somewhat late, and journals in abundance. There, with the help of the *New Statesman*, the *Observer*, the *Spectator* and the *Sunday Times*, one kept up, competitively, with what was happening in the literary world.

'Every time you look up, you see something beautiful,' said the young, blond Jonathan Ezekiel, living at the Bartolini, the son of a senior executive of the Food Agricultural Organisation in Rome, and who could disagree? There was Brunelleschi's Dome, on the cathedral; Giotto's tower, soaring beside it; and that other marvellous tower of the Palazzo Vecchio, in Piazza della Signoria, with its sublime loggia, and its marvellous array of statuary and fountains. Even sitting in the press seats, at the Stadio Comunale, watching Fiorentina, you could look up at the hillside of Fiesole, with its cypresses and villas. Cypresses, cypresses everywhere, looming in regiments over the city. It was shocking, late in the 1990s, to hear that diseases were attacking them. Cypresses, and vistas of the ghost-grey olives.

I still often went for walks. I would walk the long route to the stadium when I wanted to pick up my press pass from the friendly secretary. Fiorentina, then, were not the power they would quite soon become, but the team was taking shape. They had a passionate goalkeeper called Costagliola, who once punched the Napoli right back, Comaschi, in the face, when he rushed out of his goal. '*E' molto attaccato ai colori*,' a journalist tolerantly explained to me. (He has a strong feeling for the colours.)

That afternoon, I was given a strong flavour of the Florentines' acerbic humour; their renowned sarcasm did not endear them to the rest of Italy, but then, as I would find out, no region of Italy liked any other.

Pesaola, the Napoli left winger, a dark, squat man who played for Italy, though an Argentine, was injured, and ran along the touchline holding his back, in pain. '*Esagerato!*' shouted a Florentine, in the strong Tuscan accent I had come to know so well, famed for its aspirated Cs. '*Non è ferito: è vecchio!*' (Exaggerated! He isn't hurt: he's old.) And the chant went up around him: '*Vecchio! Vecchio!*' Later, a Neapolitan fan stood just below the stone semicircle of the *tribuna d'onore*, the directors' box, speaking in an equally strong Neapolitan accent, with its characteristic '*sh*' sound. '*Parla italiano, parla italiano!*' (Speak Italian!) came the tart response. I had, in fact, seen Fiorentina play Inter of Milan on my first visit that year in May, a game notable for the presence in Inter's team of the long-legged Dutch inside forward, Faas Wilkes, a lineal precursor of Johan Cruyff, who had played for the Rest of Europe team against Great Britain at Hampden Park in 1947.

Fiorentina had a blond Swedish inside forward called Dan Ekner, whom I had seen playing for Portsmouth as an amateur. I found out where he lived and called on him. He was a bachelor, living as a guest of a Florentine family in Oltrarno – across the river – not far from the Bartolini. He wasn't there when I called, but later he took me out to dinner. He was a charming young man who would flit like a troubadour from country to country. France was another port of call. The last time I met him, 25 years later, he was as genial as ever and wearing the official blazer of a professional American soccer club, which he had joined as an official.

I made frequent use of my little, pink-covered guidebook, which told me, 'Florentine housewives know well how to tickle the stomach and satisfy the palate.' I presented myself at the offices of *Il Mattino*, very much the secondary paper in Florence, overshadowed by the powerful *La Nazione*. *Il Mattino* was a heavily subsidised Christian Democrat newspaper, which would before long build expensive new offices in another part of the city, but fail to stay the course, just the same. Roberto Gamucci, the sports editor, a small, middle-aged man who could sometimes be seen trying to extract his expenses from an inflexible gorgon, commissioned me to write articles. He would still be working at matches in his seventies, cheerfully indomitable.

I began to hear about Mauro Franceschini, and was given his address. He was, I was told, a well-known youth coach, a deep admirer of English football. One evening, confusing two addresses, I found myself in Rifredi, a working-class area of Florence full of factories, ringing the bell of an upstairs apartment in a modest block, believing I was calling on a young secretary from the British Consulate. The door was opened, instead, by a thin, worn, patient, grey-haired lady, who put up with my confusion and my inadequate Italian, till I realised that somehow I had come to the wrong place. In due course, I realised to whom the flat belonged; and met Mauro.

He was a blond, deep-chested, muscular Pisan, somewhere in his thirties, with that Pisan accent which is still more Tuscan than the Florentines'. His voice was stentorian. He was a force of Nature, downright, dogmatic and bombastic. He coached young, aspirant footballers, often ones he spotted in the streets, on a little pitch situated among the factories in Rifredi. Sometimes he deployed them as a team. 'I beat them!' he would cry. 'I club them! You have no idea!' His English was quite fluent, but eccentric. He had learnt it, he told me, from an English tutor, late in the war. 'I know English poetry,' he once told me, and proclaimed:

Who goes there? A Grenadier!
What you want? A glass of beer!

Where is your money?
I have forgotten!
Get away, drunken sotten!

The elderly lady who had answered the door that evening, I discovered, was his maiden aunt, his father's sister: a sad, sweet, downtrodden woman who made no demands on life. His father was a Nenni Socialist – Nenni's party, then, being closely allied to the Communists. He studiously read the party's paper, *Avanti!*, every day. In a Tuscan accent still thicker than Mauro's, he would greet me, '*E allora! Allora! Siamo tutti d'accordo! Tutti hontro (contro) gli americani!*' (Well then, we are all agreed! We're all against the Americans!) Then, 'Write something! Write something about the Americans! *Sono io per Baffoni!*' (I'm for Big Moustaches!) Meaning Stalin.

In Florence, as we have seen, I was coming into close contact with the kind of Americans I had never known existed, and found most of them greatly sympathetic, though a certain residue of xenophobia remained. Mauro would take me round and about with him. Once, near his home, we met a young Florentine who, to my amazement, began quoting to me, verbatim, articles I had written for *Calcio Illustrato*. I had had no idea of the way sports journalists could be followed, even venerated, in Italy; certainly it had no equivalent in England, least of all for somebody as young as I. But the articles in Boccali's magazine and in *Corriere dello Sport*, I discovered with delight and surprise, had found me an audience. 'Come with me,' Mauro would say. '*Mi da lustro.*' (You give me prestige.)

So I would go with him to watch games on the periphery of Florence, where a handful of knowing Florentines, friends and acquaintances of Mauro, would be watching, too. 'How old are you?' one of them asked me one day, as we stood on the touchline. I prided myself then on seeming older than my years, but there was no bluffing an Italian. 'Twenty-one? Yes, I thought so.'

Mauro roamed Florence on his white bicycle. Sometimes you would meet him carrying a clock; a peripheral job, to make ends meet. He and his family were greatly hospitable. When invited for dinner, I would usually arrive before he did, press the bell, and there would be a concerted yapping by their two tiny dogs. When Mauro arrived, they would reach a crescendo. The bell downstairs would ring. Yap, yap, yap! His aunt or father would press the button to open the door, and one would hear, counterpointed by the barking of the dogs, the tick-tick-tick of his bicycle wheel, as he ascended the stairs. 'Oh-my-dear. I had forgotten!'

Sometimes I found myself in his tiny, spartan room. Beside the bed, on a narrow shelf, was a small pile of little magazines, purveying advice about sex. Mauro told me that he encouraged his pupils to lead celibate lives, promising them that on occasion, 'I bring you to fuck!' Once he said we must go out with some girls, 'Clean girls', though we never did.

Often he talked of English football and its salient virtues. He was especially proud of having made the acquaintance, in Florence, the previous May, of Walter Winterbottom, manager of England's football team who, surviving any and every set-back, remained in office for sixteen years. There was no sign, then, of Mauro's future prosperity: the car that replaced the bicycle and the seaside villa that replaced the little flat; success that would bring its own, awful nemesis.

I was, to Mauro, it seemed to me, the emblem and the beneficiary of English soccer. This was the way to play. He did not even cease to believe the following year, when the Hungarians came to Wembley in November and smashed England's unbeaten record to atoms. Like his father, he was a man of the Left. He despised Giorgio La Pira, the extraordinary little Sicilian who became Mayor of Florence, constantly organised international congresses for peace, and preferred to live in a monk's cell. 'E' un frate! Un frate!' (He's a friar!)

Nor had Mauro any time for Fascists. Beppe Pegalotti, the football correspondent of La Nazione, a lean man with a sour smile, who had been a prisoner of war in India, was a particular object of scorn. 'Pegalotti! Stupid bastard, stupid bastard. He wrote, "Next week we'll be in Alexandria!" That week they take him prisoner. He don't come back for seven years.'

What would Pat Highsmith have made of Mauro, or Mauro of Pat? She turned up one day in the Bartolini and took a room looking out on the Arno, the kind I could not afford. She carried with her a letter from Alfred Hitchcock, telling her agent he intended to make his next picture from her novel, Strangers on a Train. I had gone with my Uncle Gerry, my father's partner, to see the film in the West End, and was intrigued. The idea was ingenious. Two strangers meet on a train and agree to swop murders. A Texan and a talented artist as well as a writer, Pat had long auburn hair and an impressively dry sense of humour. Her room was quickly invaded by Bernie, a thickly moustached American painter who had fought in Burma. He erupted, bearing gifts. 'Women like that kind of confidence in a man,' said Pat, but before long she moved out of the *pensione* complaining, with some reason, of 'smelly johns'. We stayed in touch for years; years during which she became a kind of cult in England, and had novels filmed in France. It was in Switzerland, though, that she eventually died.

'Bernie's killed people,' Neil would say, with unease. Neil too was a painter, though he didn't live at the Bartolini. He was tall, dark-haired and flamboyantly handsome, and spoke – a great deal – in a strong Brooklyn accent. One day he went to Venice to see if he could enlist the patronage of the celebrated and immensely rich Peggy Guggenheim.

'She looked at me, and she said, "You don't look real. You're like something from another world."

'I said, "Why don't you make one for me?"

'She said, "I don't think that's a very clever thing to say." I said, "I didn't think your remark was too intelligent."

'Then she takes me into another room and shows me this picture she's just bought. And here's this horse, with a colossal erection. I said to her, "What's this horse going to do? Piss on Venice?" '

I finished writing *Henry Sows the Wind* and sent it to David Farrer, at Secker. There was plenty of freelance work to do, and I was busy on a new version of my *Footballers' Who's Who*, to be serialised in a magazine called *Charles Buchan's Football Monthly*. It had offices in The Strand where Charlie and his partner, John Thompson, formerly the football correspondent of the *Daily Mirror*, promised me it would reappear the following year as a book. I should have got it in writing. In the words of Arthur Miller's Willy Loman, 'There were promises made across this desk.' But they were not kept. When in the summer I returned to London, John Thompson shook his head sadly and said they could not print the book. I was still very young, and I accepted it. In retrospect, it seems shabby behaviour hardly worthy of such an icon of the game as Charlie.

Wandering around Florence, I usually wore a comfortable, soft, sports jacket light brown in colour, made by Uncle Wolf. He was my mother's uncle, the husband of her Aunt Frances, a rotund little woman renowned in her community as a fixer; of matrimony, meetings and deals. 'I could do something for you, Marilyn,' she once said to my rebellious sister, 'but you'd have to change!'

Uncle Wolf was known in his family as a failed tailor whom Auntie Frances kept afloat; and in comfort, in their stifling flat in Maida Vale. One Saturday evening, on the way back from a football match, my father and I stopped by for tea. I asked, rather insistently, if we could listen to the radio for football news. Uncle Wolf's voice rose above the biscuits: 'There isn't a living in that.'

Close to Christmas, I heard from Secker and Warburg. They liked the book! Revisions were required, but they liked it. I was overjoyed and invited three Americans I did not like, from the *pensione*, for cocktails at the Excelsior Hotel, just off the Arno. David Farrer wrote that he could hear Henry, the protagonist, sniffing all the way through the book. I worked on the revisions. Some time later, in the spring, the manuscript came back to me; it still wasn't right. David Farrer suggested I try Peter Davies, 'a publisher of quality, because you are going to be a writer of quality'. But I didn't want to go to Peter Davies; I had set my heart on Secker. That day, I sat in the sunshine at a table in the broad Piazza della Repubblica – hacked out of the historic centre, whatever the words on its huge arch might boastfully say – and talked to Tony about it.

Tony was an English friend, a Cantab., who taught at the British Institute. The tales he told showed the abyss between Italian and English expectations. Girls he had caught cheating in exams for instance, whom he had thrown out of the class with a cry of '*Signorina!*' Their fathers would then come pleading for them: 'I hid British prisoners in the war.' The abyss was huge. I already knew by then that, much though I loved to live in Florence, I could never stay in Italy, as I had believed. Sooner or later, I would go home. Already I was passing through the second stage of the expatriate's reaction to Italy, which went from enchantment to disillusion to a *modus vivendi*. Italy supplied so much of what England lacked: colour, light, beauty, spontaneity. And it lacked so much of what one was accustomed to, of what one took for granted and relied on. Here, the house was so often built on sand, and on connections.

'The Italians,' said David, an American composer, 'spend so much time blowing the whistle, they can never get up enough steam to make the train go.' David, who had followed his eminent Italian teacher to the Val d'Aosta, lived a while in Rome, then moved to Florence. He came from a patrician American family on whose grounds the University of Princeton had been built, had a private income that might be seen as the salvation or the ruination of him, wrote lapidary English, and spoke superbly idiomatic Italian though, as he admitted himself, with an accent that was still American.

I had met him on Christmas Eve, 1952, at a table near the back wall of the front room in Camillo's trattoria, just across from the Ponte Santa Trinità. He had offered me a *carciofo* from his dish, and I had accepted it. He and I and the little Roman journalist who was with us – who later wrote scurrilously of us both – had repaired to his apartment across the Arno, and listened to harpsichord music played by Wanda Landowska.

By then, I had completely given up eating anything but breakfast in the Bartolini, which stood close to Camillo's. In that period, any number of expatriates gathered there, many of them American, most of them unusual. There was Peter, a Hungarian, a Protestant – which was also unusual – who wore a small crown on his shirt, spoke in a curiously high voice, was a master of many languages, and had an exotic, plump mother who looked as if she had come straight out of an operetta by Franz Lehar. She had left his father in Budapest and married a devoted Italian businessman called Mariani, for whom Peter now worked.

Aaron had turned up one cold January day in the *pensione*; his voice had boomed across the room when I entered it for lunch. To my delight, he agreed to go for a walk with me. Most other denizens of the *pensione* went no more than once; I was still striding at my Mundesley pace, but Aaron, lean and cerebral, walked still faster than I.

That afternoon, we went up the Costa San Giorgio, tried without success to get off the cobbled roads, eventually turned into someone's property, sat on a stone wall, and were invited in for tea by an American woman who had married an Italian, and who told us that she sometimes found it hard to relate to her own children. Aaron was the New York intellectual *par excellence*, though he came originally from Utica in New York State. 'If they ever wanted to give the United States an enema,' said a Fulbright scholar who arrived that summer at the *pensione*, 'that's where they'd put the tube.'

Aaron was a devout Freudian, a heavy smoker, and had, in David's words, eyes like 'two angry assholes, staring out of a snowbank'. For his part, Aaron thought David's diligently composed work to be 'film music'. He was sexually voracious, something of a shock to a young and still romantic former public school boy: 'When you aren't working, you ought to be screwing.' At the end of each dinner at Camillo's, usually served by the massive young Bruno, a part-time boxer, we would all, for some strange reason, sing 'I've Got a Lovely Bunch of Coconuts'. Aaron was particularly delighted to hear Peter grapple with the words 'There stands me wife, the idol of my life'. We never talked about football. Only Peter, as a Hungarian, knew anything about it; and Hungary's time was coming. Their extraordinary team, kept under Iron Curtain wraps for so long, had recently won the Olympic football title, in Helsinki. The names of

Puskas and Kocsis were already in vogue; later, when Peter's Italian wife, whom he had been so reluctant to marry, presented him with twins, these were the names I chose as nicknames for them.

Famous teams came to Florence and were encouragingly available. Not for them, then, the so-called *ritiri* at some spot far out of town. Juventus, of Turin, for example, arrived in Florence not long after I had arrived myself, and stayed, as teams did, at the Grand Hotel, opposite the Excelsior, in Piazza Ognissanti. I went to visit them; they had no fewer than three Danish internationals: John Hansen, Karl Aage Hansen and Carl Praest, the outside left who had made the only goal for Gunnar Nordahl of Sweden when Britain beat the Rest of Europe. Karl Hansen had played as an amateur for Huddersfield Town.

Speaking to them in the foyer of the Grand Hotel, I was given an odd insight into the ways of the Italian male. John Hansen, a tall, lean figure, clever on the ground, formidable in the air, an inside left of high renown, was sitting in an armchair when a middle-aged autograph hunter approached him and knelt down by John's chair to proffer his album. At that moment, a photographer arrived to take a picture of John. As he pointed his camera, the man whipped round to stare it straight in the lens.

The Juventus manager at that time was Gyorgy Sarosi, a pre-war footballer of great versatility and fame; he had played for Hungary in two World Cups, and had been their centre forward in the 1938 World Cup Final in Paris, where he had scored a goal. He had also been just as effective as a centre half, had played numerous other sports besides, and had a Ph.D. into the bargain. It was he, indeed, who, when the team's leader said in 1938 that he would walk back to Budapest were Hungary to lose a certain game, replied, '*Scripta manet, verba volant*,' the Latin meaning, roughly, 'words fly away, writing remains'. The official was obliged to sign a document; but in the event, Hungary won.

Walking along the Arno, John Hansen complained of how hard the Juventus training had been under the English manager Jesse Carver who had won them the Championship in his first season there, a couple of years before. 'My face was like this,' said John, indicating with his fingers his sunken cheeks.

In that Juventus team, too, was the *jeune premier* of Italian football, the blond and blue-eyed Giampiero Boniperti, who would captain club and country, become the Juventus President, and play a salient part, years afterwards, in the vexed affair of Lobo, Solti and the club's attempt to buy referees. Then, he was a genially boyish figure. I had seen him play dashingly at outside right against England in the Tottenham fog, in November 1949.

The game occurred only months after the appalling tragedy of Superga, when a team returning from Lisbon crashed into the wall of a church above Turin wiping out Torino, the champions of Italy for the previous four seasons, and with them almost the whole of the Italian international side. That Italy would so soon be able to field a team that embarrassed England for much of the match, and would surely have won had it not been for the inspired goalkeeping of Wolves' Bert Williams, was a tremendous testimony to their resources. When England eventually broke the deadlock, late in the match, it was largely because the fog and gloom – no floodlights then – deceived Giuseppe Moro, the keeper of whom Finizio spoke, into letting a lob by Billy Wright pass over his head.

Back, though, to that sad and sunny morning in Piazza della Repubblica. Tony was a Catholic convert whose ambition, at the time, was to go into a monastery, though he eventually went into a Catholic bookshop, and became a successful publisher. He had, somewhat surprisingly, done his military service in the Palestine police, carrying a revolver and arresting illegal immigrants. He was typically sympathetic to my misery.

Then a tall, beefy, loud American loomed over our table, someone Tony seemed to know, and began to talk, unsolicited, about women. 'Florentine women are bad women for men,' he assured us, then told of his seduction technique. 'Brandy and benedictine. Brandy and benedictine. Give 'em a glass of that, and they're really ready to roll.' Who could contradict him? Oh, God, wouldn't he go? Eventually, he did, and I was left with Tony, and my gloom.

I wrote, later, to David Farrer, telling him I had no desire to go to Peter Davies as I had set my heart on Secker and wanted another chance to revise the novel. He, in due course, agreed, and told me he would be coming to Rome in May. It fitted perfectly; that was the time the Olympic Stadium was due at last to open, near the Tiber, with Italy playing host to Hungary's renowned team.

Aaron left Florence to continue his European wandering. In the room he had opposite my own on the top floor of the Bartolini, he packed, while Peter and I helped him. Show us one of your poems, we begged him. We had never seen one. At length he was prevailed on to give us a typed sheet of yellow paper. We looked and looked at it in vain.

'Aaron, what does it mean?'

He was displeased. 'Ur, I don't see what's so complicated.'

'But what's it *about*?'

'Ur, all of my friends can understand it.'

'Aaron, what does it *mean*?'

'Well . . . It's about me, sitting by the fire; and listening to birds shitting down the chimney.'

From Paris he sent us a postcard of Le Sacré, that famous painting with three women, one touching another's naked breast, the third impassively sewing, and ignoring them. His message was full of allusions; one to a woman shopkeeper Peter had fancied hopelessly, on the Ponte Vecchio. 'But she is married and she has an official lover. Also another lover.'

'The woman on the right,' Aaron wrote, 'is saying, "Tesoro [My treasure]," to which the woman on the left is replying, "Bo! [a characteristic Florentine ejaculation]." The official lover is knitting in the background. The sun never sets on Saint Germain de Près. It just hides its face in shame.'

Later, when he was back in the States and Peter was working in Milan, he wrote from New York on his familiar yellow paper: 'I have bought a map of the city with principal monuments, which are, of course, the employment exchanges. I sit there, massaging the inside of my left thigh with my right forefinger, not too aggressively, mind you, and when they ask me what my principal interests are, I look down at the inscrutable obelisk in my lap and know, as one crucified, that my passions have betrayed me.'

British managers, then, were still in vogue in Italy, and were largely recommended by the Football Association coaching department; few of them were well known in England. One, Leslie Lievesley, described admiringly by Vittorio Pozzo to me as 'a clean man', had perished in the Superga disaster. Jesse Carver, who would eventually manage half a dozen major Italian clubs, was back in Turin, but with much-diminished Torino. Ted Crawford, having had charge of Bologna and Livorno, was still living in the Tuscan port, where I went to visit him.

He was a tall, gaunt, forthright Yorkshireman, born in what was then the fishing village of Filey. As a centre forward, or inside left, he had played for Halifax, Liverpool and Clapton Orient where, it transpired, he operated for six years with a fractured ankle. He was bitterly disenchanted by his experiences in Italy, which he recounted as we walked along the sea front, while he pushed his little son Teddy in a pram.

'They told me they'd give me a nice house. Nice house! Shit house!' Another old-school, pre-war, professional, though he had played through the war and once kicked Eddie Hapgood – guilty of making him look foolish – he was a glorious mine of anecdote and reminiscence. Both teams he managed had been relegated, but through no fault of his own. Bologna had been in deep trouble when he took them over, and he had almost saved them from departing the Championship division, Serie A. Livorno had been struggling to keep their place in Serie B, and would almost surely have done so were it not for a shocking story of attempted corruption that returned to plague the inventor.

At Bologna, Crawford had been embroiled with the club president, the notoriously wily Dall'Ara, after whom its stadium is now named. When things were going badly wrong, Dall'Ara told him, 'The public are blaming *you*; you could be in danger,' to which Crawford sturdily replied, 'No, it's *you* they'll blame. They know that you're responsible.'

He spoke with wry amusement of an end of season game against the Tuscan team, Lucchese. Gino Capello, a tall, lanky inside left with grey-flecked hair, exceptional skill, Italian international caps and a dire reputation for finagling, approached Crawford and suggested that the game be drawn: 'We need a point, Lucchese need a point.' Crawford would have nothing to do with it. In the dressing-room before the game, he talked to his two Danish wing halves, Pilmark and Jensen, and to some of the younger players, urging them to take the game seriously. Matteoli, the outside left, took him at his word and scored the opening goal, whereupon Capello and other players turned on him in fury, demanding to know why he had done that.

For the rest of the game, said Crawford, he had sat roaring with laughter on the bench, watching the deliberately clumsy antics of his defenders, as they tried to miss the ball and give away the equaliser. They finally succeeded.

At Livorno, things went even worse. The team's relegation depended on the final game, and the word went round that the opposition had been bribed. The club secretary had put the fix in. In the dressing-room beforehand, Crawford harangued his players: 'You think this game has been fixed. I'm telling you it hasn't been fixed.' But just then the secretary entered the room and went round the players, whispering. 'Yes, mister, yes, yes, mister,' they told Crawford, patronisingly. In Italy, a tribute to the early British coaches, managers are still known as Mister.

So the teams went out on the field; and Livorno lost. It turned out that the secretary had divided the bribery money with the manager of the other team. Crawford was sacked, and lingered on, in Livorno waiting for his money.

He told me many other stories. One concerned the match on Christmas morning, away to Bournemouth, where the whole Clapton Orient team turned up drunk on Waterloo Station. The manager was there to meet them with a barrel of beer: 'Hallo, boys!' Each time in the game that Crawford went up for a header, he saw two footballs. At one point he collapsed, and the referee rushed up to him, alarmed, while a knowing fan shouted, 'There's another of them drunk.' Orient drew.

There was a time when a devoted fan gave parties for the players. There were drinks and girls; unlimited hospitality. It went on for weeks till one day the fellow was arrested. He turned out to be a humble council employee who had been embezzling money.

Arthur Rigby played for Orient at that time. He was a former Blackburn Rovers and England forward who had come down in the world. When he got drunk, which happened often, he would see the ghost of the famous Yorkshire witch, Mother Shipton: 'There's bloody Mother Shipton in the corner!' Smoking was discouraged by the management, but Rigby was defiant. 'Smoked when I was playing for England, I'll smoke at the bloody Orient.' One Saturday, when Orient were playing at home, kickoff was approaching and still Rigby wasn't there.

At last, he turned up; very drunk. The other players hustled him into the shower and drenched him. The referee looked into the dressing-room. 'Everything all right?'

'Just Rigby, Sir.'

'What, is he drunk again?'

Eventually, Ted and the other players got Rigby on to the pitch, where Crawford told him, 'Go out on the left wing, Arthur. I'll keep the ball away from you.' This he successfully did, till, late in the game, he had no alternative but to push the ball out left to Rigby who promptly banged it into the net. He went on to score twice more.

I confess to having used Ted's anecdotes as the basis for future short stories. He had already coached in Sweden, at Degerfors, and our paths would later cross again, in Athens; but in England he would be a prophet without honour, who would spend his last working years as a disillusioned storeman.

That season I also met, for the first time, Jesse Carver and Gigi Peronace. Carver brought his Torino team to Florence to play Fiorentina. They did not stay in the Grand Hotel, but in a smaller, more humble one, not far from the railway station. We sat and spoke in its narrow foyer. Carver was then in early middle age, a compact, rubicund man who had clearly taken pains to lose his Liverpool accent, which might now be described as semi-genteel. He often punctuated his statements with the words 'you know', smiled quite a lot, and once, to emphasise a point, poked his forefinger in my ear.

Though only of average height, he had played as a centre half for Newcastle and Blackburn, had spent the war as a policeman, and previously had coached the Dutch national team. He was, as I would discover when I came to know him better in Rome, a closed and complex man, but there was no doubt about his abilities as a coach. His appalling Italian – '*Lui parlare me lo stesso*,' he would say, which means literally 'he to speak me the same' – was no barrier to his rapport with Italian players. They admired him and responded to him eagerly.

Having won the Championship in his first Italian season, he lost his job at Juventus in what might be called 'conventional circumstances'. A journalist from the pink sports daily, *La Gazzetta dello Sport*, came to interview him and, in the course of the conversation, Carver criticised the club's directors. The journalist, Emilio Volante, put this in the paper, and Carver was dismissed.

Some weeks later, when I was in Rome and visiting the Juventus players in their hotel before a match, Karl Aage Hansen, the Danish inside right, trenchantly observed, 'Juventus have thirty directors, and they want all the players to be gentlemen. The only trouble is, they are not gentlemen themselves.'

With a smile, Carver remarked that Gigi Peronace, who was sitting beside him, had suffered, too. He, too, had lost his job. On this occasion, Gigi was quite subdued. It would have been hard, then, to predict his flamboyant future, the snakes and ladders of his turbulent career. He was a short, plump Calabrian who spoke fluent English, of an explosive kind. During the war, he had organised games in his native town for British troops; despite his stature, he had been a goalkeeper. The war over, he went north to Turin to study engineering, but took the opportunity to become interpreter to the Scottish manager of Juventus, William Chalmers. When Carver became the club's manager, Peronace continued to interpret, but his ambitions went far beyond that.

In May, I went down to Rome to meet David Farrer of Secker, and to watch the Italy versus Hungary match at the Olympic Stadium. David was staying with an old friend, Harry Morris, a foreign office diplomat attached to the British Embassy in Rome. Both were, in the

parlance of the times, confirmed bachelors. David smoked a great deal, was given to shapeless brown hats, and spoke, often caustically, in a curious, public school twang, which tempted imitation. Like Harry's his hair was grey. During the war, he had worked as secretary to the formidable Lord Beaverbrook, and eventually wrote a rather disappointing book about it, called *G for God the Father*. He was given to pungent and dismissive statements. Alberto Moravia, the popular Italian novelist whom Secker profitably published, was a bitter man 'because he's crippled, and he has a wife (Elsa Morante) who's a much better novelist than he is. I don't know which is his best novel, but I'm sure *The Woman of Rome* (a book about a prostitute which had sold very well) is his worst.'

Harry, who was rumoured to have ties with MI6, was a tall, slim, urbane man, the most amiable of hosts, though capable of tart observation. 'The Italian male is spoilt. He's spoilt by his mother; he's spoilt by his sisters; he's spoilt by his wife; he's spoilt by his mistresses; and if there's something he wants and he can't get it, he sits down and he cries, whether he's six or whether he's sixty.'

David was largely positive about my revisions to *Henry Sows the Wind*. It seemed that I might be with Secker after all.

The Olympic Stadium, now at last to be inaugurated, was essentially the creation of Benito Mussolini; its approaches, just across the river, had all the bombastic self-assertion of Fascism. Grandiose and bloated statuary stood around the Foro Italico, and, up the Olympic way, there were huge blocks of marble and slogans carved into the paving. DUCE, DUCE, DUCE! MOLTI NEMICI, MOLTO ONORE! (Many enemies, much honour.) The stadium itself, however, was a delight, its sweeping terraces open to the skies, and no ill-considered grandstand roofs, then, to block the view of Monte Mario, with its regiment of inclining trees.

To play Hungary, the Italians, in some turmoil at that time, had decided to pick what was termed *una squadra del cuore* (a team of the heart), largely made up by players of the two Roman clubs, Roma and Lazio. It found life hard against the Hungarians, but then, so would almost any team of the time. Playing in white, Hungary were simply irresistible. Their technique was refined, their movement inspired, their tactics devastating. Nandor Hidegkuti, who would score in the first ninety seconds against England the following November and go on to a hat trick, was a new kind of centre forward, dropping deep behind the front line, making bullets for the strikers to fire, but always ready to strike, himself. He did, in fact, score the first Hungarian goal shortly before half-time, but was replaced in the second half by Palotas. Ferenc Puskas then scored twice more.

Puskas and Kocsis were the dynamic spearhead, players of contrasting style and physique, but a marvellously complementary pair. Puskas's nickname, 'The Galloping Major' – a reference to his putative Army rank – was hardly descriptive, though shift he certainly and surprisingly could, when the need arose. He would show as much, as late as May 1962, when he ran half the length of the field to score in the European Cup Final for Real Madrid against Benfica. On this occasion, his goals came from less protracted solos. Stockily built, even tubby – his stomach would assume vast proportions after he retired – Puskas had a left foot that was astonishing in its power, and in its dexterity. 'With a left foot like that,' Danny Blanchflower, the captain of Spurs and Northern Ireland, once remarked to me, 'you don't need a right foot!' Puskas's right foot, indeed, was the merest adjunct, suggesting that a great player, against all orthodoxy, had no need to be two-footed.

Puskas was an imperious figure: the dominant player in his side. Indeed, it might be argued that this very dominance subverted Hungary's bid to win the World Cup the following year, when Puskas insisted on playing in the Final though he wasn't fully fit. He was, though, wily enough to know when discretion was the better part, if not of valour, then of hegemony. When, eventually, he joined Real Madrid, he realised he had met his match in the authoritarian Di Stefano, the Argentine centre forward who inspired Real to victory in the first five European Cup Finals. Di Stefano brooked no rival on the podium, as such stars as Didì of Brazil and Simonsson of Sweden had found out.

The word was that, in the last match of his first season in Spain, Puskas could have scored the goal that would have made him top scorer, but diplomatically passed the ball to Di Stefano, who thus led the goalscorers, in his stead.

On that sunny day in Rome, Puskas largely called the tune, and Sandor Kocsis strongly supported him. Nicknamed 'Golden Head' for his remarkable power in the air, Kocsis was slighter than Puskas, and not very tall, yet his jumping was extraordinary and the force of his headers formidable. He was equally good on the ground, controlling the ball with ease and frequently scoring with his right foot. Italy lost 3–0, but they emphatically did not disgrace themselves. The subsequent lamentations seemed quite excessive to me at the time, and they, and the defeat, were put into sharp perspective in November, when the Hungarians destroyed England's unbeaten record against foreign teams, at Wembley.

This, however, was the tense time of the 1953 elections in which the ruling Christian Democrats were turning every trick in order to win. Fearful that they would not achieve an absolute majority, they brought in what the opposition called *La Legge Truffa* (the swindling law), whereby any party that obtained even the slightest advantage over the rest would automatically gain a huge majority in Parliament. There were brawls in the Chamber of Deputies at Montecitorio.

It was in these circumstances that the 3–0 defeat by Hungary engendered the so-called Andreotti Veto. Even then, that sinister politician, who would be accused in the 1990s of conspiracy with the Mafia and involvement with murder, was a powerful Christian Democrat figure. Then Minister of the Interior, he reacted to Italy's perfectly honourable defeat by placing a ban on the import of foreign players, as if they had been in any way responsible for what had happened. What team on earth could have countered the wiles of Hidegkuti, the incursions of Puskas and Kocsis, the driving sallies from the right of midfield by Josef Bozsik a member, for what it was worth, of the Hungarian Parliament?

It was about this time that another Hungarian, Peter, found himself on business near Naples, where Achille Lauro was all but king. A multimillionaire shipowner, he was not only Mayor of Naples and prime mover of the now defunct Monarchist Party, he even had, on festive occasions, packets of pasta delivered to the grateful citizenry. Needless to say, he was President and the grand patron of Napoli Football Club.

In a little town near the city, Peter chanced to go into a restaurant for lunch. 'Suddenly, outside, arrives this huge car. And out of this car gets Lauro, with two magnificent whores! They come into the restaurant and sit down at a table. This stupid young man sees them, and he goes to a telephone, and he starts making calls: "*C'è Lauro, c'è Lauro!*" (Lauro's here!) And after a while people start arriving. Women come up to Lauro and they kiss his hand: "*Onorevole; onorevole!*" And Lauro sits there with these two magnificent whores. And after a time, they get up, they leave, and go back into the car.'

Almost all the major politicians came to speak in Florence, most of them from the famous *loggia* in Piazza della Signoria. Alcide De Gasperi, the Christian Democrat Presidente del Consiglio, or Prime Minister, who had seen out the war as a librarian in the Vatican, spoke simply and modestly, and for the first time made public secrets about, as I recall, American bases. Saragat, the leader of the Social Democrats, future President of the Republic, spoke in a cinema; he was a large, grey-haired man with an impressive delivery. 'Because here in Italy we have a scandal,' he boomed. 'It's where the rich don't pay what they ought to pay.' Clamorous applause; but the rich went on happily evading taxes.

Though eating at Camillo's in the evening, I now lunched each day in Piazza del Carmine, just off the working-class zone of Borgo San Frediano. There, you might well meet a *barista* (a bar owner), as I did, who would tell you that Fiorentina's play was not 'aesthetically pleasing'. Over the square loomed the massive, rough-hewn bulk of the church of Santa Maria del Carmine, inside which, in one of its chapels, could be found the sublime, innovative frescoes of Masaccio. Irreverent young Florentines sometimes played giant games of football in the square, dribbling heedlessly though skilfully along the steps of the church.

The *trattoria* where I ate, usually with David, was run by a small, dark, wiry, ever cheerful Florentine called Angiolino, helped by his plump, calm wife and his two young sons. '*Capitano, si va a pesci!*' he would greet me. (Captain, you've joined the fishes!) Quite why I was given the soubriquet of captain I don't know, but capitano I remained for all the years I ate in his restaurants. The original one, in Piazza del Carmine, had two rooms. In the outer room, little old men played some abstruse kind of card game, slamming their cards down on the table with a kind of empty defiance. Notices on the wall prohibited the playing of certain card games, notably *Naso* (The Nose), and *Bestia* (The Animal). The smaller inner room had tables ranged along each wall, and a clientele that, unlike Camillo's, cared about football in general and Fiorentina in particular. Signor Rolando, as we always called him, was a young Florentine with a book barrow, devoted to his team, though he could be humorously detached about their fortunes and misfortunes. 'Bacchetti', as he was nicknamed, was a huge, elderly man, often dressed in a singlet, who worked in a slaughterhouse. 'Oh, Bacchetti,' they would greet him. 'How many of the beasts have you killed today?'

Before I left Florence for the summer, I would meet one more manager, through Mauro Franceschini. Mauro continued to coach his youngsters intensively on the scrub grass of Rifredi, and continued to sell them, in *comproprietà*, to bigger and bigger professional clubs. This meant that when the players signed for a team, Mauro retained an interest in them; then, if they were transferred, he would take a cut of the fee. For the moment he was still riding his bicycle, but things would radically change.

Now and again, watching his teams play from the touchline, I would venture a joke. This would provoke instant silence and blank faces, till at last one of the spectators would say, '*Umorismo inglese*' (English humour), as if this at once explained and excused it.

The manager to whom he introduced me was Luigi Bonizzoni, a small, dark, round-faced man nicknamed 'Cina', for his supposedly Chinese appearance. His club, then, was Como, one of those which led a fleeting existence in the Championship division, Serie A, but seldom lasted more than a season. He was an honest, serious, dedicated man, keen to study English football. A few weeks later he arrived in London, and I took him to Highbury to watch the Arsenal training. There were no such things as training grounds, then. Arsenal's own training seemed to consist largely of endless games of head tennis on the hard court. We watched them at it, talking the while to Alf Fields, now an Arsenal coach, and discussing English tactics.

Bonizzoni went back to Italy, not to manage Como, but to take charge of Brescia, a club then subsidised by its president, Beretta, the millionaire gunmaker. Later still, when I turned up at the last moment at San Siro to attend a Milan game, it was Bonizzoni who came down the steps, genially to hand me and a friend our tickets. By then he was assistant manager of Milan. '*Un secondo*' a cynical Italian journalist once called him; but to me, an essential number two, and a straightforward and decent one, in a labyrinthine world.

4

I N LONDON, THAT SUMMER, I began work on a new book, to be called *British Soccer and the Foreign Challenge*. Its theme was to be the gradual decline of the British game as it was steadily overtaken by European and South American football. A theme that, had I known it, would be given all too great a relevance in November, when the Hungarians came to Wembley.

This meant a return to the British Newspaper Library at Colindale; an absolute cornucopia of rich material. I went all the way back to the late nineteenth century and the *Athletic News*, a paper edited by the formidable Jimmy Catton, a tiny man who wore bowler hats, and who was astonishingly prescient about the future of the game, and Britain's role in it.

It was as early as 1899 that the Football Association sent its first party on tour to the Continent; specifically, to Germany. The formidable N Lane 'Pa' Jackson, founder of the celebrated amateur Corinthian team with its ethos of fair play and its abundance of internationals, expressed foreboding and, in the process, exemplified the snobbery and scepticism of the upper classes that would do such harm to football in England for so many years. A distant cry indeed from the game's present modishness.

The touring party, warned 'Pa' Jackson, 'was not made up of University men'. Worse still, it included professionals. Given that the opposition would be made up of German student teams, full of young aristocrats, it was plain that the professionals would be boycotted. Nothing of the sort occurred. The tour was an immense success even if, at one bizarre moment, the defender assigned to man-mark Billy Bassett, the famous outside right – a large young man called Westerdorp with a duelling scar on his cheek – took his duties a little too literally. When Bassett whimsically strolled off the field, round the back of the goal and on to the pitch again, Westerdorp followed his every step.

After the first match, there was an exuberant *commerse*, at which the German team marched round the room in file singing its drinking song and concluding with a cry of, 'Hoch, hoch, hoch!' before disappearing underneath the tables. This, it was explained, was traditional.

At the end of a most congenial tour, in which all the games were won with some ease, the *Athletic News* ironically observed: 'Strange as it may seem, the pros somehow managed to behave themselves.'

In 1923, when Britannia continued to rule not only the waves but, it seemed, the world of football, James Catton wrote in his paper: 'If England is to retain her prestige in the face of the advance of other nations, all players, whether they be forwards or backs, must use more intelligence, and by constant practice obtain control of and power over the ball with the inside and outside of each foot. Unless players get out of the rut into which they have fallen, the game will lose its popularity and Great Britain her fame. Call me a pessimist, shake with Homeric laughter, and write me down senile and silly, but the truth will prevail and this is the truth.' Which it was.

Ivan Sharpe, once a notable amateur outside left for Derby County and the gold-medal-winning British Olympic team of 1912, ably succeeded Catton as editor of the *Athletic News*, and was equally pungent. 'They coach, we don't,' he wrote, 'and until we do coach – and coach properly – we shall not control the ball and play high class football. We shall just muddle through.'

Those were the days, and they lasted till well after the Second World War, when training for British professionals consisted chiefly of running round and round the pitch. The rationale for their not even touching the ball during the week was that they would be all the more eager to have it on the Saturday!

One of those who for so many years did coach, and coach properly, was, by an irony, an Englishman, a little Lancastrian from Nelson who originally intended to become a clergyman. When Hungary thrashed England at Wembley in November 1953, Jimmy Hogan was their honoured guest in the royal box. He had long been forgotten in England, though he had briefly managed Aston Villa (who dismissed him while he was ill in hospital) and had been appointed by the Football Association Secretary, Stanley Rous, to preside over the first coaching courses, shortly before the Second World War.

I had been lucky to catch up with Hogan not long before I left for

Italy. A little, grey-haired man, he had been giving coaching lessons in London schools, and I attended one of them. There was a scant evening audience of small boys and disgruntled adults. Hogan, dressed in a smart, green Glasgow Celtic track suit – he had much impressed Tommy Docherty, then a young wing half back, when he coached there – was almost seventy but irrepressibly lively and enthusiastic.

He called his audience 'my dear friends'. He kicked a ball against the same spot on the wall seven times in succession; then the audience finally applauded. He said that when he was born 'I don't know if my father heaved a sigh or heaved a brick.' He told of a session that he held for troops in France in 1940 where he kept talking about keeping the ball 'on the carpet', till a soldier asked, 'What happens if you come to a ground where they haven't got a carpet?'

His record as a coach on the Continent was extraordinary. He had been inspired by Scottish professionals whom he met when he was playing as an inside right for Fulham. It was after all the Scots who invented the passing game; the Scots who were the first professionals in England, finding 'money in their boots' at Lancastrian clubs; and the Scots who developed and perfected a style based on skill, ball control and close combination, which would be taken up by the world beyond, only to be gradually abandoned in Scotland in time to come.

Hogan first coached abroad before the First World War, in Holland, at Dordrecht, but the turning point came in 1912 when he was sent to Vienna to coach the Austrian Olympic team, and various clubs. His first day, at the Amateur Sports club, was an embarrassing failure. 'I was standing there,' he lamented, 'and I could see that everybody was disappointed, but what could I do? I had showed them what I showed people at home.'

To the rescue came Hugo Meisl, father figure of Austrian football, the dynamic Jewish banker who seldom had time for banking. Later in the day, he and Hogan spoke for hours. It was the rebirth of Hogan as a coach, and the dawn of the so-called Vienna School of football, which in time would entrance the game and so nearly, in 1932 at Chelsea, result in England's first home defeat by a foreign team.

In only six weeks, Hogan had moulded an Austrian team good enough to beat Spurs 1–0. Then he took them to Stockholm where they did reasonably well. When he told the President of the Austrian FA that he wanted the players to have more green vegetables and stewed fruit, the president, a medical doctor, took him literally enough to fill a large jar with fruit salad, which he fed to the players in their rooms each night, on the end of a toothpick.

In 1913, Hogan, by then a Bolton player, injured a knee so badly – there was scant recuperation then – as to end his playing career. The Germans wanted him, but Hugo Meisl kept him. Thus he was in Vienna when war broke out in 1914 and he found himself interned. It's an ill wind . . . for Hogan and for Hungary. In 1916, he was allowed to move to Budapest, where he coached the MTK club and laid the basis for Hungary's future success. Thence to Germany, and a job, in the mid 1920s, with the Central German Football Association, after which he managed the Dresden Sport club, and nurtured the exceptional talents of Richard Hofmann, a forward who would score a hat trick against England.

In 1936, after guiding a half-starved Austrian Olympic team to the Final in Berlin, he took over at Aston Villa. Employing the 'W' formation much against his will – the directors insisted – he took the relegated team back into the First Division, and to the semi-finals of the FA Cup.

'I've no time for all these theories about football,' said the chairman of a club whose fortunes had been built on classic Scottish players. 'Get the ball in the bloody net; that's what I want.' Hogan tried in vain to persuade him otherwise. 'I still say get the ball in the bloody net,' said the chairman, and eventually sacked Hogan, who was in hospital.

By the early 1950s, the Football Association coaching scheme was up and away, presided over by Walter Winterbottom. Significantly, Winterbottom was wont to say that this, of his two jobs, was the more important; the other being that of managing the England team. 'Coaching,' he once told me, modestly, when I visited him at Lancaster Gate, 'is a means of showing how to practise.' He always talked eloquently and cogently about the game, stressing, on that occasion, the basic difference between soccer and sports such as basketball, i.e. that in soccer it was relatively difficult to score a goal.

The coaching scheme was no doubt well intentioned and, in its earlier years, unquestionably produced some expert coaches. Its lurking nemesis, however, was always orthodoxy, and its *reductio ad absurdum*, the abysmal years in the 1980s and 1990s, when Charles Hughes, as Director of Coaching, imposed the heresy of long-ball 'direct' football, would do terrible harm to the game.

In Winterbottom's own day, jargon worked its way in. 'Peripheral vision' was a popular term. 'You know what that means?' asked

Arthur Rowe, mentor of Tottenham's famous push and run teams, and once a coach in Hungary, himself. 'It means seeing out of your arse.' John Arlott, the celebrated cricket commentator, and a notable expert on football, once told me how he spoke to Winterbottom about the ability of certain players to size up a game, even before they received the ball. 'Yes, we know about that,' Walter had replied. 'We call it environmental awareness.'

I lunched down the road from the library at a kind of busman's shelter. It was almost wholly patronised by bus crews, who had their terminus there; a plump, taciturn man cut sandwiches at the counter, and coped patiently with the banter.

'Hurry up! I've waited twenty minutes for them sandwiches.'

'Well, I've waited longer than that for a bus.'

I had lost a lot of weight. My friend Clive's matriarchal grand-mother, a handsome woman interested in marriages, was heard to remark, 'Brian looks like a ghost.' I should probably have gone to see my physician, Andrew Moreland, but I didn't; and in any case, what would he have told me? Professor Rosenheim, the grand guru, had spoken.

At least I managed to be paid for my Arsenal book. It had been published the previous year in cardboard covers with a big red and white crest on its cover at five bob. I had spoken to a good many people in research, notably to Harry Homer, the former programme editor, and a wine merchant called Reg Arbiter, who lived in St John's Wood and was close to the players. The prose was peppered with exclamation marks. It had been published under the imprint Convoy in a series of books about football clubs, this firm being a dependent of another called Grey Walls Press. Under that name had appeared a number of very welcome but rather poorly produced novels by Scott Fitzgerald, who was only just coming back into vogue. The presiding genius of the house was a young publisher with a distinguished war record of whom great things were expected, only for him to fall from the skies, convicted of fraud, and to go to gaol.

Convoy owed me my £100 advance, which was, to me at least, important money, then. I telephoned them and found myself speaking to one of the directors, a forthright, military figure who advised me, 'If I were you, I'd go in hard.' I did, not long before the firms collapsed, as he had adumbrated. A solicitor got me my £100, for a £6 fee. Latterly, I have heard, that book, like Bastin's, sells at £40 a time. 'Habent sua fata libelli.' (Books have their own fates.)

At Secker, David Farrer told me I would 'have to contain my soul in patience' for a decision on the revised *Henry Sows the Wind*, but later, more reassuringly, said that, if they didn't publish it, it would be 'over his dead body'. At last, it was accepted.

So I went back to Florence for my second spell, knowing that I was but a transient, and if I did write fiction about Italy it would involve expatriates. Peter had gone. Aaron had gone. Tony had gone. David was going – he was going to spend time in Germany. He himself looked classically Germanic. Short, stout, with a wide, handsome face, hair rather longer than the usual, grey eyes, his was the stately progression of the maestro, as they called him in restaurants and bars. His dedication was immense. Woe betide you if you chanced to interrupt him in what he called 'a work streak'. Classical he was, indeed, in his adherence to the 'Great Musical Tradition', of which his teacher, Professor Scalero, had been one of the last exemplars. He despised what was going on in the Italian conservatories, had studied flute as well as composition in the States, at Juillard, and had spent the war playing in a naval band: 'I was a crab in the crotch of Jesus.' He was pungently, even ruthlessly, funny. Where Peter detested Italy and Italians – 'He is a nice fellow; there is only one thing wrong with him; he is Italian' – David stayed sceptically detached. Not that he had much more time for his fellow Americans.

Thanks to Mauro, I changed newspapers. He was keen for me to write for *La Nazione*, the chief Tuscan newspaper, and brought me along to meet its sports editor, Giordano Goggioli. Giordano was a large, handsome, curly-headed Florentine in early middle age, with a genial smile and a strong Tuscan accent. He had been captain of the Italian international water polo team, and remembered a pre-war visit to London when, he recalled, the English had been tolerant with the swaggering of his players.

He commissioned me to write an article every week about Fiorentina in the evening paper, *La Nazione Sera*, and, when the team played at home, an article for the sports section of the paper proper, about the match. These might be described as *sui generis*. We always followed the same pattern. After the game, I would visit the paper's offices, and Giordano would take me down to the nearby café in Via Ricasoli, near the Duomo, and tell me what he thought about the game. 'When a team has such physical superiority as Inter, with Neri and Nesti as wing halves, there isn't much the other team can do. Do you agree?' he would rumble at me. Yes, I agreed, and tried somewhat unassertively to put a point or two of my own. Thus satisfied, Giordano would return to *La Nazione*, write up our conversation, and put my name at the bottom.

Perhaps my favourite memory of him, though, derives from the

Olympic Games in Tokyo in 1964. I had arrived the previous day, visited the press centre, and entered the so-called Olivetti room, with its array of typewriters, the whole a fantasy in blue: blue walls, blue carpets, blue accessories. There, huge hands poised above a machine, sat Giordano. Looking up at me, he growled, Tuscan as ever, '*Brian, c'incontriamo nei luoghi più impensabili!*' (Brian, we meet in the most unthinkable places!)

The season of 1953–54 was an exciting one for Fiorentina. For the first time for many years, *puntavano allo scudetto*, as the saying went; they challenged for the Championship. They had an excellent pair of Italian international full backs in the hefty, amiable Tuscan, Magnini, who lived *en famille* in an apartment near the stadium, and Sergio Cervato, of the furious free kicks. With Magnini lived his old father, who sat mute in a corner, treated by his son rather like Dickens' Aged P. '*Eh, Babbo?*' Magnini would chuckle at the old fellow. '*Eh, Babbo?*' expecting no reply.

The half back line of Chiapella, chunky and tough, Rosetta, an elegant centre back, and the lean Segato, was formidable. With Costagliola, the goalkeeper, these five were known as *il blocco viola* (the violets' block), after the colours of the club, and, indeed, they played *en bloc* for Italy in several games, notably on a bitterly cold day in Milan when I was at the San Siro stadium to see Italy win with some difficulty in a World Cup eliminator against Egypt. I still remember the inspired resistance of a jet black Egyptian centre half called Hanif, as his team shivered in the cold.

As I was still working on *British Soccer and the Foreign Challenge*, I went to Turin to talk to Vittorio Pozzo. I went up overnight by train, third class; it still existed in those days. The seats were wooden. The journey took eight hours. All around me, plump, dark, southern women appeared to be feeding their children out of jars of seaweed. I slept very little, but the day I spent with Pozzo was so fascinating and so memorable that I was never less than wide awake.

We spoke, mostly, in a room in his apartment, a room full of books and football memorabilia. He told me of the early days, last century, of football in Turin when one of the founders of the Juventus club, his friend, told him that he looked so foolish as a runner, running after nothing; why didn't he run after a ball? This Pozzo did, helping to found the rival Torino club.

As a student, he came to England to study the language and decided to move out of London, where, he said, there were 'too many Italians, looking for each other'. So he went to the Midlands and began to watch football there. After a while, his parents told him to come home. He refused. He was, he said, a stubborn Piedmontese. His parents retaliated by cutting off his stipend. Pozzo responded by teaching languages all over the Midlands. On Saturdays he would go to watch teams such as Derby County and Manchester United. Then he would wait patiently outside the ground, to seek conversation with such as Steve Bloomer, the prolific inside right of Derby County, and Charlie Roberts, the attacking centre half of Manchester United, who, intransigent in the professionals' cause, would never receive his full due as an England player. With them, Pozzo would discuss tactics, and thus lay the strategic basis of the Italian teams that went on to win the World Cups of 1934 and 1938.

He always wanted a centre half like Roberts, one who would launch attacks with sweeping passes; which was why he discarded the elegant, technically adroit, Fulvio Bernardini, a Roman with a law degree, and much admired in Italy for his skill, in favour of the ruthless Argentine, Luisito Monti. 'The crowd say, "Clever Bernardini,"' Pozzo admonished him, 'but you are holding up the play.'

That very season, 'clever' Bernardini was the manager of Fiorentina, and I met him quite often. I found him to be a man of charm and some sophistication, with a belief in attacking football and adroit players, an honest approach to the game and a contempt for chicanery. When the notorious Italo Allodi, who had been accused, as we shall see, of suborning referees when with Inter and Juventus, was put in charge of the Centro Tecnico or coaching centre, in Florence, Bernardini remarked, scathingly, 'All he knows is how to give gold watches to referees.'

So anxious was Pozzo to acquaint himself with English life that he even, as a Catholic, attended Church of England services. When, eventually, he did go back to Italy, it was because his parents tricked him. They sent him a return ticket to attend his sister's wedding. When he went back for the wedding, they refused to let him leave. 'I still have the other half of that ticket,' he told me.

In 1912, he was persuaded at the last moment by the Italian Federation to take a team to the Stockholm Olympics. There he met and befriended Austria's Hugo Meisl, later arranging a friendly game in Turin that caused the city's prefect to send for him and ask him whether he was mad; in many Italian minds, Austria, who had ruled so much of Italy for so long, was still the enemy. But the game went off well, and Herbert Chapman in due course completed the triumvirate of Titans with Meisl and Pozzo.

During the First World War, Pozzo served as a major in the Alpine regiment, a suitable enough role for one who loved the mountains. He resumed his role with Italy in 1924, but resigned after the death of his wife, eventually taking it up again in 1929. It would last for another twenty years. 'Kind, with a strong hand,' he told me, of his managerial policy. 'If I let them make mistakes, I lose my authority.' Pozzo's job was unpaid; he made his living as a journalist.

English players, he told me, could be dealt with collectively; Italians had to be treated individually. Long before the so-called 'sporting psychologists', in an old Italian term, 'invented hot water', Pozzo was the practical psychologist *par excellence*. If a player refused to do what he wanted in a training game, he would not confront him. Instead he would walk away, return a little later, and tell him, 'You know, you were right: you *should* do so and so,' this being exactly what Pozzo had asked him to do in the first place.

If two players had quarrelled in a league match, Pozzo would simply put them in the same bedroom. If one or the other complained he would tell them that he knew all about it, 'But we are trying to build a team. You must convince yourself this man is not an enemy, but a friend.'

Next morning, he would poke his teddy bear round the door and ask, 'Well cannibals, have you eaten each other, yet?' to which the response would be embarrassed grunts. Then, usually, the players would come to him and say, said Pozzo, 'You know, he isn't really such a bad fellow. The public set me against him.'

Italy duly won the 1934 World Cup, played on its home soil, though, as the celebrated Belgian referee John Langenus, he of the cloth cap and leggings, would write, it was not a popular victory outside Italy itself; the Fascist spirit of the times had imbued the tournament. It was a little too obvious that Italy wanted to win. Pozzo himself, though an authoritarian, was not a Fascist, but it was an epoch in which The Leader ruled.

When Italy played their opening match against Norway in the French World Cup of 1938 in Marseilles, and the players gave the customary Fascist salute, they were jeered to the echo by the Italian refugees and dissidents in the crowd. Pozzo ordered them to maintain the salute till the noise died, which it eventually did. During the war, he played no part in the Resistance. As he reasonably said, he was far too well known a figure to avoid recognition. And there is no doubt that his Anglophilia remained till the end. This despite the notorious 'Battle of Highbury'.

It took place at Arsenal Stadium in November, 1934, some six months after Italy had become World Champions. England, still out of the international body, FIFA, had not participated. Seven Arsenal men lined up for England, though some had replaced injured first choices. After ninety seconds, Luisito Monti, the Argentine centre half, clashed with the England centre forward Ted Drake, broke a bone in his foot and limped off the field in agonising pain saying, 'He kicked me deliberately.' This Drake always denied when I spoke to him about it in future years, but the Italian players were convinced of it. They then, in Pozzo's words, set out 'retaliating'. Eddie Hapgood had his nose broken. England, having missed a penalty, went 3–0 ahead.

For twenty minutes, Drake would tell me, 'We were playing the best football it was possible to play. You couldn't play any better.' In the second half, however, the Italians largely gave up 'retaliating', and started to play football. 'Players who had previously run wild,' wrote *The Times*, tracked down at Colindale, 'began to run into position.' I also found a cartoon by the *Daily Mail*'s Tom Webster in which he wrote in the caption that 'you never knew when this Latin temperament would come off the field and start setting about the spectators'. To this effect, he drew a picture of a huge boot kicking a tiny spectator, who is saying, 'May I go, now? You've kicked me twice!'

Pozzo was an endearing egotist. Later he would give me a copy of his handsomely produced book, *Campioni del Mondo* (World Champions), on which he appears, photographed, on almost every page, often in heroic poses. I have two memories of him at World Cups. He ceased to be Italy's mentor some months after England, in tremendous form, with Stanley Matthews supreme (Geoffrey Simpson of the *Daily Mail* had wondered, after the Battle of Highbury, whether Matthews had the big-match temperament), had thrashed Italy 4–0 in Turin. Pozzo had never really come to terms with the Third Back Game, though he had to adopt it in the end. On retiring from the Italian national team, he continued to work as a journalist.

He was much put out in Gothenburg, in 1958, by England's choice of the big, blond West Bromwich centre forward, Derek Kevan, who actually headed a spectacular goal against Russia in the opening game. 'To choose a player like Kevan is paving the way to brute force,' said Pozzo, censoriously. 'He scored a goal with the *outside* of his head.'

Four years later, in Santiago, after Chile had won the third-place match in the World Cup, there were ecstatic celebrations in the streets of the city. I saw Ferenc Puskas, who had played for Spain, watching, grinning, and eating monkey nuts, in a doorway. Then I saw Pozzo, the old lion, strolling through the crowds, silent, dignified, and quite unrecognised.

That season, 1953–54, processions of exalted Fiorentina fans with banners went past the windows of my ground floor apartment in the Via Romana, singing anthems. '*Ah, Fiorentin-i-i-na!*' they began, reaching a climax: '*E scrive anche del calcio nella storia!*' (And write of football, too, in history!) Somewhat superior to the obscenities which for years have poured from English stands and terraces.

England's defeat by Hungary at Wembley produced, in *Nazione Sera*, a paean of scorn and invective from Beppe Pegalotti, still smarting from his prison years in India. E CROLLATO UN MITO read his headline (a myth has crumbled). He used the defeat of the England team to broaden his argument into a critique of the British Empire.

At Angiolino's, in the Piazza del Carmine, I was overwhelmed with cheerful derision, and had to buy a number of lunches for those with whom I had bet on an English win. There was more jocular abuse to come when, early the following year, England played the first ever under-23 international against Italy in Bologna, and lost it 3–0.

I travelled up for the game, staying overnight, and was struck by the contrast between the English and the Italian players. The Italians looked like mature men. The English team, some in their Army or RAF uniforms, as conscripts, looked like uncertain boys, now and again joining in a ragged chorus. Duncan Edwards, who would die so wretchedly after Manchester United's Munich air crash, just four years later, was the team's left half, at the age of seventeen.

It was exciting to be there, however. I remember speaking at length to Walter Winterbottom, and, with Mrs Rosamund Mallmann, to Alan Brown, then the assistant coach, later manager of Burnley, Sheffield Wednesday and Sunderland. Mrs Mallmann, somewhat surprisingly, had also decided to come from Florence for the game; she had long shown some interest in football. Alan Brown, a Northumbrian of unpredictable moods, spoke about the possibility of Christ having set foot in his country.

Then there was the Graydon Affair. John Graydon was a plump, pale journalist who worked for what was then Kemsley Newspapers. He was a man who put himself constantly about, a dull writer but a considerable operator. He 'ghosted' flat autobiographies – Billy Wright, Alf Ramsey – was notable for putting up floods of ideas, whatever their quality, and even, in time, for talking his way into being the first sports correspondent of commercial television. Briefly. He was also the main motivator of the recently formed Football Writers' Association.

When I went round to the headquarters of the Emilian Football Federation, where the press passes for the game were to be issued, I wondered whether it might help were I to bring back the passes for the other reporters involved. With this in mind, I telephoned the hotel and asked to speak to Bob Ferrier, the accomplished football correspondent, then, of the *Daily Mirror*, and son of a famous Scottish outside left. We were cut off. I tried again. Once more, we were cut off.

Dilemma. To bring the tickets with me, or leave them. I decided to bring them. Not long afterwards, I was accosted in the foyer of the hotel by an irate John Graydon. '*You* had no right to bring those tickets! The FWA had everything arranged.' I answered, in the Italian phrase, *per le rime* (with equal heat), and Graydon, as was his way, backed down. I vowed then that I would never join that organisation and, rightly or wrongly, I never have.

Later, I found that Graydon had some strange propensities, notably a predilection, on foreign tours, for accompanying young footballers to a brothel, arranging an 'exhibition' between a couple of the whores, and watching the players who were watching.

This seemed to me the stuff of potential fiction, and indeed I wrote a short story about it called 'I'll Fix You Up', which was published in a men's magazine. As a result of this, I was asked to adapt it as a play for a commercial television station, which I did. I was generously paid for it, but it never saw the screen. The editor involved wanted me to compromise by changing something that I thought fundamental. The odd thing was that the editor was none other than the American writer, Ruben Ship, famous for a lacerating radio play called *The Investigator*, a satire on the nefarious deeds of Senator Joe McCarthy, busy, then, in hounding liberals with the aid of his sinister committee. At the end, the senator indicts God, and is promptly blown to smithereens.

Shades of the pungent line in an anecdote told by Lenny Bruce: 'The producer said, "Be a man! Sell out!" ' So the play never got off the page.

I wasn't well. My back, which gave me agony again that winter, was catching up on me. I often felt very tired, and took to having the kind of bed rests I had been used to in Mundesley. I drank a lot of milk, ate white chocolate, but still my weight went plummeting down, till it was barely ten stone. A phase of denial?

Certainly I didn't dare to admit to myself that tuberculosis was back, again. But eventually I went to David, my medical preceptor in a beret, from a family of doctors himself, who sent me to a

Russian lady physician. She pronounced my condition 'interesting', did not specifically diagnose it, but sent me to a strange practitioner of X-ray therapy, who, wearing black goggles, laid me down beneath clanking machines.

My parents visited, saw the lump on my back – perhaps I wanted them to see it – and appealed to David. I made arrangements to have an operation in the Casa di Cura, on the outskirts of the city, but when David found 'it was a bone', he immediately sent for his Belgian doctor, in Rome. The doctor, a brisk and breezy man, diagnosed TB, told me I needed an instant operation, and suggested I go to a clinic in Switzerland. It meant leaving almost instantly. The shock was immense. David stood by me loyally, offering to clear out my effects from the apartment, which he capably did. Dr Rouette, a Rabelaisian fellow, ate dinner with us at Angiolino's and predicted I would be fit again: 'You will be top man!' I was hardly in the mood for jokes.

An extra complication was that I was in the middle of writing a new novel, about Florence, *Along the Arno*, which I had started at the beginning of the year. I had carefully drawn a diagram, inside a circle, to decide how the book might develop from its characters. There would be one based on Peter, one on an American girl from the finishing school for rich people, up on the hill of Bellosguardo, and one loosely based on an expatriate friend on the GI Bill. By then, I was well into the book and had no intention of abandoning it. I wrote it as usual by hand, typing it up later. In the restaurant of a Swiss railway station, a kindly Italian waiter asked me what I was writing, and we spoke. In my present agitation, I was grateful for the human contact.

At the aseptic hospital in Zurich, they were less forthcoming and less responsive. A cool secretary read the doctor's note, went away with it, returned, and told me that a specialist would not be available for weeks. So I got back on the train and returned to London, finding myself, eventually, where I had been before: on the fourth floor of the private wing of University College Hospital. This time, however, cost what it might, I was paying for myself.

Cecil Fleming, a sympathetic and accomplished surgeon, came to see me, told me that, judged from the X-rays, I had almost cured the bone myself, but it would need two minor operations to drain the abscess, plus a major one to install the bone-graft. Dr Moreland came to see me. He did not apologise, but apology was implicit in his demeanour. After a few weeks in UCH, he had me moved to a room nearby, which was gratis. There was, however, a catch in it. I had to allow myself to be examined by his students as an example of a remarkable cure of chest TB. This was simply too much; too great an irony. I refused and promptly found myself back in the paying wing at UCH.

The first two, draining, operations were carried out under a local anaesthetic. The bone-graft necessitated a general anaesthetic. That evening, back in my room, immobilised on the plaster bed where I would lie for eight weeks, I was in fearful pain. A small, sturdy, cheery New Zealand nurse had been looking after me. She was not much comfort. 'Well, I'm not worried about it, Brian,' she told me, as I lay in agony, 'so I don't think you should be.'

In due course, the hospital's engineers rigged up a sloping board for me, so that I was able to type, and could so proceed with *Along the Arno*. *Henry Sows the Wind* was published and, for several weeks, got no reviews. Suddenly it was praised both in the *Times Literary Supplement* – 'He has a beguiling sympathy for the less successful, especially if they be modest at heart' – and the *Spectator*, where Kingsley Amis wrote, 'Mr Glanville, who is only 22 years old, has an enviable future.'

The prospect of which, oddly enough, plunged me into a strange kind of dismay. The book had hardly set the Thames on fire – 'It's made its little mark,' as David Farrer would say – but, lying on my plaster bed, I somehow convinced myself that I had prematurely arrived, that doors everywhere would fly open, and it depressed me. In the event, I had two more years to wait before *Along the Arno* would make that kind of an impact, but the novel had still to be finished and to pass through all kinds of hoops, before then.

I owed much to Peter Marchant. He was a large, dark, impulsive, exuberant figure, who still wore his Cambridge University Judo Club sweater. He had, with great enterprise, founded a short-story magazine called *Chance*, persuading such celebrities as Elizabeth Bowen, Joyce Cary and Frank Tuohy to write introductions for it, or to contribute. He became an assistant editor on *Encounter*, the cultural–political monthly that, eventually, to large embarrassment, turned out for all its prestige and splendour to have been bankrolled indirectly by the CIA; but he had long since left by then.

He was enormously taken with *Along the Arno* when he read it in manuscript. Of my juvenile *Reluctant Dictator*, he had insisted that the most powerful scene, between the South American dictator General Augusto and the English footballer, Morton, had really been between me and my mother.

Gwenda David, the chief reader for Secker, wrote quite a

favourable report on *Along the Arno*. David Farrer returned it to me saying that I was not nearly ready, yet, to attempt such a book. Bolstered by Peter and his enthusiasm, I held out against this. In the end we reached a compromise. I allowed David Farrer to cut the book, which he did, severely, and Secker accepted it.

Some two years passed. David would tell me that, in such and such a publishing season, they could not possibly publish *Arno*, 'because we've got a new Thomas Mann, and a new CHB Kitchin that we consider a near masterpiece, and you'd be absolutely swamped'. So I gritted my teeth and waited. When the book did at last come out, in July 1956, it blew up in Secker's face. The reviews were too good to be true. Far from keeping me away from Kitchin, a veteran homosexual writer, and his masterpiece, Secker published them the same day, only to find Kitchin's novel brusquely dismissed as dull. I confess that I could never feel quite the same about Secker or David Farrer, though I would have numerous other books published by them. Twice we had parted company; the second time, quite bitterly, for good.

David the composer came over to London and stayed in my parents' flat in Oakwood Court. Carla, whom Peter had now, with scant enthusiasm, prepared to marry, came too, heavily pregnant with twins. An Anglophile as ever, Peter wanted them to have British nationality. When he arrived, the marriage would take place in Kensington Register Office. Carla was short, plain and somewhat shrewish. Yet when Peter, a few years later, was so cruelly killed, falling, asleep, out of his car, while a client was driving, Carla showed that strength and resilience with which Italians can so often respond to disaster. By then she had three small children to bring up – Adam, Nikki and Clari – and bring them up she did, in the same flat in Milan she had shared with Peter.

After the wedding, conducted by a large, red-faced man with a buttonhole, we went to the Kensington Palace Hotel, nearby, to see if we could get a drink. My father had watched it go up, brick by brick. He had bought shares in it, and for a long time it looked as if he would lose all his money, since it remained but a derelict site. 'Can we get a drink?' my sister Marilyn asked. 'My father has shares in this hotel.' We were refused.

In November, I felt strong and well enough to go back to Italy. To Florence, first, but only in transit; I had decided that this, my third and last spell, should be in Rome, even though the city and its heavy atmosphere had never, for all its beauties and glories, attracted me. I stayed with David on the way down, and remember sitting with

Giordano Goggioli in his car while he, as a good Tuscan, warned me about it. '*Sono strafotenti, i romani,*' he told me. (The Romans are arrogant.) Peter was censorious, too. 'It's not just corruption,' he told me, 'it is *Latin* corruption.' David, who had lived there, told astonishing tales of plot, counterplot and almost Feydeau-esque farce.

It turned out to be an extraordinary winter, not least because, for the first time ever, both Roman clubs had an English manager: Jesse Carver at Roma, George Raynor at Lazio. And I was working for Rome's *Corriere dello Sport*; an English journalist.

Carver and Raynor could hardly have been more sharply contrasted. Carver we have already met. Though in the sun of springtime he liked to lie out, dressed only in shorts, on a bench in the Stadio Torino, down the road from the Olimpico, where Roma trained, I remember him best tightly and symbolically buttoned and belted into his fawn raincoat. The man himself was buttoned up and closed. His smile was always knowing, rather than amiable. He assured me when I arrived in the city that there was a clause in his contract that forbade him to give interviews to the press. It eventually transpired that no such clause existed. He lived, childless, with his wife in an apartment on the ground floor of a building near the football ground. It was rumoured that, from time to time, she would cross into Switzerland, carrying paper bags. Did they have cash inside them? It was never proved.

She was a small, lively, voluble woman who seemed to be kept on a very tight rein. 'I often think Jess will bring you back here when you've been at the stadium,' she told me, wistfully, once. 'But he never does.' On one occasion, she did, indeed, invite me over, only to telephone me shortly before I was due to tell me she had to go to the dressmaker.

'The number of times I've heard about that dressmaker,' said George Raynor. He was a tiny Yorkshireman, from the village of Hoyland. When he joined Sheffield United as a young professional, he replied, when asked where he came from, ' 'Oyland.'

'So you come from Ireland, do you, son?' asked Jimmy Dunne, the team's blond Irish international centre forward, extending a large hand. 'Put it there, if it weighs a ton!'

Raynor had had much success with the Swedish international team, and would have still more in the 1958 World Cup. The side with which he won the Olympic tournament in 1948 at Wembley was an exceptional one, containing players such as the Nordahl brothers, Gunnar Gren, Nils Liedholm and Garvis Carlsson. Alas for

Sweden and for Raynor, most of these stars decamped for foreign climes, thus becoming ineligible for an international team which, technically at least, remained amateur. Raynor managed to qualify his team for the 1950 World Cup Finals in Brazil, unearthing a particular talent in the little, flaxen-haired attacker, Nacka Skoglund, who would later join Internazionale, but the team was thrashed 7–1 by Brazil in the final pool.

A few weeks before Hungary routed England at Wembley, Raynor took his Swedish side to Budapest, telling them that, if they won, 'I'll paint Stalin's moustache red!' They didn't win but, using shrewd containing tactics, they did achieve a 2–2 draw. Walter Winterbottom's England, alas, had no such strategies. Not only did it lose 6–3 at Wembley but, learning nothing from the defeat, it was thrashed again, 7–1, in Budapest the following May. I remember lying in my hospital bed – the free one – listening sadly to the radio commentary, which was peppered with doleful interjections by Charlie Buchan, who had not realised his microphone was on.

Very briefly, that 1954–55 season, Raynor had been in charge of Juventus, but, when things went wrong, the Turin club let him go to Lazio. There, he found a team in chaos. For obscure reasons, the club had put its whole transfer policy in the hands of Gigi Peronace, who had turned it into a kind of elephants' graveyard. He had bought two elderly defenders of previous renown: the 32-year-old Carlo Parola, once famed for his spectacular bicycle kicks, though he put through his own goal playing for the Rest of Europe against Britain at Hampden in 1947, and the 30-year-old Attilio Giovannini, from Inter.

When results went wrong, the Roman sporting press, ever ready to swoop and savage, turned furiously on Peronace. It was all his fault. He had bought crocks. It would have been fairer to ask why a club as prominent as Lazio should put all their eggs in the basket of one so inexperienced in the transfer market. A tearful Peronace ran for solace to Mrs Carver, whom he had known well in Turin, swearing that he would give up football, and go back to the building trade, where he had been working.

Not only did Raynor have to contend with an inadequate roster; he also had to battle with subversives within the club itself, notably with the Count Vaselli. The Count, the scion of a family that had enriched itself building roads and the like, had opposed the choice of Raynor, and did all he could to eject him. He was a noisy, voluble, overbearing, middle-aged man, addicted to wide-brimmed black hats. On match days at the Olympic Stadium, he was far more in evidence than the club's actual president, Tessarolo, a gentler and more dignified figure. '*Abbia la cortesia di non scrivere!*' he shouted at me, in the dressing-room after a lost game, angrily tapping my notepad. '*Ha giocato bene Giovannini, e basta!*' (Have the courtesy not to write! Giovannini played well, and that's enough!)

Raynor, altogether more hospitable than Carver, inviting one to his apartment in a new block in Via delle Medaglie d'Oro – one of those featureless if expensive developments going up around Rome at the time – was deeply unhappy. His pleasant wife once heard him muttering to himself, 'And I always thought football was a game for gentlemen.'

He did, however, have his supporters, notably Tessarolo and his grey eminence, Captain Guaitini, of the Air Force. Guaitini was the epitome of seriousness and rectitude. He cared deeply not only about Lazio but about football in general and football tactics in particular. Dark-haired, of suitably upright carriage, sturdily built, he would, at the dinner table, make elaborate strategic patterns with toothpicks. He lived in Spartan austerity in an Air Force barracks. His judgements were considered and lapidary; not least, quite charitably, on the subject of Gigi Peronace.

'Given the profession he follows,' he told me, in his room at the barracks, 'Gigi Peronace is not a dishonest person.'

Then there was Domenico Biti, who would become a long-standing friend. Born in Umbria but largely domiciled in Rome, Biti had been presented to me by his fellow youth coach, Mauro Franceschini. Less driven, more humorous, more detached than Mauro, he liked to recount the first time he met him. He was sitting at a café table in Piazza della Repubblica in Florence with Fulvio Bernardini, Fiorentina's manager, when Mauro came striding across the square, jacket thrown over his shoulders. 'If you could see this colt!' he roared. 'He kicks like this with his back legs!'

'What are you?' asked Biti. 'A trainer of horses?'

'*Macché!*' cried an outraged Mauro. 'I'm a football coach!'

Biti himself was a youth coach of great competence. Then in charge of the Lazio juniors, he was subsequently engaged to run the football school established by the Italian Football Federation in Rome, then persuaded, for a high salary, to coach the juniors of Roma. Later, not wanting to leave the Roman area, he became manager of a string of clubs up and down the coast, causing the wags at *Corriere dello Sport* to nickname him *Il Mago del Tirreno* (the magician of the Mediterranean). He was also number three coach of the Italian under-21 side which contested the 1960 Olympic tournament in Italy, and at one point had no fewer than fourteen of his players in Serie A and Serie B of the Italian League. Best known of them was the right winger, Bruno Conti, whom he coached while managing Anzio, and who, in 1982, would be picked by Pele as the outstanding player of the 1982 World Cup, in Spain.

Despite his years in Rome, there was always something of the countryman about Biti, with his round face, his ruddy complexion and his sly smile. He worked under the aegis of Prince Gianni Borghese, a tall, imposing aristocrat who used to tease him and call him *finto tonto* (feigned simpleton). Borghese, who spoke flawless English, had an estate at Scarperia in Tuscany to which he invited me one weekend. This enabled me to write to my father – who was wont to respond to anything I said that displeased him with 'Keep that for your footballing friends' – saying that I had been staying on the estate of Prince Borghese, 'who is, of course, one of my footballing friends'.

The Prince had a gracious, elegant wife and several delightful children. It was a fearful shock to hear, a few years later, that the youngest of them, the pretty little Gwendoline, had died in great pain from a mysterious ailment.

Biti himself was a mine of anecdote and reminiscence, not least about the war, in which he had served in North Africa in the Italian Army, in a platoon given to playing harsh practical jokes on fellow soldiers, such as erupting on them in the middle of the night pretending to be British troops.

The best of his tales, however, concerned the time when they were all, in fact, taken prisoner by the British. Most of them were packed off to see out the war in India, but Biti and a Neapolitan conceived a plan whereby they stayed. It was the Neapolitan's idea. The English captain in charge of the camp was an ardent football fan, who ran his own team. Biti then was himself a footballer. 'I,' the Neapolitan told the captain, 'am his personal trainer. I have to massage his legs with a special liniment; otherwise he cannot play.'

The captain accepted this, and Biti had to undergo the massage. Whatever concoction the Neapolitan was using, it burned the legs agonisingly. Biti gritted his teeth, and managed to put up with it. He and the Neapolitan thus stayed in North Africa, avoiding transfer to India, till one day the Germans counter-attacked, overran the camp, and both Biti and the Neapolitan were freed.

Carver was better off than Raynor, but not entirely. He had a stronger squad of players, thus obtaining more impressive results. His footballers enjoyed his training methods, which placed much emphasis on loosening exercises; they would walk up and down vigorously swinging their arms in a way that would probably have invited scorn in English clubs of that time.

Carver, indeed, in a short spell at West Bromwich Albion, before joining Roma, had revolutionised the training, putting a strong emphasis on ball skills which, bizarrely, was largely unknown in British football then. Jimmy Hogan's methods at Celtic had merely been the exception that proved the rule, however much they appealed to the players.

Albion's players were greatly enthusiastic, and their results while Carver was there were excellent. But doing well with Roma in Serie A had its dangers, as well as its advantages. The better the results, the more the club's directors, its fans, and the demanding Roman press expected. They wanted Roma to win a Championship that they'd won just once in their history, back in 1941. So while Lazio battled against relegation, Roma battled against such expectations.

As the season wore on, however, they found it hard to rise above third place. Milan dominated the Championship, followed by unfashionable Udinese, inspired by a blond Swede called Arne Selmosson, who was nicknamed 'The Ray of Moonlight'. But even managing Milan, with its array of stars, was something of a two-edged sword. When, in mid-season, it lost two matches in succession, Bela Guttman, its Hungarian manager, was promptly fired.

He turned up one day in the restaurant in Via Frattina, near the Piazza di Spagna, where Biti and I ate lunch, at the time. 'In my next contract,' he said, 'I intend to have a clause: not to be dismissed when the team is top of the League.' Then he told us a significant tale.

'Once Lucchese (a little Tuscan team, briefly playing in Serie A) were due to meet Juventus, in Turin. On the way there, their manager, poor fellow, died. How could an Italian team take the field without a manager? They phoned all over the country, till at last they found a manager to join them. The team drew the game and carried the manager off the field on their shoulders!'

I published an interview with him next day in *Corriere dello Sport*, and we met once more at lunch. 'Only an Englishman could have written that article,' he said, which was at once encouraging to hear and, in its implications, sad.

So Carver was criticised, and justifiably resented it. Relations with his president, Sacerdoti, a large, flamboyant, pompous man, degenerated. Carver still refused to talk to the press. Frequently, I attended Roma's training. Sometimes Carver and I would stand behind the goal in the Stadio Torino, and watch Roma's reserves play. There were days when they deployed two international wingers: Chico Ghiggia, who had scored the winning goal for Uruguay in 1950 when they beat Brazil before 200,000 fans in the World Cup decider, and Stefan Nyers, who had played for Hungary. Each, felt Carver, was trying to upstage the other; '*Insiste, insiste!*' he would cry. At a certain point, a cohort of huge, chuckling, joshing men would surge among us, a badge in their lapels marking them as players for Rugby Roma. Carver gave me a Roma badge to wear in my lapel. Absent-mindedly, I wore it one day at the Stadio Torino when I went into the Lazio dressing-room, at another game, to be rebuked by the massive Lazio centre half, Malacarne: 'That badge doesn't go down well, here.'

Carver talked often about players he had coached, players he had developed, players who, by implication, owed their careers to him. Could there really be so many? There was no doubt, though, of the respect he enjoyed. Once, insisting that I should not publish it, he showed me a letter from the Roma right back, the Italian international, Alberto Berticelli, who had played for him at Juventus when the Championship was won. It was a paean of fulsome gratitude and admiration. But enemies lurked in ambush, even among the officials of the club, ready to strike when things went wrong.

Among them was *avvocato* Colalucci, the lawyer Colalucci, nominally Roma's press officer. In the weekly column of barbed items that he wrote for the evening paper, *Giornale d'Italia*, he frequently sniped at Carver, and sometimes even at myself. He was a man in his fifties, with a round, roguish face, silver hair, and a monocle that, said Vittorio Finizio, he used to see round corners. It was rumoured, though never confirmed, that in Fascist times he had been a police spy.

I spent much of my time in the offices of the *Corriere dello Sport*, then ideally situated in an eighteenth-century, brown-walled palazzo, in the Largo dei Lombardi, right on the Via del Corso in central 'historical' Rome. The atmosphere at the paper was described by some as *studentesco* (student-like). There was much banter, much playing of rather puerile games such as rolling up a ball of paper that a football journalist would whack with his hand, while another went in 'goal'.

There were several Fascists on the staff. Cencelli, the virtual editor – Bruno Roghi, a respected writer, seldom was there – blinked endlessly and would sometimes cry, 'But in England, there are the sanctions!' a throwback to Mussolini's invasion of Abyssinia. Molinari, a stocky, middle-aged, disaffected man with a moustache, saw most of those he spoke about as *stronzi* (turds), a favourite Roman expression. It was said that in Florence, one learned blasphemy; in Rome, *parolaccie* (dirty language). When a senior journalist left, Molinari remarked, 'Now we're one *stronzo* less.'

Alberto Marchesi was more genial and generous than that. A tall, bronzed, handsome man (who had been a notable oarsman), silver-haired and exuberant, Roman to the core, he spoke admiringly of the sporting spirit English enemies had shown in the war. A committed Roma fan, he spoke English with an appalling accent, and wanted to translate Joyce's *Ulysses* into Italian.

The football editor was Giuseppe Melillo, a pale, plump, red-haired man of slightly bird-like features who enjoyed joining in the games with paper balls. When pressure was brought on him to stop publishing my work, because I had been critical of one or other Roman club, he had the courage to resist, asking what kind of an editor would he be if he succumbed. It was something he never told me about himself. Some years later, he hoped to become editor of the paper and was keenly distressed when he was passed over. In the late 1990s, I would still see him, from time to time, eating lunch in the little family *trattoria* in Piazzale Flaminio, just opposite the tram stop; always at a corner table, always alone.

Ezio was one of the chief football writers. Though originally from Livorno, he had assumed the noisy mannerisms of a *romanaccio*, a very basic Roman. Tall, dark, vulgar, with a prominent nose, he was known to be a ladies' man. Once, in the office, he clutched his cock and proclaimed, 'If you knew the satisfaction this has given me!' Yet there was a residual kindness there. When Vittorio Finizio, who, with his slightly spinsterish ways could not have been a greater contrast, fell so ill, it was Ezio who visited him in hospital, every day.

It was a friendly, warm, convivial office, yet all the time I was there, not one of them invited me to his home. I recalled a line I had read in Florence, in the British reading room, written by a young Italian poet: 'The Italian is a ferocious family-loving animal.'

For a while, before Biti introduced me to the delights of Via Frattina and its Trattoria Romana, then a waiters' co-operative – getting me, typically, a good deal on my bills – I would eat at the Taverna Margutta, not far from Piazza di Spagna. There, the food was cheap and bad, the expatriates plentiful. A young man with a guitar and a fearful indentation on his temple would come and sing

'*Ti voglio bene, tanto, tanto*', a song popular at the time. Cheap and bad, too, was the food at a restaurant where I would eat dinner: the Vicolo dei Serpenti, just across the Via Nazionale. There, however, the expatriates were an unusually interesting lot.

Seamus Walsh, a small, grey-haired Irishman in his forties, had got extremely lucky. A teacher at an American school, he had met Alden Hatch, a writer of hack biographies such as *General Ike* and *Red Carpet for Mamie*, and got himself commissioned to write a biography of the Pope (Pius XII). He would often talk about the money, asking John, an impecunious Australian, also a teacher, who was sharp, quick, clever and self-defeating, 'Should I take it in dollars, John, or would it be better in lire?'

Harold Norse was a New York poet of some standing; short, stocky and dark, a wearer of berets. He would read us his clever, Brooklynese translations of the sonnets of Gioachino Belli, an anti-clerical poet who had lived at the turn of the eighteenth and nineteenth centuries. One especially Rabelaisian sonnet Harold saw as the acme of Christian charity. Called 'La Santaccia di Piazza Montanara' (the holy whore of Piazza Montanara), it described how a prostitute was being penetrated at almost every possible orifice by several men while a country hick watched from a corner. Eventually, she called across to him, asking why he didn't join in, to which he replied, 'I haven't got a ducat.'

'Then take any hole you can find!' she cried. 'For the blessed love of Christ, our redeemer!'

One day I telephoned Seamus at his *pensione*, put on an Irish accent, and said, 'This is Father O'Flynn of the Vatican Special Squad. We're puttin' the finger on you this afternoon. There's something you wrote we didn't like on page two hundred and thirty-two.'

Seamus was alarmed until I disabused him. Not long after this, his plump landlady rushed to his room and cried, '*Dottore: il Vaticano al telefono.*' (The Vatican are on the phone.) Seamus went reluctantly to the telephone and demanded in a surly voice, 'What do you want this time, blast you?' eliciting the reply, '*Scusi, non ho capito.*' It was indeed the Vatican.

Later still, when the book had been completed, life imitated art. Seamus was kept in a car outside the Vatican for several hours by a couple of Irish priests who went through the typescript page by page. 'And we don't like this. You take this out, do you understand? If you don't do what we want, you won't work anywhere. You'll starve!'

'I realised,' said Seamus, bitterly, 'that my life wouldn't have been worth living.'

The book duly appeared under the title *Crown of Glory*, and by strange chance I was asked to review it for the weekly magazine *Truth*. A Freudian slip induced me to call it *No Crown of Glory*, the title of an earlier book. It was a hagiography, but it had made Seamus wealthy.

I stayed first, in Rome, in a *pensione* near the Porta Pinciana. Called the California, it had been recommended to me by Aaron, who had found the fact that it was centrally heated a useful way of enticing women to his room. Eventually, with the help of Ed, a tall, good-looking, muscular Ivy League American who roared round Rome on his motor bike with myself on the pillion, I found an apartment; but not before vicissitudes. There was one place particularly, just near the Stazione Termini. A rather gloomy, middle-aged man showed us around. I asked if I could see the bathroom. There was a pause. '*Ho dovuto sacrificare qualcosa*,' he replied, at last. (I had to sacrifice something.) But there was, he added, an Albergo Diurno across the way, where one could get a bath.

The apartment I found was in Prati, a dull, lower-middle-class area close to the Vatican. I was the tenant of a sad, elderly lady called Olga Vedova Tedesco (Olga the Widow Tedesco), who shuffled round the flat in carpet slippers and had long, self-pitying telephone conversations in the hall with her equally despondent friends. Years later, I used my landlady and the flat as background for a novella, *A Roman Marriage*, which sold to a surprising number of foreign countries and provoked much interest, even before it came out, from film producers. Sam Goldwyn Junior summoned me to the States, where we walked for hours while he tried to persuade me to adulterate it. 'He's in the son business,' a man in cinema said. In the end, I sold the rights to what turned out to be the wrong one of three Hollywood companies; but was there ever a right one?

As Lazio struggled to survive, so Raynor came under increasing pressure. Several of the players stood by Raynor loyally, notably John Hansen, the tall, accomplished Danish inside left whom I had first met when he was playing for Juventus. John, then, was coming to the end of his Italian career, but he still had clever feet and was formidable with his head, not least when he stooped to make contact.

One midweek, Lazio surprisingly beat Inter at the Stadio Olimpico. I was in their dressing-room when John said how pleased he was for George Raynor. When the interview was broadcast that evening, the line was cut out.

Carver, too, had his troubles. Roma were doing far better than Lazio, but the Championship was a mirage. My own pieces in *Corriere dello Sport*, sometimes critical of one or the other club, inevitably whipped up controversy in that Byzantium of football. *Tifone*, a popular, aggressive football weekly, made a full-scale attack on me: ANCHE LA ROME HA IL SUO PERONACE (Roma too has its Peronace). In his malicious column, the ineffable, monocled Colalucci referred to me as *'l'ormai quasi celebre'* (the now almost celebrated), which I suppose might serve as a kind of epitaph.

One morning, Carver asked me – 'It might do you some good' – to accompany him to meet the Football Association's powerful secretary, Stanley Rous, at the Hotel Quirinale in Via Nazionale, where Rous always stayed. I had in fact met Rous before, and asked him if he had had a good journey. 'Yes, yes, yes, yes; who are *you*?' Very tall, very large, white-haired, of rubicund complexion, he was the very model of a successful autocrat. Not till *Along the Arno* had been published with success, the following year, did I really make the grade with him; he told me he was buying it to give to his friends. To enter Sir Stanley's good graces it was always important to achieve something outside the game that had made him what he was, a presence in royal boxes.

To my surprise, he proceeded, virtually, to offer Carver the job of England's team manager, in succession to its incumbent, Walter Winterbottom: 'It's time we brought Walter into the office.' It probably was, but it didn't happen. Carver promised to think about it, took off briefly for Coventry with Raynor at his side, at the season's end, then went back to Italy and Inter. I deemed the conversation private, and did not write about it for some thirty-odd years.

Carver was forever changing horses and, in the end, it would catch up with him. After Juventus, Marzotto, Torino, Roma, Inter, Lazio, Sampdoria and Genoa, even Peronace could no longer get him a club. I learned during the 1958 World Cup from Karel Lotsy, a Dutch administrator as tall as Rous, that Carver had walked out on Holland, too.

On his return to Italy, he was met at Ciampino airport by Count Vaselli, the then President of Lazio (before his building firm went bust), who presented Mrs Carver with a bouquet of roses. 'The thorns,' *Calcio Illustrato* captioned its photo of the presentation, 'were for Lazio,' since Carver promptly took off for Milan and signed for Inter. Lazio in due course would forgive him and appoint him.

Gradually, meanwhile, George Raynor pulled his Lazio team together by various means, not always tactical.

He had a Scandinavian winger who was playing poorly, and heard rumours that the man was indulging in *la dolce vita*. Raynor engaged a private detective who followed the player to night clubs. Raynor called him in and threatened to tell his wife; the forward changed his ways and began to play well.

Another Scandinavian, the chunky Swede, Sigge Lofgren, was used by Raynor as, what he called, his 'G-man', close-marking the most dangerous attacker in the opposition. Typically Roman jokes went around. Lazio, said one of them, had signed a new Chinese player, '*Va in B*' (go down to Serie B).

Carver was not immune, and nor was I. At Epiphany (Befana – the turn of the year), Colalucci, in his column, wished us as Befana presents a ticket each to return to England.

When Roma played Lazio in the ever febrile Roman derby at the Olimpico, the result seemed a foregone conclusion. Lazio wallowed in mediocrity. Roma were fresh from an impressive win at Bologna, where Carver had used his international left half, Giuliano, as a pseudo outside right, dropping back into defence. Quite unexpectedly, in a game where Roma were surely going to force the pace, Carver picked the same team, and it foundered. Under drenching rain, John Hansen stooped to head an early goal, and Lazio won, 3–1, to the joy of their fans. '*Andiamo in botti–i–i–ia, ah, ah, ah!*' they chorused on their terracing. (Let's go down to the *bottiglieria*.)

I wrote, in the *Corriere dello Sport*, that I thought Carver had got his tactics wrong. He rang me to expostulate. I told him I didn't think he should have used Giuliano as a deep right winger. 'Ah,' said Carver, triumphantly, 'but didn't you know? Giuliano played outside right for Torino juniors.'

Strolling through the Via del Corso with Carver, one afternoon, I was surprised when he accosted a large, grey-haired, good-looking Roman, and engaged in a protracted argument about Roma and the Championship. 'Mister,' said the Roma fan, 'it's thanks to you that we're not going to win the Championship.' Carver strongly disagreed. Neither convinced the other. As we walked away, he told me he wanted to challenge the man, who had spoken out against him at club meetings. There was, in fact, no catching Milan, nor even Udinese, but Roma in the end took second place, Udinese being relegated for having bought a game the season before.

In early spring, I went to Athens for a fortnight. Ted Crawford was there, coaching the AEK club, then a much humbler entity than it later became, with a modest stadium in the suburbs. He was living in digs, and doing pretty well. Most of his players, then, were part-timers who would turn up in the evening for training. Crawford would stand in the middle of the field, while high above they walked round the perimeter of the terraces. 'Come on, shithouse!' Crawford would call to them while his interpreter, a young naval officer, standing beside him, would tactfully stay mute.

But Crawford's luck deserted him again. The practical, tactical lessons he gave his players were absorbing and effective. He stationed them around the field in various situations and asked them what they thought they should do. The team did well in the League, but then came ENOSIS, the campaign to unite Cyprus with Greece. The President of AEK told Crawford he could no longer guarantee his safety, or that of his family – who were by then with him – and back he went once more to England, and to anonymity.

For a little while he had a job with Barnet, still, then, an amateur club. I went along one Saturday morning to see him coaching on the muddy, steeply sloping, Underhill ground. Alas, he did not keep the job for long. The chairman sacked him, to the displeasure of the club's virtual icon, Lester Finch, an amateur and Olympic international of renown, who even had a game, during the war, for the full England team. But Finch could do nothing. Crawford would never work again in football.

In early summer, Juventus, Raynor's former club, came down to play his present team, Lazio. Lofgren, Raynor's 'G-man', was assigned to mark Giampiero Boniperti, then operating as Juve's centre forward. 'Boni', not always the most passive of players, ultimately became exasperated, and felled the Swede with an elbow to the stomach. Sacchi, Lazio's dark, rugged, generally unshaven left half, instantly knocked down Boniperti with an elbow to the jaw. Antonazzi, the Lazio right back, came rushing forward to intervene, only himself to be flattened by the elbow of Juventus' big centre half, Ferrario. There were so many bodies lying on the ground, I wrote in *Sport Express*, that one awaited the arrival of Young Fortinbras and his army.

Afterwards, in the dressing-room corridor, Ferrario came up to Raynor. '*Che peccato, mister*,' he cried. '*Dieci minuti dalla fine era una partita tranquilla, tranquilla.*' (What a pity. Ten minutes from the end, it had been a quiet game.)

Next day, on the sunlit Spanish Steps, in company with Biti, I ran into Sacchi. 'Just because he's the captain of Italy!' he said.

Roma, briefly flourishing again, received Fiorentina at the stadium.

TUTTI ALLO STADIO PER APPLAUDIRE LA ROMA exhorted *Tifone*. (Everyone to the stadium to applaud Roma.) But in a game of many goals, Bernardini's Fiorentina won. I could not contain my amusement, and a large Roman journalist sitting beside me, pointedly changed seats.

Having put aside *British Soccer and the Foreign Challenge*, which George Greenfield thought too long to sell, I had rewritten it, by hand, under the title *Soccer Nemesis*; in retrospect, not the perfect title. Secker accepted it, and it appeared, to some enthusiasm, some six months after I had left Rome. The theme was the same: the far-from-inevitable decline of the British game as football matured in Europe and South America. England 3, Hungary 6. Hungary 7, England 1. There was no need, by now, to underline the theme.

Towards the end of the football season, a well-known journalist, Antonio Ghirelli, took up the cudgels for me in the weekly *Sport Sud*, describing me as 'an Englishman rich in humour and culture'.

A lively Neapolitan of left-wing persuasion, Ghirelli would eventually become editor of the *Corriere dello Sport*, and of *Tuttosport* of Turin, after a spell in charge of *Calcio Illustrato*.

That admirable weekly moved to Rome when Boccali retired, but it would never be the same. Maurizio Barendson, another Neapolitan and a great friend of Ghirelli, would also edit it. Both had a charm and humour denied to Leone Boccali, but neither had his deep dedication.

Barendson, a small, bright, impulsive man, would subsequently flourish in television, but my lasting memory of him is in the press area at the delightful Piazza di Siena, in the middle of the Villa Borghese, where the showjumping events were taking place in the Olympic Games of 1960. Maurizio knew nothing of showjumping and cared less. His paper, then the *Giornale d'Italia*, had assigned him to the event, and he was in a black temper, unsure of what to write.

His problem seemed to be solved for him when Piero D'Inzeo, one of two brothers, officers in the *carabinieri* and great horsemen both, came to the press area to use a telephone. Unlike his more expansive brother, Raimondo, Piero was stony-faced and dour.

'Whom did you phone?' demanded Maurizio, scenting a story.

'It was a private matter,' answered D'Inzeo, stonily.

'I'm a journalist!' cried Maurizio, outraged.

'*Ha fatto male il suo mestiere,*' was the answer. (You've practised your profession badly.)

In years to come, Ghirelli would become right-hand man to the Prime Minister of Italy, Bettino Craxi, who ultimately decamped to

Tunisia in a welter of financial scandals. 'Go and see Melillo,' Ghirelli asked me, when he, and not the football editor of *Corriere dello Sport*, had been made editor, '*è molto giù.*' (He's very down.) As for *Calcio Illustrato*, it died. Boccali was irreplaceable.

5

HARSH THINGS HAVE BEEN SAID about 1950s England and London. We are led to believe that it was a kind of chrysalis time, the aftermath of war and austerity before the bright, beautiful butterfly of the 'swinging sixties' broke out to transform all our lives. Did not Philip Larkin, aside from telling us that 'they fuck you up, your mum and dad', also assert that sex began in 1963?

London, when I returned to it, seemed a pretty lively place to me, even if the correspondents of *Time Magazine*, ensconced in their Mayfair offices, had not yet informed us that it 'swung'. There were plenty of parties to go to, not least on Saturday nights in Notting Hill. But it was hard to come down from the heady peaks of the Olympic Stadium, with Lazio or Roma to report on every Sunday, to the banalities of Third Division football, which I covered for the old *Empire News*.

This was a Sunday paper which had flourished, essentially, in the North. I had first known it through my Mancunian friends, the Kesslys. It was famous for coming out quickly on a Saturday night, when it was rumoured to sell as many as 600,000 copies. Now, however, its owners, Kemsley Newspapers, were trying to promote it in the South, which made my eventual fiasco at the Goldstone Ground, Brighton, the less forgivable.

Thanks to George Greenfield and their sports editor, Harold Mayes, the *Empire News* had taken over my *Footballers' Who's Who*, publishing two editions. Not long after I returned to London, Mayes was succeeded by the more genial Sid Bailey. I might have been a denizen of the Olympic Stadium in Rome, I might have edited and compiled the *Footballers' Who's Who*, but, so far as Sid and the *Empire News* were concerned, the Third Division (South) it was.

My first assignment was at Southend, not far from where Eddie Estherby had tried to teach me tennis. It was the day that Roots Hall, the new Southend United ground, was opened, with a lively match against Norwich City. My Monday pieces for *La Nazione* and *Corriere dello Sport* were one thing; match reports on the dot for an English Sunday paper quite another. Reporting from Southend always meant a desperate rush up a mud bank to get to the phone in the local post office. The *Empire News* in those days never supplied one.

I fretted and cogitated a great deal about this report. Sid Bailey wrote to me and said he thought it 'rather wordy', and I am sure he was right. Now, my beat was Brentford, Leyton Orient, Southend, Brighton and Aldershot. In the press room at Brentford, where I would sometimes come across Stanley Halsey, reports had to be phoned in under the baleful eye of Bob, the press steward, who took it much amiss when I spoke about 'such threadbare stuff'. I told him I had been used to Italian football. He implied that perhaps I should have stayed there.

It was, however, always fun to go to Orient, where Harry Zussman was the buoyant, irrepressible chairman. Short, fat, bespectacled, a shoe manufacturer given to long black overcoats and Homburg hats, he caricatured the caricature of an East End *nouveau riche*: quick, generous, funny and an inspiring chairman. The apple of his eye was his manager, Alec Stock, for whom he was prepared to go to any lengths in order to keep, or lure back, if he went away.

Stock had made his name as player-manager of little Yeovil Town, another non-league club with a notable slope. At inside forward he had led them to a sensational FA Cup success against mighty Sunderland. During the war, as a tank captain, he had been wounded in Normandy. A Somerset man himself, he was supremely at ease running clubs at this level and skilful in getting the best out of modest performers. Higher up the scale, at Arsenal, and with Roma, he found life less easy. Under pressure, he tended to succumb to asthma attacks. 'Quite honestly,' he would say. 'Quite honestly.'

He had two chief adjuncts: Les Gore, a cheerful Londoner who would stand in for him on those occasions when he briefly went elsewhere, and the chief scout, Sid Hobbins. Hobbins it was who had kept goal for Charlton when Arsenal put seven goals past them in the 1943 League South Cup Final. I still have a picture in my mind of Ted Drake, who scored two excellent goals that day, chasing a ball in vain and ending up with one arm round Hobbins's shoulders, the other held comically aloft.

Hobbins by now was a huge, heavy man with a high-pitched London voice, a great red face, and a penchant for boots rather than shoes. He lived in a prefab from which, once, it was said, the club's precious allocation of FA Cup Final tickets had, surprisingly, been stolen. We shall hear of him again.

I was also able to take over as chief writer for *Sport Express*, Reg Drury having moved upwards and onwards to *Reynolds News*, the Sunday paper then owned by the Co-op. It was manifestly a promotion and a deeply deserved one, but the situation he found himself in had a Jacob and Laban aspect about it. *Reynolds* – for whom I would happily find myself writing literary interviews, from Graves to Golding to Koestler – was honest, but *Reynolds* was poor. While other national papers sent their main men abroad, Reg was obliged to stay at home. There, he was a celebrity, known to every manager and major player in the land. But when at last they let him go abroad, he was like a man who had just been released from solitary confinement, blinking in the light. I recall him on his first England tour abroad, in a frenzy of anxiety, fearing he had lost all his luggage, when in fact it was on the bus behind us. In time, but it was a long time, he joined the *News of the World* and was treated more as his abilities deserved. But he was always happy to escape early from World Cups.

Sport Express paid me three guineas a week for my articles, which seemed very fair at the time. I had a lot of freelance work besides, continued to write for the Italian press, and made a fairly decent living. Nemesis arrived when I went down to Brighton on a foggy winter's day to cover a game at the old Goldstone Ground.

The press-box then, absurdly, was situated behind one of the goals. In the enshrouding fog, it was hard to see what happened at the other end. A figure in a blue-and-white-striped Brighton shirt headed two goals from an inside-right position. I assumed it must be the inside right, Albert Mundy. It was absurd not to check, absurd not to ask, but I knew no one there and was too embarrassed. Not only was I quite wrong, but the goals had in fact been scored by Frankie Howard, whom I had actually watched after cycling in from Charterhouse to see him play outside left for Guildford City. This was the time when the *Empire News*, as we know, was trying to expand in the South. I left them, soon, by mutual agreement. I had had enough of Third Division football; they had had enough of me. But not before another nightmare.

I was due to cover a game at Aldershot's Recreation Ground, oddly enough against Brighton. This was a ground I knew well; on a number of occasions I had cycled the ten miles along the Hog's Back from school, left my bike in one of those convenient sheds for a few pence, and watched a game. Twice it was to see Tommy Lawton playing for Notts County; once it was to watch Arsenal's reserves, for whom Arthur Milton was playing.

That morning, Louis Blom-Cooper, making his way, by then, at the Bar, had come to see me in the service flat I had at the White House, a block of flats that faced Great Portland Street Station. My mother, always active on my behalf, had found it for me, and I had stayed there a while after my operations.

Eventually, Louis drove me to Waterloo Station, and it was only when he had left me there that I found I had come out with scarcely any money: just enough to get me to Aldershot. Except that, in my agitation, I got on the wrong train and did not arrive till near to half-time. How would I ever get back? Again, I knew no one in the press-box. I needed to borrow six shillings, and promised I would pay them back. Nobody would help me. One large young man with a moustache, I remember, muttered that I should try the club's office.

So anxious was I not to err again that I went into the Brighton dressing-room to check who had scored. Then I made my way to the station, and begged the help of an elderly lady working behind a counter. Amiably, and without hesitation, she lent me the money. I sent it back, with a letter saying she had restored my faith in human nature.

I often visited the hospitable Lou, and his wife, Miriam, in their home in Richmond. Many years and much hard work lay between him and the laurels of his later career: a QC famous for his loyalty to lost causes and a formidable chairman of tribunals and commissions.

Jerry Weinstein, too, was a barrister, famously brusque, unfailingly kind, loyalist of friends and immensely versatile. He had won scholarships to Oxford, Harvard and Cambridge, and then the Harmsworth Law Scholarship. He had written a bibliography of Strindberg. He had played football during the war for Ayr United, while serving in the RAF. But, alas, he had developed polio, had an iron brace on his leg, and walked with the help of a stick. *Inter alia*, he had been a founder member of the refulgent Pegasus club, where he carried rather more weight than his office of assistant treasurer would suggest.

Fools were never suffered gladly. I remember going once with him to Earl's Court for some kind of football show. A surly member of the Corps of Commissionaires, in blue uniform and white cap, had been foolish enough to treat him arrogantly. 'All right, thank you very much, *Corporal*!' said Jerry, and left an enraged commissionaire behind him. Jerry was tall and dark, a good-looking man, who wore horn-rimmed glasses. He was very quick and very funny, a notable teller of Jewish jokes, and proud of his friendship with his fellow Old Pauline, Peter Shaffer, whose career as a playwright would take wing so remarkably in 1958. 'My best friend,' Jerry would say.

So long as he stayed in England, he was able to temper the curmudgeonly excesses of Professor Sir Harold Thompson FRS, at once the founder and the ultimate destroyer of the Pegasus club. A Yorkshireman, once a soccer blue himself, and a distinguished expert in infrared spectroscopy, 'Tommy' was a compulsive intriguer, and a domineering figure, given to perverse changes of front. This I would discover for myself, long afterwards, in the Lobo–Solti Affair, when his behaviour was paranoid in its illogicality. Women, at public functions – and on aeroplanes – were known to complain of his attentions.

The members of the original Pegasus team were mostly grown men who had returned from courageous service in the war. There was no way for Thompson to dominate them. Later, with younger players straight from school, Thompson's authoritarianism and irrationality simply drove them away, and the club gradually died.

Thompson's right-hand man was John Tanner, whom I remembered well from watching his incisive displays at centre forward in Godalming for the Old Carthusians, in the Arthur Dunn Cup. Tanner was not much more tactful or sensitive than Thompson. The episode in which they discarded one of their finest, most committed, most gentlemanly players, Tony Pawson, an Olympic footballer who had played right wing for Charlton, was unpleasantly emblematic. Once, exasperated beyond measure by Thompson's obduracy, Tanner hit him. Thompson walked round the pitch during the ensuing game, pointing to the bruise and saying, 'Look what Tanner did.'

While Stanley Rous remained in office, there was little harm Thompson could do in the counsels of the Football Association; Rous was simply too strong and would swat him like a fly. Thompson, however, had his revenge when Rous retired in 1962 to become President of FIFA, the international body.

It had been generally expected that Rous would be succeeded by his protégé, Walter Winterbottom. Thompson, though, exploited a newspaper article by the future Liberal MP Clement Freud, in the *Observer*, trumpeting Winterbottom's virtues. Thompson took the paper to each member of the FA selection committee in turn, asking them if they were willing to let themselves be influenced by a newspaper. So it was that they chose a compromise candidate in Denis Follows, the FA treasurer, much disliked by Rous, an animus which he reciprocated.

On the night he was elected – when, to Rous's disgust, he spoke for the first time ever to a cleaning woman at Lancaster Gate, telling her how happy he was – I had to interview him at Broadcasting House. 'The Secretary,' he said, pompously, 'is meant to be the servant of the Association, and we all know what happened. The servant became the master.'

Which, one reflected at the time, was just as well. For all his faults, his snobbery, his social climbing, his autocratic ways, his indifference to the troops on the ground, Rous was still a force for progress and for good not only in English but in international football. As for Follows, he would soon be acquainted with the darker side of Harold Thompson, whose perpetual hectoring interference was generally believed to be the cause of his heart attack.

Jerry, like Lou Blom-Cooper, began to write for *Sport Express*. The magazine had fallen on hard times. Based, now, in offices near Moorgate, it had lost Sid Silver, its original proprietor, it had lost Alex Lee, and was being run by an accountant called Freddy, a weightlifter who could box and tear telephone directories in two, but who gave as much time (or more) to his business, as he did to the ailing magazine.

So it was that I brought in Gordon Watson. Gordon by then had come down from Oxford, had taken articles as a solicitor, and would eventually become a merchant banker. His admirable, refreshingly acerbic, mother provided what had been a dingy office with carpets and curtains. Duns from the railways and other companies would appear at the magazine with their demands, expecting to find some evasive and embarrassed supplicant. Instead they found the large figure of Gordon, dressed in an expensive suit, his feet on the desk, puffing a big cigar and treating them with condescension. 'I shall pay you when it's your turn, and *only* when it's your turn,' he would inform them. They would leave the office cowed.

Money, though, was desperately short, and desperation led us to Eddie Calvert, known then as 'The Man with the Golden Trumpet'. We managed somehow to get support from him, in return for running a column under his name entitled 'My Friends In Sport'. Eric Butler, a lanky Londoner who had been sports editor of the communist *Daily Worker*, took over the editorship of the magazine and found it hard work to deal with Calvert and his sidekick, Basil Foster. 'Fuckin' hopeless, mate!' he would say on the phone to me on a Sunday morning at the White House. 'Calvert copy still ain't turned up. That Basil Foster's a bloody old woman. Oh, well. Mind how you go.'

We could not hold out for ever. In the end, the magazine went broke. We gave Jerry his cheque as priority, but as a member of the Bar, he said, he could not go ahead and cash it. So eventually it bounced. The magazine was taken over by its chief creditor, its printers, the South London Press, who kept it going until the 1957 Cup Final, when Paul Trevillion's caricatures of both teams appeared on the shiny green-and-white front cover. Lou Blom-Cooper was still writing on amateur football as Lew Cullis. Jerry was still writing, too. I had written the last leading article and, in retrospect, not very elegantly. It was very sad to see the magazine disappear and I shall always look back on it with gratitude and affection. In its time, it enjoyed a good deal of respect within the game, which was probably the ultimate criterion.

Jerry now left London for Paris, to the great regret of all his friends. Not, however, before he had introduced me, at a lunch in Simpson's of the Strand, to Michael Davie, the sports editor of the *Observer*, which would be my next port of call. I remember Jerry asking Davie about Chris Brasher, then known as a British steeplechaser. Davie's reply was that Brasher wanted to be a sports journalist, but he wasn't sure he would be able to crack it. By the end of the year, Brasher had won the gold medal in the Melbourne Olympics and succeeded Davie as sports editor of the *Observer*.

In the summer of 1956, I went back to Italy for six weeks, had 20,000 lire pinched from my trouser pocket on a Roman bus, and spent two mistaken weeks in the Adriatic resort of Cattolica, then largely a German colony. In the middle of July, by which time I was living in a single room with a threadbare carpet in Egerton Gardens, South Kensington – my mother had found it, again – *Along the Arno* appeared. The Sunday before its publication, it had an ecstatic review in the *Observer* from John Wain. 'I am still astonished at the publisher's statement that the author is only 24,' he wrote. 'How can so young a man understand so much?' I reflected somewhat wryly that Secker had kept the book so long that I had in fact written it when I was 22.

Most of the other reviews were almost as good, and new doors began to open. The book was published in the States, but did not sell a single foreign right. It did not make me rich, but then from the very beginning I had hedged my bets, believing that my football journalism would underpin my fiction.

Working for the *Observer* was at once a joy and a frustration. In those remote, pre-floodlight days, with kickoffs at 2.15 p.m., there was plenty of time to write a measured report. The *Observer* paid six guineas a match, which was enough to pay the rent, but I was never sure I would be used. Those were the days of the first flourishing of the intelligentsia. Professor AJ (Freddie) Ayer, the eminent philosopher, and John Sparrow, Warden of All Souls and expert on the buggery in *Lady Chatterley's Lover*, wrote reports, rather badly. I was, as likely as not, when I rang Michael Davie, early in the week, to be told, 'Good report, but we're not using you this week. We're using John Jones.'

'Who's he?' I would ask, in disappointment.

A short, uneasy pause. 'A friend of mine.' He was, in fact, another Oxonian don, author of a well-regarded book on Wordsworth. His match reports read like kick-by-kick pieces from the provincial Saturday-night pinks.

'Go upstairs!' Davie shouted at me once, from the 'stone', in what appeared to be a moment of crisis when, back from a game, I looked into the room.

'I was hoping for instructions.'

'Then go upstairs without instructions.'

I wrote to tell him I thought his behaviour was appalling. He did not reply, and I don't think I ever set eyes on him again. The excellent book he and his wife wrote about the rascally Beaverbrook reconciled me.

It was the year 1956 that I first met my wife, perhaps inevitably at a party, held in her own home. She was working just off Fleet Street, for the monthly magazine *Housewife* – a Hulton's publication – as chief sub-editor and, later, as beauty and features editor. Fleet Street remained the magic canyon; newspapers here, the Temple there – and the much mourned Kardomah café, where journalists and lawyers mingled over coffee.

Jerry left his chambers to join Euratom, the European Atomic Agency, where he would rise to become the deputy director-general. We collaborated on a history of the World Cup which was published by Robert Hale in 1958; from Paris, he bombarded me with questions, corrections and objections, till one morning – I was by now living in Sloane Avenue, Chelsea – I refused, exasperated, to take the call. His life was never easy. Pain from his crippled leg necessitated painkillers, which in turn kept him awake, so necessitating soporifics. He remained as cheerfully acerbic as ever.

Visiting him in Paris, some five years later, I coincided with the arrival of the company of Joan Littlewood's *Oh What a Lovely War!*, which I had seen and admired in Stratford. In Jerry's car, we bowled across the airport at Orly, to meet his friend Victor Spinetti, the star of the show. 'There he is!' cried Jerry. 'The Welsh Wop. The Welsh Wop.' Victor smiled. It was not long afterwards that poor Jerry collapsed over a restaurant lunch table in Paris, afflicted by a cerebral haemorrhage, and died at the pitifully early age of 36. We all missed him more than ever. At his bleak suburban funeral, a dim rabbi talked nonsense about him and his supposed religious interest. Pegasus players wore yamulkas.

It was through the *Observer*, indirectly, that I would meet John Moynihan, be lured back to playing football again, and thus become a founder member of Chelsea Casuals, the Sunday team with no basis in reality, which is still flourishing after 40 years.

The *Observer* had assigned me to cover a match at Tottenham, but since they also planned to run an article, by me, about international football, decided that David Sylvester would cover the game instead. So I met David for the first time. A huge, dark, plump polymath and a substantial art critic who in the future would actually win the Venice Biennale, David was a lover of many sports, which he practised with limited success. In his perfectly modulated voice, he would speak – at places like the Knightsbridge Soup Kitchen restaurant – of the cricket team he ran, the Eclectics. 'We're so strong this year,' he would say, without a trace of irony, 'that when we're at full strength, *I* can't get a place.'

The tale was told that once, when he was fielding for the Eclectics, a member of the team consistently ignored his instructions, till David turned to him and said, 'If you don't do what I want you to do, I shall be forced to intimidate you physically.'

He played rugby for the Slade School of Art. A mutual friend, in Rome, Lorenza Mazzetti, novelist, documentary-maker with Lindsay Anderson, psychologist and puppeteer, told me once in her quaint English, 'I remember David Sylvester playing football, and *never* getting the ball, *always* missing it.'

He was reputed to play a good game of tennis, but once, it was said, turned up at the Royal College of Art, where he was then teaching, and held up a hand to stop the ping-pong game. With him he had brought a fine new set of bats, balls and a net. It was duly installed, and he played, losing 21–2. 'How stupid of me,' he said. 'I was playing on your backhand. I should have been playing on your forehand.' They played again. He lost 21–1.

He was always, however, a benign and encouraging presence. It was alleged that his brother-in-law, the playwright Frank Marcus, once wanted to portray him in a play, where he would be shown as threatening somebody with one of those anorexic Giacometti statuettes. To this, however, David objected, and to this alone. He would never, he said, threaten anybody with a Giacometti sculpture.

After the Tottenham match, we repaired to one of those white-tiled, anonymous fish and chip parlours in the High Road, where David, inauthentically calling the woman in charge 'dear', proceeded with his report, reading me bits of it now and then. 'Stokes was backheeling like a schoolboy who has been watching Shackleton.'

Then we travelled across London together, arguing fiercely and endlessly about some arcane fact of football history about which I knew I wasn't wrong, finally striking an enormous bet. 'No, you're right,' sighed David in the end, as we sat in a taxi from South Kensington Station, on the way to Chelsea. 'I'll pay you.'

'No, no,' I said, 'just pay for the taxi.'

'Do you know John Moynihan?' he asked.

'No,' I said. In retrospect, it astonishes me that, at any given time, I did not know John Moynihan.

'Do you play Subbuteo?'

'No.'

We stopped at a house in Old Church Street, where the door was opened by a tall, languid, good-looking young man, with a thatch of black hair. John Moynihan. The house belonged to his parents, who were both distinguished painters. He and David set about playing Subbuteo, the table-football game. David, in what I later, perhaps unkindly, described as paunch and braces, rushed around the table crying, 'Fuck, oh, fuck!' while John effortlessly scored goal after goal.

Some weeks later, I was visiting the *Evening Standard* to see their film critic, Philip Oakes. An accomplished poet, he had given me a generous review in the *Standard* for *Along the Arno*, and I had met him through Gordon Watson, from whom he lived not far away. Looking around, I spied a bushy black head above a desk partition. John Moynihan. I greeted him.

'Do you play football?' he asked, in his slow drawl.

'What, that game on the table?' I asked.

'No, the real thing.'

'I've not played for eight years.'

'Well, some of us have never played at all.'

Which was how it started: the germ of Chelsea Casuals, the little Sunday club with no basis in reality, still going strong after more than forty years; the club that John, I and the painter Keith Critchlow, later an adviser to Prince Charles on such things as futuristic domes, would found, and which I would run, through joy and disaster, misery and triumph, for thirty extraordinary years.

That Sunday, I turned up, as invited, at John's basement flat in South Kensington. Keith Critchlow was there. Frank Bowling, the West Indian painter, who would become so fashionable in the nineties, was there. So was Jeff Bernard, who was the only one who did not play. I had borrowed a large, brown, old-style pair of boots from my brother-in-law, Bernard, an academic and an economist, who himself still played. We went up to Hyde Park where, somewhere near the centre, was the preferred pitch, and the opposition.

Later, I would write that 'it all started as a rout in Hyde Park. The editor of *London Last Night* (John) captained one side; the future literary editor of the *Spectator* and the *New Statesman* the other. There was a centre half who had played Cassio at the Old Vic, and won, and the best player was a tree. Eventually, the tree dropped out. He found it difficult to get to away games.'

How John managed to play football at all, given the nocturnal demands of his job, I never knew. He would be up until the small hours chronicling the doings of the fashionable: a grand repository of gossip. He saw himself as a centre forward, used his height to good purpose in the air, and ran very well if you gave him the time and the space, preferably on the flank.

The future literary editor, and professor of literature, was a Scot, Karl Miller; neat on the ball, but a perpetual protester who would complain his way through every game. Famed, or notorious, for his description of Paul Gascoigne as a 'priapic monolith', after the 1990 World Cup, he was in fact a genuine fan, from his Edinburgh and Hibernian-following days, rather than one who jumped on the bandwagon in the post Nick Hornby 1990s. 'Can you imagine yourself doing this in twenty years?' he once asked me, as we sat on a tube, after a match.

'Yes,' I said.

'So can I,' he answered.

He was the original Chelsea Casuals inside right. The actor, Tony White, was the original centre half. He was a complex character, handsome, talented, oddly self-destructive, occasionally violent and doomed to a horrible, early and absurd death – a heart attack, after breaking a leg on Tottenham Marshes. Tall, dark, well-built and good-looking, the son of an elderly English father, who would often limp along on a stick to see him play in Hyde Park, and a French mother, Tony was himself bilingual and later translated books from the French. At Cambridge, he had been an outstanding *jeune premier*, and his progression into the theatre proper seemed natural and irresistible. Perhaps too much so, for him. Suddenly, when his career seemed in full motion, he gave it all up. He became . . . a lamplighter.

Picture Post, then a celebrated weekly magazine, devoted a complete article to him. Later, he would appear in a variety of different guises. I remember, when I was living in Sloane Avenue, coming out of Sloane Square Station early on a misty morning, walking along King's Road, and seeing in front of me a large figure in a leather jacket inscribed MAC'S NAPPY SERVICE. Walking a little faster, I found that it was Tony, and invited him round for a cup of tea.

He had charm as well as talent, but it was hard to get anywhere near to him. When he played football, there was a strange disproportion between the quantum of violence and the insignificance of the event. He was at his most aggressive in pick-up park games. Once, playing such a game in Battersea Park, he went hell for leather into a young boy, injuring him. This annoyed me so much that, when next we went for a ball, I tackled as hard as I could – I was not a gentle player myself in those days – and we both came down in a heap. Tony rose menacingly to his feet and I thought, wearily, well, if we must, we must, but then he simply turned away and went on with the game.

The matches in Hyde Park grew rougher and rougher; inevitable perhaps when the same two groups keep playing each other every Sunday, and there is no referee. Jonathan Miller came along a few times, refulgent star of that marvellous revue, *Beyond the Fringe*, and, red-haired and lanky, would introduce a welcome note of comedy, sometimes lying down in the goalmouth. But Assheton Gorton, an outstanding television and theatrical designer, a well-spoken rugby player who resembled a small tank, was made in Tony's mould. He turned to me one day, after we had thundered into one another several times, gave me a little smile, and said, 'We haven't really clashed yet, Brian, have we?'

The two groups got together to pick a team for the first match ever played by what came to be known as Chelsea Casuals. The opposition, on that day in November 1957, was fashionable if not formidable: a King's College Cambridge dining club, who met us in a match in the lea of that superb building.

We won it, 5–1. I played at left half and had the first shot in the club's history, which whistled past a post. I would seldom shoot again. I played much of the game on a pulled muscle in the left-hand groin, having no idea then what I had done. Knowledge and awareness of remedies would come much later. 'Che lusso,' I sighed, exulting in a hot bath after the game; the worst thing possible for a pulled muscle. 'Che lusso,' (what luxury) came a reply from the next cubicle, where John Moynihan was wallowing, in his turn. Tony and Assheton had for some strange reasons worn red shirts, while the rest of us wore white shirts of one kind or another. We were photographed before the game, sending up a nineteenth-century team, sprawling about in various obsolescent poses.

At the suggestion of our right half, the author and film writer David Stone, who himself would die a sadly premature death on the operating table, we called ourselves Chelsea Casuals, and played together eight matches that season. The chief problem proved to be in reaching a *modus vivendi* between the two groups, each of whom wanted as many of their own people to play as possible. Tony was by then working in a garage in Manresa Road, opposite the Chelsea library, and it was there that we would meet to thrash out team selection. Meanwhile, the two groups were developing two very different currents of thought. John Moynihan, Keith and I were all for having more full-fledged, eleven-a-side, games. The other group regarded this as 'too serious'. We in turn thought that nothing could be more serious than being maltreated every week by reckless opponents, with no help from a referee.

If our playing resources then were limited, John's social contacts were abundant. He even arranged a fixture at Eton against the Old Etonians some weeks after we had gone all the way to Oxford to play a team which never turned up. Kim Caborn Waterfield, known to the popular prints then as 'Dandy Kim', was then a member of the team. A good-looking, debonair, well-dressed young man, he drove up to Oxford in a luxurious car, and, when we couldn't find the ground where we were meant to play, drove whimsically three times round a roundabout, an exquisitely dressed and groomed blonde beside him. We had had lunch in a pub where the drinkers seemed to find us funny. Tony muttered that 'there'll be fisticuffs in a minute'. The locals laughed. The moment passed.

In another pub, I found myself drinking next to Dom Moraes, the young Indian poet, then an undergraduate, pretty and precious. 'Talk to *him*,' he said, as I lamented what was happening, as he gestured to someone farther down the bar. 'He knows lots and lots about football.' Eventually we found ourselves playing against the Christchurch College Hockey Club, and winning by a goal.

Kim Waterfield spent some years avoiding extradition to France, where he was accused of taking large sums of money out of the safe of the Hollywood movie mogul, Jack Warner, with whose daughter he was having an affair. In the end, however, he had to go back and face the music.

I believe he played that day at Eton. I didn't. It was a Saturday, and I had to work for the *Observer*. Our outside right was a 36-year-old master baker, Phil Isaacs, who had served in India with the RAF. He seemed very old to us – but he had a car. In due time he would run bingo in Burnt Oak, then become proprietor of the Sportsman gaming club, on a corner of Tottenham Court Road. He was the best treasurer the club ever had. At the end of each season he would give a little party complete with tea and his own brand of cakes, in his flat in St John's Wood, and present the meticulous accounts.

'The first thing I see,' he said, of Eton, 'is that the referee has a broken leg. I'm not kidding. A broken leg. I go up to their captain and I say, "I don't think much of this. Old Etonians, hundreds and hundreds of you, and the only referee you can find has a broken leg." He said, "I don't think that's a very sporting attitude." I said, "No, please don't misunderstand me; I've got nothing against him and I hope his leg gets better, but is this the only referee you could find?" '

Not a very strong team at the time, a weakened Chelsea Casuals were pulverised that day, scoring only once, when several players seemed to rush the ball in. One Etonian turned to another: 'Like a pack of hounds, old boy,' he said, 'like a pack of hounds!'

Gradually, the Other Side dropped out, leaving Chelsea Casuals to John, Keith, Phil and myself. On the Maccabi ground in Hendon, which was heavy with mud – and was where I learnt inadvertently to slide tackle – we were thrashed by the Show Biz eleven, which included one of my former idols in Walley Barnes, the Arsenal and Welsh international full back who used to coach the Sandhurst team that came down to play at Charterhouse, where he would talk to me on the touchline.

In the summer of 1957, while lying on my bed in my little service flat (the service would eventually disappear; my rakish Uncle Gerry lived a few floors below), I received a telephone call. A high-pitched London voice addressed me from the other end. It was Sid Hobbins, of Leyton Orient, and late of Charlton. Round and round the mulberry bush he went, for a very long time. If a certain English manager, as if I couldn't guess who, wanted to work in Italy, what would be the chances, how should he go about it and whom should he talk to? After half an hour or so of this, I was suddenly told: 'That manager is AWA Stock.' I tried to sound surprised.

I answered that I could not do anything directly myself, but that Gigi Peronace, by then a players' agent and the man whose great coup that year was to take John Charles from Leeds to Juventus, was in London at the moment. I could talk to him. This I did. For some secretive reason – listening devices, after all, were in their infancy then – Gigi and I repaired to the middle of Green Park, and sat on two deck-chairs. It was a time when he was busy reinventing himself, for English purposes. In Italy, though in later years he would achieve a role and a grandiose title from the Italian Football Federation, he never really established himself at his own valuation. He was still the *meridionale*, fighting, with some desperation, for his place in the sun, or the north, a faintly comic character, a tolerated vulgarian.

In the lower-middle- and working-class world of English professional football, it was infinitely easier to be accepted for what he wanted to be. He was exuberant, generous – presents were part of the act, but he still liked giving them – and extrovert. 'Because with Gigi, *si diverte*, you enjoy yourself,' he would sometimes cry. 'With Gigi you laugh; with Gigi you sing.'

There were times, in our relationship, when we would meet in some hotel room, often the Mount Royal, at Marble Arch, and sit silently; there was nothing to be said. '*E allora*, Brian,' Gigi would say at last, '*eccoci*! Well then, Brian, here we are,' which was undeniable. Or, at other times, 'If you don't want to see me . . .'

In Rome, a few summers later, I found myself dining in Piazza Navona with the ineffable Colalucci and several young members of his tennis club, who were indulging, amidst much mirth, in drinking games. The old satyr was as shamelessly amoral as ever. At that point he was trying to persuade Fulham to sell their star and talisman, Johnny Haynes, to Roma, and had visited me in South Kensington, where, by then, I lived with Pam, who had become my wife. At a certain moment, Colalucci looked at me and asked, 'Brian: *come guadagna la vita Peronace?*' (How does Peronace earn a living?)

That sunny day, in Green Park, Gigi asked me what I thought of Stock. I said he could get a team fit and knew how to organise a defence. Gigi said he would do what he could. Sid Hobbins had told me that if Stock did find an Italian club I would, of course, be looked after.

The amazing thing was that it happened: happened as high up as

Roma, the club that Gigi went to first. They were looking for a new manager and the President, Sacerdoti, as much the Grand Panjandrum as ever, allowed himself to be convinced that Stock was his man. But Harry Zussman was still more strongly convinced that Stock, whom, after all, he had plucked out of the chorus, was *his* man. Zussman and Sacerdoti, as it happened, were both Jewish, but the contrast was absolute. Sacerdoti was tall, studiously dignified and orotund. Harry made a virtue of being down to earth, unaffected and exuberant: a joyfully unreconstructed East-Ender. He had an irrepressible sense of humour. Sacerdoti had none at all. Sacerdoti clearly saw himself as a Roman aristocrat in everything but birth. Harry Zussman was what he was and had no ambition to be anything else. So the harder Sacerdoti pushed, the harder Harry Zussman pulled.

I was in Rome in the middle of it all, in Roma's offices, then down by the Tiber, the evening when Sacerdoti swept in and announced with dramatic certitude, '*Stock viene alla Roma.*' (Stock is coming to Roma.) He wasn't, for a while. The tug of war went on, till at last Alec decided he would leave London. He called his staff together, told them he would be going and said to Hobbins, 'As for you, Sid, if you go down to the bank you'll find there's something there for you, and if I were you, I'd take my wife and family on holiday.'

Sid duly went down to the bank and found that what was waiting for him was £40. He was not too pleased, and became disaffected there and then. In later months, he would spend much time and energy trying to expose Orient's alleged finagling, though it never came to anything.

I was in Rome, as was Peronace, when Stock arrived. We sat in a car outside the Hotel Quirinale. 'How much do you want?' Stock asked us.

'I don't know,' said Gigi.

'I don't know,' I said.

Alec got out of the car and went into the hotel. 'How much *do* you want?' I asked Gigi.

'At least a million,' he said, meaning lire. The rate then was some 1,700 to the pound, but of course the pound was worth a great deal more than now.

'Then I'll ask half a million,' I said.

Up in his room, Stock stripped to have a shower. 'Quite honestly,' he said. 'Quite honestly.'

I realised he would have trouble when it was announced that Roma had appointed Busoni as their chief executive, a man who had briefly been one of the three who ran the Italian national team, and who had a formidable fame as an intriguer. Back in London, I spoke to Sacerdoti on the phone.

'*Ma Lei parla un italiano perfetto,*' he exclaimed, '*perfetto!*' (You speak perfect Italian.) Which may or may not have been true; it was no different from the Italian I had spoken to him on other occasions. He then told me, with some anxiety, 'Carver says that Stock isn't *un allenatore*', which can best be translated here as 'a coach'. I said I thought he was, and spoke about it to Bob Findlay, then the sports editor of the *Daily Express*. Findlay blew it up into a piece under the headline WAR BETWEEN TWO ENGLISH MANAGERS. I got the blame from both of them; Stock expostulated bitterly when I telephoned him.

Alas, he did not stay long. Roma were due to play their so-called 'derby' match in Naples. Stock and his interpreter missed the train that the team was on and came down later. By the time they arrived, Busoni and his cronies had picked the side. Stock refused to take charge of it on the bench; sat in the stand; and was sacked.

Many weeks passed. No half a million lire. Eventually, one hot day in Richmond Park, I asked Louis Blom-Cooper, as a barrister, what he thought I should do. 'Write him a letter,' he said. I did. There was no reply. But the next time I saw Gigi in the Mount Royal Hotel, he reproached me, 'How could you ask that poor man for money?' That did it. Gigi, affecting moral superiority! Never again, I thought, never again.

I spent three months in Italy that summer, some of it clopping around the stony mountains of Calabria, pursuing the story of a *mafioso* mayor who had kidnapped a schoolteacher. Mauro Franceschini was flourishing now; at long last all his hard work on the training ground at Rifredi was paying off. Bigger and bigger clubs were acquiring his players *in comproprietà*. The bicycle had gone; a powerful car had taken its place. In it he drove me to the seaside, to Viareggio, Paradise of Florentines. One of his pupils, the red-haired full back, Angiolini, sat in the rear seat.

Zooming in and out of the traffic, Mauro exhorted Angiolini, 'How many cars have we passed? Keep the score, Angiolini, keep the score.' Zoom, zoom. 'If I'd only started earlier, I'd have been another Musso!' – the motor-racing star of the moment. 'How many cars, Angiolini?'

'Ninety-two.'

'Keep the score.' Zoom! Another car overtaken. 'Because, in Italy, there's no discipline.' A lorry would loom in front of us. '*Quell'armadio!*' (That wardrobe!) Eventually he passed it; on we zoomed.

In Viareggio he had a squad of his boys on holiday in a *pensione*, sniffing the sea breezes. At lunch he sat at the head of a long table, roaring out his views. A well-known manager had been to Rio to study Brazilian methods. 'That charlatan! What did he find? That in Rio there's a beach where everybody plays: old men, women, cripples!'

After lunch, we all repaired to a nearby pine wood and lay there, under the trees, for a siesta. Mauro had an invitation from Walter Winterbottom himself – or 'Meester Bottom', as a huge fishmonger known as the 'Big Carp' used to call him – to visit the Football Association training course. Mauro was sceptical about the Big Carp, a burly presence at the stadium and round the Bar Gol, where Fiorentina fans gathered to argue near the post office, and where I once saw a *tifoso* laughingly pile one coloured newspaper after another into the hands of another to emphasise his point. 'He talks about women,' cried Mauro. 'But I know him; he likes small boys.'

Driving back to Florence that evening, the traffic heavier than ever, Mauro continued to overtake, cut in and exploit the smallest space, until at last he was stymied at a traffic light, boxed in as he tried to make a third line of cars. One car after another drove past him in the adjacent lane, their occupants jeering out of the windows. '*Dio boia, la milizia!*' he suddenly exclaimed. (God the hangman – a famous Florentine expression – the traffic police!)

A huge, khaki-uniformed copper on a motor bike, formidably helmeted, appeared beside us and looked in at Mauro's window. 'What would happen if a lorry came along?' he asked mildly, and made room for Mauro to slip into the line.

After admiring English football and speaking so passionately of English football for so long, the idea of actually leaving Italy for England disconcerted Mauro. He was a Tuscan through and through. We sat in his car outside the Pensione Bartolini one evening while I drafted, at his behest, a letter to Walter Winterbottom explaining, untruly, that he had to do his military service. England never saw him.

Once, we drove to Viareggio with a girl, rather than a footballer, in the car. She was a plump, raucous Florentine brunette whom Mauro would refer to as *una donuccia* – a dirty great lady, you might roughly translate it. On arrival, he and she got on a boat and disappeared out to sea; I did not see him again for many hours to come.

With Chelsea Casuals, I brought off my first great coup. Towards the end of our first season I persuaded Reg Drury to join us. He was highly sceptical. He had, after all, spent all his playing days in Hackney, whose Jewish clubs took soccer seriously. 'Duke of York's would beat you twenty goals,' he once said. But now, marrying his Irish girlfriend, Cepta, he had made the great trek northwest, to a house in Finchley. Then there was Blondie – enlisted in Hyde Park when, one Sunday morning, he joined in a game in which John Moynihan and I were playing. He was a stocky, fair-haired fellow in his twenties, and I had seen him play before when John and I had joined a larger, more committed game. He had looked very good: a strong tackler who was eager for the ball. Our own game seemed by then to have withered on the vine; there were just a few of us in the park that morning. Blondie, alias Peter Hudson, then a bank clerk, had turned up accompanied by a small boy.

'For God's sake get his phone number,' I urged John. He did, and wrote it down on a cigarette packet. So Blondie made his debut for us on the Royal Hospital pitch in our last game of the season, against formidable Chelwick, a Sunday team that 'meant it'. Thanks to Reg, we wore a Queens Park Rangers second strip of red shirts. Chelwick quite outshone us; they were wearing the dazzling equivalent of Manchester United's second strip, which was then all white, the shorts being very short indeed.

Blondie was not very tall, but his heading was formidable. 'He *flies* through the air,' said Phil Isaacs, admiringly. In goal, a laconic Scotsman, Scott Birnie, performed great feats. 'That left back comes through like Langley,' one of the opposition said of me, making an analogy with Fulham's attacking left back that was grossly flattering. All through the first half we would keep them out. But who was captain?

At the kickoff, as John moved forward to toss up, Keith went past him at a rate of knots, and tossed up instead. 'I said to John, "I thought you were captain,"' said Reg, drily. 'John said, "*I* thought I was."'

Early in the second half, their little outside right tricked me near the corner flag and put over a cross that was headed in. They rejoiced as if it were the Cup Final. With Maurice Schofield, our most dangerous forward, lamed by a harsh tackle, our chances seemed meagre. But almost at the end, Reg lunged in bravely to score the equaliser. Chelwick found it hard to believe. Casuals, at last, were well and truly launched.

The following season would show a dramatic transformation. In the first instance, we began to recruit players from the Royal College of Art, where John's father, Rodrigo, had been professor of painting.

Most of them were northern boys, studying ancillary subjects, who had been on the books of local professional clubs, though Keith Bell, once with Rochdale, was a painter. Small, skilful and adroit, he used to giggle as he slipped past opponents. Geoff Purser, another gifted inside left, had played senior amateur football.

The other great source of supply was the London School of Economics, where my brother-in-law Bernard, who had joined the club, was now teaching. Their captain, Des Cohen, who had played against us for a Jewish team, the Eagles, said he would put out a team against us at Berrylands, the LSE's ground.

'I think Des gets out a beer team,' one of the Eagles told me. Some beer team! Our opposition was late getting to the ground, and we were kicking in when they took the field, each player seeming bigger than the one before. 'Milk and orange juice,' said Bernard. 'Milk and orange juice!' This was no beer team, but the full LSE first eleven, preparing for a cup tie. They beat us 9–1.

After the game, Bernard and I spent a long time drinking with them at the bar. Friendships were formed. Several of them, sturdy and engaging northern lads, several from Lancashire, began to play for us. Bonds were forged that lasted for many years. When various LSE players left university and began to play for Ulysses, the former London University club, Ulysses footballers played for us as well. A few years after that defeat, a Chelsea Casuals team went down to Berrylands and beat the LSE first team 7–1. Norman Ackroyd, a highly talented painter and engraver from Leeds who looked a little bit like Denis Law, never stopped running. He came to us from the Royal College of Art and ironised about the fact that before the game, he had been told that nine first-teamers had been playing. Afterwards, he heard that there had been only seven: 'And two of those didn't know they'd been dropped.'

Keith wanted to be captain, and Keith wanted to play inside left. He was a good footballer who had once kept goal for Tudor Rose, the Chelsea junior team of the time. He headed the ball well (he said it gave him headaches) and had a very powerful right-foot shot with which, occasionally, he scored sensational goals from long-range. We wanted him to play left half, where we thought he was much more effective, but we didn't want him to be captain as we felt he would be divisive. There was tension.

One Sunday afternoon, sharing a motor coach, we went down to Southend with the Eagles team, their first eleven, and lost by several goals. Keith did play inside forward that day, and played well. The other inside forward was Mike Pinner, the Cambridge Blue, England amateur goalkeeper, and, at the time, Aston Villa keeper, who loved to play for us on Sundays because it re-created the ambience he had enjoyed so much with Pegasus. Socially, of course; by no means in terms of ability and prowess.

At that time, we used to have a team meeting every week, and one was held a few days later in my tiny flat in Sloane Avenue. Keith, feeling his oats, favoured us with a critique of our failings. He not only assured me I had played badly, which was true, but accused me of hitting an opponent who ran by me, which is something I have never done in my life. Reg challenged him to name names, in other contexts, which he wouldn't. John sat there, appalled. I described the meeting afterwards as group analysis without the analyst.

'John didn't sleep all night,' said Keith, regretfully, a little later. Something had to be done, and we did it. John, Phil, Reg and I decided, first, there would be no more meetings; second, Keith would not be captain; third, he would not be inside left; and fourth, the captain would be Reg.

And what a captain he was! Energetic, indomitable, ruthless. 'All right, all right,' he would cry, in the midst of battle. Hackney Marshes had left their mark. 'I don't mind shaking hands with them, Brian,' he told me, 'but I can't give three cheers. It sticks in my throat.'

When, some years later, we played on Hackney Marshes against Battersea, the team eventually formed by our old Hyde Park foes, the opposition appeared in various colours, one of them playing in jeans. We scored a lot of goals against them – games would later be much closer – and Reg knocked ten minutes or so off the time to save them from further punishment. 'I don't mind playing them again, Brian,' he said, 'but not at Hackney, 'cos there's people there that know me.'

'Before each game,' I once wrote of him, to his displeasure, 'there was the endless ritual of bandages, as though he were preparing for his own private sarcophagus.' He always played in spectacles: his football glasses. Once, on the Royal Hospital pitch, he took a nasty bang in the face, and his glasses broke. Needless to say, he played on. The following Sunday, at Colindale, playing the Royal Dental Hospital, Reg was down on his knees in the heavy North London mud, when the half-time whistle blew. We crowded round him anxiously, afraid he had been hurt again. 'No, I'm all right,' he said. 'I was looking for me gum.'

About the time we lost to Show Biz, my fourth novel, *The Bankrupts*, came out. It was a stark picture of Jewish life in Northwest London. Most of the initial reviews were positive, but then the storm broke, and it would last for years. So many letters poured into the *Jewish Chronicle*, for and against, that they eventually published them in a special supplement. Opponents of the book were broadly divided between those who thought it unkind and unfair, and those who thought that, in the delightful words of the actor David Kossoff, four years later, it could constitute 'a handbook for anti-Semites'. Broadcast words which, as we shall see, led, bitterly, to the High Court.

By then, I had begun writing football short stories. The notion had come to me that summer of 1957, in Florence, when, at siesta time, I lay on a bed at the Bartolini – I had a better, larger, room by now – reading the baseball short stories of Ring Lardner with delight. The first such story I wrote, 'Goalkeepers are Crazy', was turned down by those popular magazines I sent it to and published, eventually, by the highly literary monthly, *The London Magazine*, thanks largely, I believe, to its future editor, the poet, critic, cricketer and brave naval officer, Alan Ross.

Once I had begun, there were so many tales to tell, in so many voices; not least the marvellous anecdotes bequeathed me by Ted Crawford, which I eagerly used. In time, such stories would find a home all over the place. There would even be *Evening Standard* vans travelling London carrying a poster for them on the roof, yet it seemed both ironic and indicative that at first, only a highbrow magazine would touch them.

At Chelsea Casuals, two people taught me to play football at left back. One was Mike Pinner, who kept goal not only for Aston Villa but for Sheffield Wednesday and, once each, for Chelsea and Manchester United. Later, with Reg and myself as his proxies, he would play professionally for Queens Park Rangers and Leyton Orient. But still, so flatteringly, he played for us: first at left half, then on the left wing. His left foot was formidable. 'Come on, come on!' he would cry when we went training, *à deux*, in Hyde Park, opposite the barracks. Wiry and fit, he was a hard man to keep up with.

As a left winger, he was always calling for the ball. Norman Ackroyd would recall a game at Vincent Square against Westminster School, which we were lucky enough to have twice a season for many years, when he heard Mike yelling for a pass. 'I looked up to see him flat on the ground, with three defenders round him.'

And there was Piero: Mauro's protégé, originally. He had written to me. A long, emotional letter, telling me he was coming to London in the hope of studying English football; how he had been nicknamed 'Bozsik', after the Hungarian star; how his promising career had been ended by knee injuries; and how Mauro had ultimately let him down and disappointed him. I did not reply; the criticism of Mauro seemed, in the context, gratuitous. But one morning the bell of my Chelsea flat rang and there was Piero himself. A tall, blond, heavy Florentine with a heavy chin and a heavy Florentine accent, smiling, full of goodwill and buoyant enthusiasm. I ushered him in and eventually took him to the pub up the road for lunch. Mauro, it grew clear, had not treated him well. He was plainly more intelligent than Mauro, had a lively sense of humour, which Mauro lacked, and a manifest idealism.

I did my best for him, arranging for him to attend the training of clubs such as Arsenal and West Ham United; and enlisting him for Chelsea Casuals. So he played for us, an outraged perfectionist, shouting at us in his then rudimentary English. 'John, John. Don't go way, John' as our centre forward threatened to disappear over the horizon before the ball could come. 'Brian, Brian; take your time.' Scott would lean against the goalpost and remark, ironically, 'Tell Piero to take his time, Brian.' Reg was sceptical. 'He *talks* a good game,' he said one day, in the Tottenham car park, where you could then meet Tottenham's players as well as Johnny the Stick and One-Armed Lew, their privileged hangers-on. Danny Blanchflower, gifted and fluent captain of Northern Ireland, who was standing nearby, said he thought Reg wasn't being very fair to him. Reg had quickly to explain.

In Hyde Park, Piero coached John and myself. He had obviously been a player of impressive technique; he could bring down a high ball with easy skill. Indeed, he had been on the fringe of Italy's youth team before his knees packed up on him. It was the beginning of our first full season, and to start with, before the reinforcements came, we were a very limited team. I suggested we might play a counter-attacking game. 'With who?' asked Piero, despairingly. We continued to play frequently at Hackney Marshes, where, then, you carried your own goalposts, changed in a cramped wooden hut of Stygian gloom and washed in cold water in the equivalent of horse troughs. John and I would catch a very early bus from South Kensington Station which took us, in its own time, all the way to Hackney. It seemed an awfully long ride on the way back, after we had lost.

Indeed, we lost an early game there against a team from Western Union, full of very mobile teenagers, 2–1. 'Brian,' said Piero, sadly, '*ti sei demoralizzato!*' which alas was true; I had indeed eventually been demoralised. 'In the park, you're a lion,' he told me, 'but, in a match, I could always play against you.' Still, he and Pinner between them were helping me to improve.

1958 was a momentous year for me. Pam, my future wife, was getting her divorce, so we could marry. Casuals began to flourish. And I covered the World Cup for the *Sunday Times*.

It took many months of negotiation. Amazing, now, to think of just how casually the great broadsheets, then, took the competition. On the *Sunday Times*, rugby ruled. Football correspondents were appointed in the most haphazard way. At that time, it was an Oxford don who had met the paper's editor on a train down to London, spoken of his interest in football, and been commissioned in consequence. Later, Jim Wilson, then an Army colonel, who in fact had long experience and deep knowledge of the game, found himself at a party talking to somebody called Mortimer, who asked him whether he would like to write for the paper. Thinking he was talking to the celebrated literary critic Raymond Mortimer, Jim said he would. In fact he was talking to the racing correspondent, Roger Mortimer, and it was as football correspondent that he was taken on.

When I returned to London in 1955, Jerry Weinstein told me the *Sunday Times* were looking for a football correspondent, and that I should apply to them. I duly did, only to receive a dusty answer; I wasn't even offered a match report. So I went from the *Empire News* to the *Observer*, who, it grew plain to me, were unlikely to send me to Sweden for the World Cup Finals. Indeed, they sent Tony Pawson and, into the bargain, refused to let me use my own name in the *Sunday Times*. I therefore used my second name and reported for them as Brian Lester.

For weeks on end I spoke on the telephone to Ken Compston, the laconic Mancunian who was sports editor of the *Sunday Times*. He held out hopes of commissioning me, on a freelance basis, but for a long time the job hung in the balance. At long last, to my delight and relief, he told me I was hired. I would receive £20 an article, and no expenses. But, accredited by PA Reuters Features, I had a good deal of freelance work that would get me through, even if the £7 expenses per diem enjoyed, then, by my national newspaper colleagues seemed beyond the dreams of avarice.

England were based in Gothenburg, so that was where I went, to a hotel somewhat misleadingly called The Ritz, which stood quite near the railway station. In the room adjacent to mine stayed Wilfried Gerhardt, a charming German, working then for a press agency, later to become the grey eminence of the German Deutsche Fussball Bund, their FA, when they put him in charge of public relations. His English was exquisite, with the one exception of the double 't', which he intoned with a cockney glottal stop. The words 'bot'le' and 'rat'led' would suddenly emerge in his speech like vulgar interlopers. It was many years before I could bring myself to mention it. Wilfried was hurt. 'I thought that was how it was pronounced,' he replied. He had lived with a family in Romford.

'Isn't it a sin and a shame,' asked George Raynor, who was managing Sweden again, with great veterans such as Nils Liedholm and Gunnar Gren back in the team, 'that England stayed at the Park Avenue Hotel?' – a hotel bang in the middle of Gothenburg. Notionally, this made it convenient for journalists, but in fact doors would be shut in our faces, notably by the interpreter, a tall, blond, epicene Swede, who could be seen trotting, bare-chested, round the track when England trained at the old Gothenburg stadium.

Training, too, would be an Englishman of military demeanour, a military moustache, and the general carriage of a non-commissioned officer. He turned out to be a wealthy businessman called Chalwyn who had given Sir Stanley Rous hospitality in Australia. In the 1962 World Cup in Chile, up in the hills at Coya, he would even join in England's training games, though the players, at meal times, were said to shift their tables to avoid him. 'We're playing the Chalwyn plan,' Bernard Joy would say.

For reasons that defied reason, England had brought only 20 players rather than the permitted 22 to Sweden, omitting Bolton's Nat Lofthouse and the indestructible Stanley Matthews. The horrific disaster at Munich airport the previous February had robbed the team of three crucial Manchester United players in Roger Byrne, the left back, Duncan Edwards, the powerful young left half, and Tommy Taylor, the centre forward.

I had first got wind of the crash when visiting the offices of the publishers Stanley Paul with Jack Kelsey, the Welsh international goalkeeper whose autobiography I was then 'ghosting'. There was a tiny item in the stop press of a London evening paper which hinted at a bad landing in Munich. Jack, the publisher Bill Luscombe and I, hoped and thought it would be nothing serious.

That evening, when we all knew how cruelly serious it was, John Moynihan and I went training at the Queens Park Rangers ground, which we used to do on Tuesday nights, though it involved little more than lapping a muddy pitch. Alan, who was also present, talked endlessly of how well he knew Duncan Edwards, who by then was in hospital, fighting vainly for his life. Alan was a well-known if peripheral character at that time. I had first met him when I went to the Great Northern Hotel, near King's Cross, to speak to the players of the Northern Ireland team. Alan, a tall, blond Geordie in his twenties, suddenly arrived, dropped to one knee beside a player in an armchair, and emitted an unending stream of dropped names and cross-references. This player had told him this; the other player had told him that.

It was like a kind of smokescreen of words, behind which, and its allusions, he could shelter from any kind of rejection. Did he want tickets on that occasion? I can't remember. In ensuing years, I was to see a very great deal of him. In winter, dressed in a camel-hair coat, he assumed the mannerisms of a pop singer; to be one was one of his ambitions. He hung around a great deal with show business people, played, competently, for the Show Biz team and survived a score of snubs from Show Biz people themselves. But he was unsnubbable; it was his essential stock-in-trade.

I went up to Stockholm to watch Sweden play, and beat, a much diminished Hungary. 'Comes the revolution', and the stars had departed. Puskas, Czibor and Kocsis all settled down in Spain. Hidegkuti and Bozsik were spent forces. *Learn to Play the Hungarian Way* was the title of a book issued shortly after the Hungarians had annihilated England at Wembley. The word was that the Hungarians, with their variegated training, had 'got it right', that the world would be foolish not to follow them. Their somewhat unlucky defeat by Germany in the Final of the World Cup of 1954 in Berne suggested they were hardly invincible and now, in 1958, they looked little better than moderate.

Raynor was as delightfully ebullient as ever. 'We're the slowest team in the competition,' he confessed. 'If there was a relay race between all the teams, Sweden would finish last. But we'll still reach the Final.' Which they did.

He was scathing on the subject of Nacka Skoglund, now an outside left of skill, speed and penetration, who had been involved in some skirmishes. He would be having a word with him. 'We want no circus men in our team.'

Back in Gothenburg, one of the delights was the psychologist the Brazilians had brought with them; eclectic to a degree. He wore grey sweaters, spectacles, and what in those days was not yet known as designer stubble. He complained that everyone was writing about him, but no one sent him the articles. Some players, he said, were instinctive, some more cerebral. To find out which was which, he encouraged them to draw pictures of a player. The first category drew the equivalent of matchstick men, the cerebrals' figures were more sophisticated. The two types made good wing partnerships. Defenders should contain their aggression; attackers should project it. He did not believe in haranguing players in groups, but nor did he like to talk to them individually, because this simply magnified the problems.

Vicente Feola, the plump, rumbling manager of Brazil, was not impressed by him. Towards the end of the competition, Danny Blanchflower, fluent and polymath captain of Northern Ireland, attended a press conference at which Feola was asked about the psychologist. 'Senhor Feola,' said the interpreter, 'is not saying that he wishes the psychologist would go to hell, but he is thinking it.'

In those happy, innocent days before World Cups became a chaotic, overcrowded circus in which television ruled, it was possible to attend training sessions as one wished. Out at Hindas where the Brazilians had their training camp, one could watch their joyous training, the players yelling at each other like a male voice chorus gone berserk. When they trained in the Ullevi Stadium in Gothenburg, you could talk to Feola behind one of the goals and hear him deprecating the performance of Mazzola.

Mazzola in fact was the nickname given in Brazil to the nineteen-year-old centre forward José Altafini, who was already booked to go to Milan when the tournament ended.

'He's nineteen,' Feola rumbled, shaking his head. 'All the publicity about his transfer to Milan; how can it help but go to his head? He doesn't fit in with the team.' Mazzola, nicknamed because of his alleged resemblance to a famous captain of Italy, Valentino Mazzola, who died in the Turin air crash of 1949 and begat the equally distinguished Sandro, looked good to me; but Vavà, eventually, and effectively, replaced him.

Russian footballers, due to meet Brazil in the final group eliminating match, would lumber out of the woods like bears to watch them train. Much was said about the new *wunderkind*, the seventeen-year-old Pele, a fabulous scorer of goals, but for the moment injured and inactive.

England drew 2–2 with Russia in Gothenburg, Derek Kevan scoring that invaluable goal, from Billy Wright's lofted free kick, with the 'outside' of his head, but Tom Finney, who had tied the Russian right back Kessarev in knots, was injured and forced to drop out; a fearful blow and an irreplaceable loss. At this time the England team was still supposed to be picked by a selection committee, but it was an open secret that Walter Winterbottom, not unfairly, was now getting his way. Some of the choices, however, were contentious.

Against Brazil, though, England did commendably well, with a game plan allegedly devised by their coach, Bill Nicholson, who would have so many years of success at Tottenham Hotspur. Don Howe, the right back, operated as a second centre half and Eddie Clamp, the Wolves right half, as what we would now call an attacking wing back. All in all, Brazil's attack was smothered, though England's was seldom seen; with one exception. When Bellini, the Brazilian centre half, brought down the onrushing Kevan, there should certainly have been a penalty, but it wasn't given. Brazil now were playing with a system that would shortly dominate football: 4–4–2, with four defenders strung across the back, as opposed to the Third Back Game introduced in England by Arsenal in 1925, with a stopper centre half and pivoting full backs. This was a system that was always alien to Brazilian football, and which its teams had never really mastered.

One of my salient memories of that game was of Don Howe skying a ball that was immaculately brought down by the England left back, Tommy Banks, a robust Lancastrian famous for his physical commitment rather than his skill, but at that moment clearly determined to show the Brazilians that he could be as technically adroit as they.

We had two memorable press games in the older Ullevi Stadium: the first against the Swedes; the second against the Brazilians. Our captain was my old hero, Bernard Joy, still an imposing centre half. Tony Pawson, not so long ago an Olympic footballer, grey-haired, quick, a clever dribbler, was at outside right. Some notable stomachs were revealed. And Alan Hoby, at left half, accused me, much amused, of being one of the dirtiest players he had seen.

Alan, who had been sports columnist for the *People* and was by then on the *Sunday Express*, had been a patient of my father's and had kindly given me a plug for the Bastin book. He was a slender, elegant, highly strung, sophisticated man who had served in the Royal Marines during the war. Perceptive and humorous, there was, however, a curious dichotomy between what he said and what he wrote. Years of working for the popular press, as we knew it then, had left him, in print, with a persona which had little or nothing to do with the real man.

The Swedes, that day, had an inside forward, 57 years old, called Sven Rydell, a little, grey-haired man who had once been a famous international. Next morning in a local paper there was a photograph of him and myself tussling for the ball. I sent it to Pam, who wrote back that she enjoyed the picture of me 'bashing that poor old man'.

The truth was that I could hardly get near him; he was so quick and fit and skilful.

We managed to draw 3–3, thanks in large measure to a superbly brave performance by our goalkeeper, Alan Clark, a BBC radio commentator. So gravelly was the pitch that Harold Shepherdson, the England trainer, afterwards took a long time to remove the tiny stones from Alan's knees. One of the goals we conceded was my fault; earlier success had gone to my head and I had ignored Bernard Joy's exhortation to clear the ball, rather than hang on to it.

The Brazilians were much less formidable. At half-time, as a joke, Geoffrey Greene of *The Times* and Maurice Smith of the *People* sneaked on to the field, making us thirteen in number. In no time at all the Brazilians had some twenty-five men there! We won 5–1, with an irresistible Tony Pawson scoring four times. Jack Peart, of all unlikely people – Stanley Halsey's *bête noire* – not only turned peacemaker when I rounded on a Brazilian who had clouted me in the face, but picked his way meticulously through the defence to score our final goal. I then learnt that, in his youth, he had been a player of some substance.

Would the *Sunday Times*, I wondered, take me on when the World Cup was over? I spoke about it to Tony Stratton-Smith, then of the *Daily Sketch*, later a pop promoter, who would die sadly young. We sat in the Gothenburg park, trying our hand at describing passing clouds. Tony said that Faulkner, a favourite author of mine then, would surpass us both. He didn't think the *Sunday Times* would have me. 'They've got Jim Wilson,' he said.

The World Cup went on. England had to play-off against Russia. Members of the selection committee confided their doubts and preferences to journalists, filed into their meeting with Winterbottom and came out saying, 'No change'. But for the play-offs there would be two changes, and both seemed reckless. Peter Brabrook, the Chelsea outside right, and Peter Broadbent, the Wolves inside right, would receive their first caps in a game so vitally important.

No place for Bobby Charlton. He had clearly been traumatised by his appalling experience at Munich where he had survived almost miraculously, being catapulted out of the aeroplane still strapped into his seat. In Belgrade, on the way to the World Cup, where England had lost 5–0 in intense heat, he had had a poor game. But his promise was vast and evident. Not to use him at all seemed absurd. For much of the time he seemed understandably dejected. Just once, seated in the lounge of the Park Avenue Hotel, I heard him tell a joke. It was about a bus queue in his native northeast. A man in the queue, who could not quite get on, asked, 'How long will the next one be?'

'About as long as this one,' answered the conductor.

England lost the play-off to a single goal, and out they went. Brazil meanwhile had brought in the amazing Pele and the astonishing Garrincha, the child of Nature, the right winger with a distorted left leg which, in Adlerian fashion, he had turned into an advantage, facilitating an amazing body swerve, backed up by explosive acceleration. He would rout the Swedish defence to make two goals for Vavà in the Final, and would be even better, as an all-round performer, when Pele dropped out injured four years later in Chile.

As the World Cup went on and Sweden, to the surprise of their fans, made more and more progress, nationalism was in the air. One had already been surprised by the profusion of uniforms, as if the Swedes were somehow trying to make up for the fact that they had not fought in the war, but had merely allowed the Germans to march across their territory to Norway. War guilt seemed to be in the air still. When Sweden played Germany in the semi-final in Gothenburg, their cheerleaders pranced about the pitch with flags before the kickoff, while a man in a blazer exhorted the crowd through a microphone. 'Heja, heja, heja!' they thunderously chorused. Such licence was forbidden for the Final. Without exhortation, the Stockholm crowd was curiously quiet.

Wales had gone out gallantly. Really they should not have been there at all, but when the Arab countries refused to play Israel in a run-off decreed by FIFA, Uruguay, already knocked out, proudly refused to step in; Wales, with less pride, accepted, winning 2–0, home and away.

Resilient, they beat the Hungarians in a play-off to reach the quarter-final against Brazil – and Pele. Had the massive John Charles, King John, as he was known by worshipping Juventus fans in Turin, been fit to play, who knows what might have happened? As it was, one watched in Gothenburg as the Welsh defence put up a marvellously defiant show against Brazil's attackers, with Mel Hopkins, at left back, largely containing Garrincha, and Mel Charles, younger brother of John, a Titan at centre half.

The only, Brazilian, goal was fortuitous, even though in later years Pele would say it was the most important he had ever scored. In fact his shot would hardly have gone in had it not hit the boot of the resilient Welsh full back, Stuart Williams, and been diverted past an otherwise impeccable Jack Kelsey. After the game, I congratulated Kelsey on his handling. 'Chewing gum,' he replied. 'Always use it. Put some on my hands. Rub it well in.'

The following evening I went out drinking with Jack and several of his Welsh colleagues, who had nicknamed themselves 'The Big Five'. We sat at an outdoor table high above Gothenburg, drinking round after round of potent dark beer, till I could no longer keep up with them. There was Colin Webster, the Manchester United forward, and Derek Sullivan, the Cardiff City wing half. 'Fem beers, miss,' they kept saying, 'fem beers'. Five beers. They had earned them. Kelsey, once a blacksmith in the village of Winch Wen, had the huge hands to go with the trade. He had had a bad beginning, making his debut for Arsenal in 1951 at home to Charlton Athletic whose attack was then led by the formidable Swedish international, Hans Jeppson, who scored three out of five Charlton goals.

The following week, up the road from Highbury at the old Finsbury Park Empire – a bastion of variety – Old Mother Reilly and Kitty McShane were playing. At one point they brought on a bedraggled figure. 'Arsenal's new goalkeeper,' said Arthur Lucan, playing Old Mother Reilly, in drag. Arsenal complained, and the scene was dropped. Kelsey would go from strength to strength.

He spoke to me, while I was 'ghosting' his book, about the brief, unhappy spell of Alec Stock at Highbury, before Harry Zussman whisked him back to Orient, again. The directors plainly thought Tom Whittaker was losing his authority. Stock became assistant manager and told the players that twenty of them would soon be away. The players, said Kelsey, were shocked; 'We had never been spoken to like that before.' There was a significant moment when he and Dennis Evans, the ginger-haired left back, were smoking while Stock talked. Stock sent a younger player, Danny Clapton, over with an ashtray, to have them stub out their cigarettes. Each of them simply tapped his ash into the ashtray and continued smoking. So Stock went back to Brisbane Road and, later, had happier times at Queens Park Rangers and at Luton Town.

So to the World Cup Final in the rain, in Stockholm. 'If Brazil give away an early goal,' forecast George Raynor, 'they'll panic all over the show.' They did give away an early goal but they didn't panic. The goal was scored by 36-year-old Nils Liedholm, playing at inside left, the man who had called Raynor a good manager of a happy team. He picked his way expertly through the Brazilian penalty area, after only four minutes, to put his team ahead.

It didn't last. Two jaguar swoops by Garrincha, those two goals by Vavà, and afterwards three more, two from Pele. The first of which was a small miracle of cool juggling in the box, surrounded by tough defenders, the second his majestic header. When the tireless

Mario Lobo Zagallo, later to win the World Cup as manager as well as player, scored for Brazil, he went down on his knees in joy. 'Samba, samba!' shouted the Brazilian fans. After the final whistle, the Brazilian players ran round the field, first with their own flag then with Sweden's. The joyful psychologist ran with them.

I went on down to Milan by train and slept nearly a day when I got there. In Florence, I cut my shin open on the new metal steps on the Bartolini's roof, and David had to come to the rescue again, putting me on to a doctor in Rome who, when the wound wouldn't heal, put me on the right medicaments – and sunshine.

Back in London, the new football season was approaching and there was still no word from the *Sunday Times*. The season began and I was still, reluctantly, with the *Observer*, and hauled into the office on Saturday afternoons, as often as not, to write a football round-up anonymously, rather than to report a match.

At last, in September, the call came. I went to the *Sunday Times*' then dingy offices in Grays Inn Road, met Ken Compston for the first time, and was offered the job of joint football correspondent with Jim Wilson, who would turn out to be the most generous and genial of colleagues.

Chris Brasher, sports editor of the *Observer*, tried to make me stay, but offered me nothing attractive. Anonymous round-ups still seemed to be at the heart of it. 'They didn't ask you to come in and sweep up on a Saturday night, as well?' asked an amused colleague. 'You're determined to go, aren't you?' asked Chris, and indeed I was; the *Sunday Times* had long been my principal ambition.

So I began to work for Compston. He was a man somewhere in his fifties, laconic to a degree. 'That's all cold, dead, wet fish,' he would say. Dressed, usually, in a tweed jacket, his hair scanty, his demeanour sour, he worked with a single, female secretary and usually answered the phone himself, in his sepulchral voice. 'Sport!'

'How are you, Ken?'

'Bloody awful.'

He was most reluctant to send anybody on a foreign trip and once, when I returned from New York later than he had expected, but still in time, having flown overnight to cover that Saturday afternoon's game, he flew into a rage and refused to send me. I had a fantasy about him: I would go to him one day and say, 'Ken, I wonder if I can go to Alderney tomorrow. I've got an inside track on the Second Coming.'

At which he would, characteristically, take off his spectacles, ungum his right eye, and reply, 'I don't really see it for us, Brian. I know we're meant to be an Anglican newspaper, but strictly between thee and me, I don't think there's the religious interest. You can try it on the news side.'

It was the same year, 1958, when, thanks to the recommendation of the critic, novelist and scholar Peter Green, whose job it was, I was made literary adviser to Bodley Head. This meant reading lots of manuscripts and going into their office in Seven Dials once a week for a conference. The head of the firm was the urbane, genial, well-preserved Max Reinhardt, whose chief advantage was his ability to charm the good and the great; notably Charlie Chaplin, whose autobiography was his greatest coup. By an odd stroke, one of the firm's subsidiary titles was T Werner Laurie.

The two senior literary directors were JB Priestley and Graham Greene, both Heinemann authors then, but otherwise the sharpest of contrasts. In 1961, after I had been on tour with the England team in Vienna, I met Greene at one of Max's many cocktail parties in his elegant South Kensington house, and told Greene something I thought might amuse him. The *Sunday Times* stringer had failed to book me into my hotel for the night we arrived, and I was led round the corner to a smaller, less salubrious one.

Presiding was a large, fat woman in carpet slippers who greeted me, 'Come in, come in, do not make afraid', while a procession of what seemed like East European refugees in shiny peaked leather caps walked in with rolls of carpet on their shoulders, which she fulsomely admired.

'It was just like a scene from one of your novels,' I said.

At this, Greene bridled. 'I don't know why people write about Greeneland,' he said, huffily. 'I simply describe what I see.'

Early in 1959, Pam and I moved into the pleasant top-floor flat of a cylindrical building opposite South Kensington Station. A little later we were married in the same register office where Peter had married Carla. Later still in the year came the birth of our first child, Mark; for me, a cataclysmic event. Alas, it was also the year when my poor father fell ill with cancer of the pancreas, moving in and out of University College Hospital, and his flat in Dorset House, where Uncle Willy Warshaw had lived. Now and then, with tantalising cruelty, it seemed that there might be a remission, but the illusion never lasted long and he was often in dire pain. I saw him every day. My mother was devastated.

I saw a lot of Danny Blanchflower. He had written a lively foreword to Jerry Weinstein's and my book on the World Cup, which appeared not long before he so skilfully captained his Northern Ireland team in Sweden. He was a remarkable, refreshing maverick among those professional footballers, though his Belfast origins were no different from theirs. Late in the war, on an RAF commission course, he had attended St Andrews University in Scotland. He was as fluent a writer as he was a talker. He analysed football with tremendous flair and originality, an eagle eye for detail, and kicked steadily against the pricks of a game dominated by the uneducated, the unenlightened and the *nouveaux riches*.

He took football seriously, but could talk about it flippantly. Before Northern Ireland (who had sensationally eliminated Italy) set out for Sweden, he announced that they had got a plan: 'We're going to equalise before the other team score.' I would talk with him, fascinated, for hours; sometimes in cafés near Tottenham, sometimes, after he had given me a lift home, in the flat I occupied before I moved to Chelsea, in that odd horseshoe Newton Road, off Westbourne Grove.

He and Peter Doherty, an abundantly gifted, red-haired inside left who had been playing 'Total Football', *avant la lettre*, made Northern Ireland what they so excitingly were. Doherty, who, in his playing days, had always resented the way the Irish team were put upon and marginalised, was an inspiring manager; Danny his perfect lieutenant – or captain. Jimmy McIlroy, whom I also came to know well, was an inside forward with the same intelligence, technique and high ambitions. He played for Burnley when they were an exemplary team.

Danny's domestic life was not as serene. I had long phone calls from his wife, Betty, complaining of his neglect. 'I told him, those are your children, Danny. They're not your little brothers and sisters.' She was his second wife, having met him in her native Birmingham when he was playing for Aston Villa. It was saddening to hear of a marriage that was so clearly doomed. Danny was not a family man, but in his time he lit up the scene of football.

Had his younger brother, Jackie, not been traumatised by the Munich air crash of 1958, how much better Northern Ireland might have done in Sweden. Jackie was a player of great versatility, originally an inside forward, later a wing half, then, for Northern Ireland, a football playing centre half of skill, intelligence and resilience. He even played impressively in goal for Manchester United in the FA Cup Final of 1957, when Peter McParland's harsh challenge put Ray Wood – a goalkeeper who survived the crash – out of the game.

As Danny pointed out, the loss of his brother, and the need to put a full back, Willie Cunningham, in his place, entailed a tactical upheaval. Whereas Danny could happily leave his gifted brother to his own devices, and move upfield to link with Jimmy McIlroy and feed his right winger, Billy Bingham, Cunningham had to be protected; so Danny had to restrain his natural game.

Inevitably, he had his ups and downs with managers, who were usually far less intelligent than himself, and far less perceptive about the game. When, in an FA Cup semi-final, Spurs were losing to Manchester City, he decided, on his own account, to move the big centre half Maurice Norman into attack; Spurs still lost and the captaincy was taken away from him.

The intelligentsia rallied to him. Professor AJ 'Freddie' Ayer, the logical positivist and Tottenham fan, was a particular admirer. 'I succumb to his charm,' he told me. Once, the three of us took part in a discussion of football fiction on a television book programme, soon after I had published my first collection of short stories, *A Bad Streak*, in which the football tales had been picked out for special praise. Maurice Richardson, that idiosyncratic, very funny, writer and critic, wrote me out of the script in his *Observer* television column, in which he described Danny Blanchflower and Professor Ayer 'talking brilliantly' about the possibility of writing a football novel. I wrote it the following year.

For obscure reasons, I never got a friendly critique from Richardson for anything I wrote, though around that time, strangely enough, I was trying to persuade Bodley Head to republish his early, amusing, forgotten novels. In vain. I never met him.

Some time later, I was invited for drinks, by Freddie Ayer. The flattering reason was that he wanted his son, Julian, to play for Chelsea Casuals. This seemed to me an excellent idea. Julian was a big, strong inside forward who had played powerfully against us for Old Etonians on the Bank of England ground at Roehampton where we, then, had the privilege of occasionally appearing. Times had changed. We met the OEs quite often now; and never lost to them again.

Julian did play a game or two for us, but not with the same verve. 'They never play *for* us like they do *against* us,' said Blondie, sadly.

In 1960, I went to the Rome Olympics; despite Ken Compston. We had fallen out over a triviality. A newspaper that belonged to our organisation – in which the self-made Canadian millionaire Roy Thomson bought out Lord Kemsley – the *Aberdeen Press and Journal*, was carrying a column of mine about world football, worth seven guineas a week; very useful money, then. When I joined the *Sunday Times*, Compston and I had agreed that, for a small consideration, I would drop my byline on the same column, then running in the *Manchester Evening News*, the rival to Kemsley's *Manchester Evening Chronicle*. But the Aberdeen paper refused to run my pieces unless they could use my name. Since they were, in effect, a sister paper, it seemed reasonable to me, but not to Compston, that I should be allowed to do so. Eventually I got my way, but not before much bitter altercation; and Ken was not a man who easily forgot.

So it was that, though the Olympic Games were in Rome, which I knew so well, I was not accredited. It later emerged that Compston had farmed out the ticket to a reporter on the *Scotsman*. The *Sunday Times'* editor, HV Hodson, a decent India hand who had once, there, edited the *Round Table*, sent for me and I told him that I wanted to go. I knew Rome, I knew about a lot of sports, ergo I should be there.

Overruled, Compston sullenly agreed, but it was too late to accredit me. I could have £40 to cover tickets. No doubt my other sources would help me with the rest. I would be paid an extra £100 for my labours. But when I got there I found that I was expected to write the main feature.

To do that, access to the Olympic Village, which stood not far from the Stadio Olimpico, was essential, and to have this, I was obliged to wait every day on the official in charge, an amiable but discursive Armenian, who kept me talking for forty minutes or so, before I was granted the essential pass. Once inside the Village (in those remote and happy days), access to the athletes was delightfully easy. One talked to sprinters, swimmers, shot-putters, jumpers, hurdlers and footballers. And one spoke Italian. It was hard to go wrong.

Corriere dello Sport came blessedly to my rescue. They wanted to put out a multi-language paper for the duration of the Games, and I was co-opted to supply the English text. Presiding over the paper was a big, jolly, grey-haired Roman, Sabatini, whom I nicknamed Falstaff, so for *Corriere* the paper became *Il Giornale Falstaffiano*. Ringing the *Sunday Times* from the stadium on a Saturday afternoon, I was suddenly asked by the managing editor, Pat Murphy, to provide a news story.

I was taken aback. This was what the man from the *Scotsman* had supposedly been doing. 'What kind of a news story?' I asked.

'You're in Rome, Brian,' Pat replied, with his carefully articulated public school (Dulwich College) accent, the Rs just slightly impaired; 'I'm sitting here in London. It's for you to decide.' I thought of something.

Pat was a large, rotund and orotund figure, a practising Catholic who once told the literary editor he believed the Jews had still to expiate their guilt for the Crucifixion, yet played golf with Jewish businessmen and delighted in promoting their sons. I had, indeed, first heard of him from Peter Shaffer, riding high on the immense success of *Five Finger Exercise*.

This, I should say, in parenthesis, followed swiftly on the heels of a bleak few months at the start of the year. Peter had resigned his job as secretary to the music publishers, Boosey and Hawkes, to dedicate himself wholly to the theatre. Each weekend, he would laudably go down to Worthing to work backstage at the repertory theatre there. Meanwhile, he was living, like his twin brother Tony (later author of *Sleuth*), in Earl's Terrace, a property belonging to his wealthy father, who had known my own father for many years. An elegant, handsome, if eccentric, figure, Mr Shaffer, usually to be seen in a black Homburg hat and a long black coat, had, my father said, once flung himself on the bonnet of his car as he drove along Piccadilly and cried, 'What have I done to offend you?'

Seeing *Five Fingers* as the equivalent of a *roman-à-clef*, Mrs Shaffer, a handsome woman, had allegedly woken her husband in the middle of the night, after the first night, and cried, 'He's perfectly right; you always were impossible.'

At all events, Peter, in the February cold, was given the sinecure by his father of going round the various properties he owned near and in Edwardes Square. At one of them, the door was aggressively opened by a puce-faced old charwoman with cropped grey hair: 'Yes?'

'I've been sent round by Mr Shaffer,' Peter explained, from beneath his fur hat, 'to find out what you do.'

'Mr Shaffer knows what I do,' cried the woman. 'If Mr Shaffer wants to talk to me, he can come round himself!'

'Yes,' said Peter, 'I'm sure that whatever it is you do, you do it very well; but what is it?' Then, turning to me, *sotto voce*, 'Terrible old woman. Obviously drunk!'

One evening in Earl's Terrace, he told me, 'I knew you were going to the *Sunday Times* from the *Observer*. That man told me, what's his name? Murphy! He plays golf with my father. He said to me, "Oh, you write plays, do you, you write plays? That's your line, that's your line! Splendid."'

Which was all Peter ever said to me about Pat Murphy. Pat was once sports editor of the *Sunday Times*, himself, and later, though not for very long, editor of the company's Manchester paper, the

Daily Dispatch. Pat, however, was forever talking of Peter. 'Oh, you're going abroad, are you? You'll miss Peter Shaffer's cocktail party.' Or he would pause, portentously, in the corridors of what then was Thomson House to say, 'I wonder whether *The Royal Hunt of the Sun* will *ever* be produced.' It was.

'The trouble with Pat,' Ken Compston said, 'is that he's up everybody's arse.' Pat was, however, for all his postures, a first-rate journalist with a strong feeling for words, and I had cause to be grateful to him.

Shortly before the Olympics were over, he told me, on the phone, that he and the *Sunday Times* wanted me to write a general sports column; something the paper had never had before. I had mixed feelings. On the one hand, I was flattered and delighted. On the other, I was sharply aware of the irony of the situation. Had Compston had his way, I would not have been at the Olympics at all. As it was, I had been obliged, without benefit of accreditation or decent expenses, to take on the main coverage of the tournament; and now I was offered a column.

Meanwhile, there was the Olympic football tournament to enjoy, not least because the amateur Great Britain team was doing so well, against such odds; and its goalkeeper was Mike Pinner. It was obliged to play Italy in Rome, at what was now called, since it had been rebuilt, the Stadio Elaminio, rather than the Stadio Torino. No easy task. The Italians, with serpentine ingenuity, had managed to put out an under-21 team consisting wholly of the best young professionals in the country. The rationale was ingenious. In Italian football, a player, technically, could not turn professional till he was 21 years old. Ergo, what must he be before he reached that age? Why, an amateur! So the team included the brilliant prodigy Gianni Rivera, who had just joined Milan at a large fee from Alessandria, at seventeen – an inside forward of consummate abilities. In the half-back line there was Giovanni Trapattoni, himself a Milan half back, later to become a full international and a celebrated manager. Salvadore, the Milan centre half, was another future full international, as was Tarcisio Burgnich, the right back, who would be outjumped by Pele for Brazil's first goal in the World Cup Final of 1970 in Mexico City.

Domenico Biti was attached to the team as third man on the totem pole, behind two well-known Milan managers in Gippo Viani and Nereo Rocco. We met from time to time. And Britain survived, holding the Italians gallantly to a 2–2 draw, with Mike Pinner resilient in goal. That evening, I took him out to dinner at my favourite restaurant, Otello, in the Via della Croce. There was no trouble in finding a table. For the most part, the Romans had abandoned the city in its summer heat, and the barbarians, if you like, had remained beyond the gates, in camping sites and the like. '*Qui non girano, Signora*,' I heard an unhappy shopwoman tell a customer, above the Spanish Steps. (Here, they just don't circulate.) I must say I was glad of it.

Mike, at dinner, was not sure what he wanted to do. He was qualifying as a solicitor, but did not relish the idea of spending the rest of his life behind a desk. As it transpired, this was just what he would do, for he embarked on a successful career with London firms, eventually becoming a partner.

At the bar of the Stampa Estera, the foreign-press club, in Via della Mercede, I asked Henry Thody what he thought I should do. Did he think I could get as much as £3,000 a year out of the paper? At that time, as football correspondent, I was on £1,000. Henry, who had been in Rome for years, Kemsley's correspondent when first I knew him, laughed. He was a humorous fellow, sporting an RAF handlebar moustache, and had had his fifteen seconds of fame in Federico Fellini's *La Dolce Vita*, being among those journalists who greeted Anita Ekberg on her arrival at a press conference. 'Ah, the drinks,' said Henry, as the drinks trolley appeared. 'I don't know if you'll get it,' he told me, 'but I should have a jolly good try.'

I did. I was ushered into the presence of HV Hodson, congratulated on what I had done for the paper in Rome, and offered £2,000 to write the column, as well as my football coverage. I answered that I thought £3,000 a fairer price. This took him aback. He was a gentlemanly editor, unused to bargaining. Eventually, he said I could have £2,850, which I accepted. Then he wrote to me to say it would have to be £2,800. I wrote back to say we had agreed on £2,850. Being a gentleman, he concurred.

It was not an easy assignment. I had to cover all major, and some minor, sports, not merely soccer, and had minimal help. Ironically the best of it came from our rugby correspondent, Vivian Jenkins, formerly a Welsh international of renown. Rugby had been, for so many years, my *bête noire*, the acknowledged enemy; the minor sport posing as a major one; the violent sport posing as the moral superior of soccer.

For years, however, I had taken a fan's interest in athletics, boxing, tennis and cricket so I did have the basis on which to build. But the demands were great. Half a dozen short items at least, each of which, in the broadsheets of future years, would be the stuff of an extended article. I was endlessly on the telephone, endlessly interviewing. Ah, the interview; the great escape hatch for the uninitiated, the lazy journalist's eternal 'cop out'. Nowadays, to my amusement and sometimes my despair, the interview has been elevated into spurious prestige. Numerous journalists live by it. We have, in the various broadsheets, the Bill Bloggs Interview or the Mary Contrary Interview. God knows I have been interviewed myself, usually engendering dreadful howlers. One interviewer on a broadsheet quoted me as having said that, cycling through the picket line at Wapping, when Rupert Murdoch and the printers were at war, I had been beaten up. No word of truth in it; I had to publish letters of denial.

In a Sunday broadsheet's magazine, I was quoted as saying that, when I went to Charterhouse as a thirteen-year-old, the place was 'like Auschwitz without the Schindlers'. A screenwriter friend, who had played at times for Chelsea Casuals – is there anyone who hasn't? – called me from Hollywood to ask if he might use the phrase in a sitcom he was writing, so taken was he with it. Do by all means, I replied, especially as I never said it. What I had in fact said was, as I mentioned earlier, 'Auschwitz without the *chimneys*'. And the interviewer was using a tape recorder.

Generally speaking, responses to the column were good. 'CD Hamilton likes it,' I was told, and mentioned that to Ken Compston. 'CD Hamilton,' he told me, 'is a critic of the column in its present form.'

On a Saturday evening at the *Daily Telegraph* in Fleet Street, where the *Sunday Times*, then, used to print, I asked my colleague Robert Robinson, later to gain fame on radio and television, who CD Hamilton might be.

'CD Hamilton?' he replied. 'He's the editorial director. He has a moustache. He says nothing. Think of all the circumstances in which the only possible thing to do is to say nothing. You couldn't do it, I couldn't do it, but he does.'

By the grace of God, I had a letter from Julian Symons, author of many detective novels, and, then, a senior reviewer on the paper's book pages. 'For weeks,' he wrote, 'I have been sitting with my fingers poised above the typewriter. Can he keep it up? I asked myself, and the answer has been, triumphantly, yes.'

So when HV Hodson sent for me, I took the letter with me. He began to talk about the column, primed, quite obviously, by CD Hamilton. I passed the letter across the desk. The editor read it, stopped in his tracks, and indulged in generalities.

Denis Hamilton, to give him his full name, had apparently been demanding more controversy and more news in the column. News, as any journalist will tell you, is the hardest thing of all to find and to keep; not least when you are on a once a week Sunday paper. Tuesday's scoop – for some reason it so often seemed to be on a Tuesday – would be what Compston, in his picturesque way, would describe as 'cold, dead, wet fish' by Sunday.

My father died that September, at the age of 62. By then he was in St John and Elizabeth's Hospital in St John's Wood, reduced to skin and bone, though still brave and cheerful, despite his constant pain. I went to collect his things on a Sunday morning. 'I want them out of here by twelve!' cried a big, breezy nun. I told her, coldly, that they would be. Thirty-three years later, my eldest grandchild was born in that hospital.

In July, the following year, our twins were born: Toby and Elizabeth. Things being as they were in those somewhat primitive days, my wife did not even know there would be twins before having an X-ray – something that would never happen now – a fortnight before the births. They were not identical. Toby was a premature baby, weighing not much over four pounds and, at the Catholic hospital in Wimbledon where the delivery took place, he was whisked away from my wife and put in the 'prem' or premature ward. Three children. Two new faces. An eruption in the life of Mark, then two years old and used to being king of the castle. Parents, *pace* Larkin, who never was one, can fuck you up for the best reasons. Knowing that whatever you do will prove to be wrong and that your best is never good enough are the beginnings of wisdom.

At Bodley Head, Max Reinhardt gave me a rise each year and told me how pleased he was with me. In 1962, when I was in Chile and the States, he sacked me with compensation but no notice; he wanted a permanent 'adviser'. I was away at my second World Cup. In Santiago, where there was smog but no industry and where Bob Ferrier and myself briefly shared a small single room at the Emperador Hotel on the central Avenida O'Higgins, players and teams were still accessible. After Argentina had lost 3–1 to England in the ramshackle Copper Company stadium in Rancagua, you could go into their dressing-room to see their officials giving the manager, belligerent Juan Carlos Lorenzo, a kiss on the cheek and saying, '*Muy bien, Juan Carlos!*' By the time the World Cup came to Argentina in 1978, you couldn't get into a press conference.

Though, like Bernard Joy and others, I became violently, painfully ill – we were tyros, then, so far as South American bugs were concerned – it was a World Cup I enjoyed immensely. A group of us, including Bob and Bernard, used to share a taxi to drive up into the mountains to the England camp at Coya. 'One of the players,' said a disgusted Jimmy Adamson, then England's coach and Burnley's captain, 'sat down on his suitcase the day we arrived and said, "I'm homesick already." ' Santiago was an endearingly hospitable city. Chile, then, may have been far from the perfect democracy, but under Frey's Christian Democrat Government, the balance was being held. Going too fast, too far, Allende was sure to bring about a brutal reaction, and so he did later on, leading to the cruel years of repression under General Pinochet, when hundreds were slaughtered in that very national stadium where we had watched so much exciting football.

The win against Argentina apart, England did not play very well. They stuttered in Rancagua against Hungary, could do no better than draw 0–0 against Bulgaria, and seldom found a rhythm. Jimmy Greaves, so prolific a goalscorer in England, made scant impact. He once remarked to me that there were 'a lot of good players out here who are afraid of getting killed'. Johnny Haynes, the captain of Fulham, and the first £100-a-week player in the history of English football, pursued by Colalucci and Roma at one time, was a sullen captain.

'Don't tell me you're going to give us to beat Brazil?' he asked, with irony, in the dressing-room, after the dull draw with Bulgaria. It seemed unlikely, even though Pele had been forced to drop out of the Brazilian team. In the pretty little stadium of Viña del Mar, where you could see pelicans on the rocks, the sea wrack swirled over the ground, and the Brazilian fans kept up a constant samba chant, England could do nothing with Garrincha.

In Pele's absence, Garrincha grew into a protean player. He out-jumped the huge Maurice Norman to score a goal from a corner. He shot furiously from afar with both left foot and right foot. His swerve and burst of speed when he went to the right wing were as irresistible as ever. Brazil won, 3–1.

I had been down already to Viña del Mar to see the Spanish team, under the command of that formidable autocrat, Helenio Herrera. The word was that Alfredo Di Stefano, the inspiration and leader of Real Madrid, who had long dominated the European Cup, wouldn't play for him. A naturalised Argentine, he had often been capped by Spain, but now he was said to be injured. His elderly father, once a player himself, was there. He had brought with him a secret liniment, which he was sure could cure his son's pulled muscle. 'Use it, use it! I tell him, but he won't.'

Gerry Hitchens, the former Shropshire miner who had played that season under Herrera for Inter of Milan, would have understood. 'Like coming out of the fucking army!' he said, when transferred to Torino, a few months later.

Wherever I went in Santiago, I seemed to come across the tall, blond, sonorous Ken Aston, who had refereed the appallingly violent match between Chile and Italy in Santiago. Neither he nor his linesmen had apparently seen Leonel Sanchez, the Chilean outside left, break the nose of Humberto Maschio, the Argentine who was playing inside right for Italy. Aston eventually sent off two Italians, pronounced the game 'uncontrollable', and limped out of the tournament with a strained Achilles' tendon. A cheerful fan from Peterborough played Sancho Panza to his Don Quixote, accompanying him everywhere.

Once, having scaled many steps to a small park overlooking the city – the smog reached even there – I assumed that I would be alone, but no. Ken and his loyal Sancho Panza arrived. From that point, Ken Aston's career as a refereeing official went from strength to strength. The 1966 tournament in England found him presiding over the FIFA referees. A primary school headmaster from Ilford, Aston was one of those who stepped between Herr Kreitlein, the little German referee, and the incensed Argentine players at the end of their torrid quarter-final against England at Wembley, four years later.

Once, he even refereed a Chelsea Casuals match. *Sub specie aeternitatis*, it was surely negligible, but it mattered quite a bit to us, since it pitted us, on the smaller pitch of the Royal Hospital, against a strong team put out by Ulysses, the club of the London University alumni. Very much the underdogs, we would in fact have won it but for two decisions by Ken; an offside goal that he gave against us and a penalty that he refused us when Phil Jacobson, a journalist who usually played for us, blatantly handled the ball, and later admitted it. 'Well, it made it a more interesting game,' said Ken.

Garrincha was sent off in the semi-final against Chile, retaliating with a kick at Eladio Rojas, who had been kicking *him* consistently. Landa, the Chilean centre forward, was sent off, too. Would Garrincha be cleared to play in the final? The world of football waited. The President of Brazil listened to the news on headphones during mass. Kenneth Wolstenholme, the television commentator, who was also staying at the Emperador, said that he would phone Stanley Rous, by then the President of FIFA.

'The disciplinary committee met this morning,' Rous informed him.

'What did they decide?'

'Just a minute. I've got my papers here. Seven and nine. Seven and nine. Seven was cautioned and nine was suspended.' Which was how we found out that Garrincha would play.

On my way back, fortified by a cable of congratulation from the editor that turned out to be dictated by a minion, I stopped in New York. It was a revelation. Aaron and his wife met me at the airport. I stayed on West 57th street in a duplex apartment, the guest of Stanley Moss, the huge poet and art dealer whom I had initially met on the Spanish Steps in Rome. He was on his beam ends, then, but with extreme ingenuity had, in the meantime, laid the basis of a fortune as an art dealer, while his poetry got better and better. Moreover, my novel, *Diamond*, was just about to be published in the States by Farrar Straus. Roger Straus, the president, greeted me in his offices: 'Hi! You look like you look!'

He gave a luncheon for me. The *Sunday Times* had commissioned a series of interviews with famous novelists, so that I met James Purdy, Issac Bashevis Singer and Philip Roth. I was initially refused entrance to the King Cole bar at the St Regis Hotel, because I was wearing – knowing nothing of the place – an open-necked aertex shirt. Roth had suggested we meet there. 'The King Cole bar?' reflected Stanley, when I went back to change. 'I think that's a pretty shitty thing for one writer to do to another writer.'

Roth had invited his publisher along as an extra guest. He gave me an excellent interview. When next I saw him at the enormous bash given in Harlem for James Baldwin's novel, *Another Country*, he went past with a curt nod. I had evidently served my purpose.

The news from Bodley Head was depressing, but in the autumn there was new adventure. Ned Sherrin and David Frost invited me to lunch at Bertorelli's on the Green, in Shepherd's Bush. They were planning their new, satirical BBC TV programme, *That Was The Week That Was*, and seeking writers. I was taken on board, and had ten sketches performed. Bliss was it in that dawn. Then things went sour. Ned brought in another echelon of writers and turned down a sketch called 'You Must Come Round When We're Settled', based on the little street behind Notting Hill Gate where I was living; it had been gentrified. The *donnée* was that one last working-class family was holding out. 'Don't think it really works,' said Ned.

In due course, I sold the sketch again and again. June Whitfield and Peter Jones performed it on television. It was put on at a short-lived City nightclub called The Poor Millionaire. I was there with my wife when Ned Sherrin walked in, roared with laughter throughout the sketch, came up to me after the show and said, 'That was yours, wasn't it, the Chelsea one? Thought it worked very well.'

Diamond was spitefully reviewed on BBC radio by David Kossoff. I demanded an apology, which didn't come. Kossoff suggested we should settle it 'like gentlemen, in a duel, on television'. I agreed. The BBC wouldn't have it. Then by lucky chance I discovered, at a reception given by the Israeli Embassy, that the BBC had wiped the tape, with its invaluable evidence. How could they now go ahead? They did; I had two years of *angst* ahead of me. For my lawyers, I went back to Herbert Oppenheimer's; the avuncular Mr Connett, the litigation management clerk, was still there and was put in charge. Try as I might, I couldn't see the defence's case. How could they maintain it when I had been writing, all this time, for the *Jewish Chronicle*? The mystery, ultimately, would be solved, demonstrating for the umpteenth time that the law is an ass. A short, bald, elderly managing clerk – this is the way things go in the law – had taken over the case for Kossoff and the mighty BBC. And he, it transpired, had not forgiven Connett for taking him to the cleaners for £150,000, a fortune, then, in a recent case.

In the new year of 1963, we moved house again, westwards, to a Victorian home in Holland Park Avenue, with all the concomitant expense. A fourth child was on the way; the libel case was eating money and, if it did come to court and I lost, I would be wiped out. 'They can't take away your talent,' said big Frank Cvitanovic, the talented Canadian documentary director; but at the time it was scant reassurance. What got me off the hook, financially, was that I wrote a couple of short stories, both of which I sold for a lot of money in America: one to the *Saturday Evening Post*; the other to *Mademoiselle* magazine. But, the day we moved, everything seemed to go wrong. I lost some money; I lost my passport (the house turned out to have a very active poltergeist); and I lost my press pass to the Rotterdam Final of the European Cup-Winners' Cup, between Spurs and Atletico Madrid. Moreover, on the previous Sunday I had dislocated my shoulder, playing football, for the second time, and my arm was in a sling. 'This house will be my tomb,' I told my wife, melodramatically. She, having found the house – and a superb discovery it was – was properly disdainful.

I got to Rotterdam eventually, where Spurs had a spectacular win. Before the game, Bill Nicholson, their manager, went meticulously through the Atletico team, eulogising every player, till Danny

Blanchflower saw the heads going down. He then proceeded to give what you might call a counter team talk, lauding the merits of the Spurs. 'They've got a Jones who's fast; but we've got Cliff Jones, and he can motor a bit.' Heads went up again. Tottenham went out, even without their powerful left half Dave Mackay, and thrashed Atletico 5–1.

The Rise of Gerry Logan, my first football novel, was due to come out that year, with Secker and Warburg. Much of it had been written – handwritten and typed – during the Chilean World Cup. In those days, my philosophy was that if a novel was going well, you could write it everywhere; if it wasn't, you couldn't write it anywhere.

The central character, Gerry himself, a partial narrator, was a Scottish inside forward, based, I confess, on Danny Blanchflower. This, largely because the footballer had to be untypically intelligent and aware, as well as an accomplished performer. Danny, so fluent, so original and, in certain ways, so flawed, seemed an ideal model. Yet he, or his surrogate, could not carry the whole book. I used various voices. His wife's. My own.

It was very clear to me that in the last analysis, I was not the right person to write the book, however inventive I might be. It should have been what was called, in the thirties and forties, a proletarian novel: such as David Storey's novel of rugby league, *This Sporting Life*. When it appeared, it was generally well received, much liked within the game itself, especially by such ur-professionals as Pat Crerand of Manchester United and Scotland and Tony Knapp, the Leicester City centre half. Years later, when I flew up to Glasgow to interview the future manager of Scotland, Craig Brown, then in charge at Clyde, I gave him a copy of the book. He instantly produced another, battered and clearly much read, from his case, and told me there was a little band of managers and coaches in and around Glasgow who were aficionados of the novel. *Habent sua fata libelli*, as the dramatist Terence proclaimed. (Books have their own fates.)

Frank Cvitanovic was very keen to film it. I was persuaded to produce a script, on spec. Sean Connery, an accomplished footballer in his day, read it, but said he was too old. Peter Shaffer, with great kindness, gave my wife and myself tickets for his Shaftesbury Avenue double bill, *The Private Ear and The Public Eye*, so that we could go with Tom Courtenay. Walking along the street with him, Peter had seen him suddenly kick at an imaginary football, and discovered that he was an enthusiastic fan. Chiefly, as it turned out, of Hull City.

Tom was keen to play the part, but alas, for all his talent, we could not set up the film on him. We did, however, become very friendly. He would join John Moynihan and me for practice in Hyde Park, arrange a spirited pick-up game opposite his house in Hurlingham Park – he had rented it from David Niven – and once brought a string of actors to Hyde Park in midweek to join in a game. One of them was Rod Steiger, who had never played soccer in his life but, bulky in a green track suit, did his noisy best to run the game. 'Oh, yeah: you got that homosexual penalty!'

Hull City was Tom's passion, then. He was from Hull himself, and his father had been a fish porter on Hull docks. One evening, when Hull were playing at Millwall down at The Den, he drove Mike Pinner and me there in the new Ferrari of which he was so proud. He was then charmingly shy; the actor's carapace had yet to grow. We went into the directors' room, and I introduced him to Cliff Britton, the former England right half, who was then managing Hull. 'He seems to know what he's doing,' Tom said, as though wishing to be reassured.

After the game, outside the dressing-rooms, we met the Hull players, including their captain, Mike Milner, who had been at school with Tom. 'Quite the star, now, aren't you, Tom?' said Milner. 'I remember you running around; little short arse!'

'We played football together,' said Tom, conciliatorily.

'You were never in the same team as me, Tom. You weren't good enough. Here; here's half a crown; go and get your hair cut.'

On the first of September our fourth child, Josephine, was born in the Royal Holloway Hospital, which had been the recognised Arsenal hospital before the war, where the players went for their operations. It was the first of the births I had attended, and when she emerged, I thought it was a boy; and was glad to find it was a girl!

In 1963 the BBC televised *European Centre Forward*, which Stephen Hearst had directed and I had devised and written. Later it won the Silver Bear award at the Berlin Film Festival. Its hero was Gerry Hitchens, who had led England's attack against Brazil, in the World Cup. The original plan was to shoot the film in Milan, where Gerry was playing for Inter. The problem was that there were rumours he would be transferred when the Italian transfer market briefly reopened in November. I telephoned Helenio Herrera and asked him whether this would happen. Categorically he said it wouldn't. Shortly afterwards, with our whole effort planned for Milan, Gerry was transferred to Torino. To Turin we would go.

It rained for most of the time we were there. It rained when we filmed Gerry playing in a practice game for Torino against a youth team, in their old Stadio Filadelfia. Stephen, pale, red-haired, intense, middle-aged, brought up in Vienna on the pre-war Austrian *Wunderteam*, paced up and down behind the goal. 'Gerry Hitchens,' he said, in his slightly accented voice. 'Nice fellow, nice fellow, but he can't play football; he doesn't understand.'

By comparison with some of the British players who had lately come and gone in Italian football, there might have been some truth in this. Hitchens could hardly be compared with Denis Law, who had preceded him at Torino, or with Jimmy Greaves, who had also arrived simultaneously in Italy at Milan, after a tremendous wrangle, for the 1961–62 season.

I had watched with fascination, and some amusement, the battle for Greaves between Milan and his original team, Chelsea. Acting as agent for Milan, in England, was an Italian whom I had known and liked ever since he interviewed me one Sunday evening after a Fiorentina–Milan game, in the restaurant of the Florentine railway station. His name: Roberto Favilla. He was a sharp contrast with Peronace, a northerner, where Gigi was so classically *meridionale*. But Favilla was a dark, intense, nervous, quite unflamboyant man, with a long, straight nose, a pale complexion, none of the panache and bravado of the usual agent.

Greaves, he made it quite clear to me, had signed for Milan. But a journalistic battle broke out between Jim Manning, son of LV, on the *Daily Mail*, and Bob Findlay, on the *Daily Express*. Manning, who was reckoned by Fleet Street at large to have had the better of it, wanted Greaves to stay; Findlay insisted he must go.

After England had beaten Italy 3–2 in Rome in May 1961, the English party, myself included, flew to Vienna for the next match. Greaves gave a mid-air press conference, to say that he was staying with Chelsea. Stanley Rous, dozing in his seat like an old turtle in the sun, looked up and muttered, 'I don't know how he thinks he can.' And indeed, he couldn't.

In very little time at all, Greaves, after many vicissitudes, many a clash with Milan's manager, the big dark, formidable, *catenaccio*-favouring Nereo Rocco, went back to England, and to Tottenham; but not before he had scored nine goals in no time. Later that season I sat with Rocco on a train coming back from Cardiff. '*Ha rovinato il mio Campionato*,' he grumbled of Greaves (he's ruined my Championship). But in the event Milan signed the Brazilian Dino Sani, and won it.

Denis Law and Joe Baker, the Hibernian centre forward, a Scot who, by accident of birth, played for England, detested it in Turin. Law, once, at half-time in the dressing-room, threw his jersey into a corner in disgust, and Baker knocked down an over-persistent photographer by a Venetian canal. Eventually they ran their car into a road island in Turin in the small hours of the morning. None of this prevented the blond, wiry, infinitely versatile Law from making a colossal impact in Turin. Indeed, when we were making the film and I spoke to an elderly Torino fan outside the Stadio Filadelfia, he told me that Law was the finest inside forward the club had ever had.

'Even better than Valentino Mazzola?' (the former captain of Torino and of Italy) I asked. 'Yes,' was the reply.

Hitchens may not have been in that class, but he was a far more resilient and integrated personality. And he had in Meriel a supportive wife; Greaves's wife hated it in Milan. '*Un buon minatore*' was how I heard one Italian critic describe Hitchens, and it was relevant enough. Gerry had begun his working life down a Shropshire mine, where, indeed, we filmed. 'A proper little turell!' – a word I've never heard before or since – was how he was described to me by one who had worked with him in adolescence, and whose green eye was plainly flashing. The discipline of the mines was far harder to endure than anything Hitchens suffered under Helenio Herrera, with his bombast and his slogans. Making the most of physical strength, courage and persistence, Hitchens scored freely for both Inter and Torino, and four years later, for Atalanta, where I visited him again. On that occasion he scored the winning goal against Napoli. 'I've had more kisses from rough beards!' he said.

People constantly asked me on whom I had based Gerry Logan. Denis Law was the favourite – reasonably enough, since he was both Scottish and an inside forward – and Hitchens himself was mentioned. Karl Miller, our former Chelsea Casuals inside right was, by then, literary editor of the *New Statesman*, where Danny Blanchflower was writing a lively column. I begged Karl not to give the book to Danny, so of course he did. An acid review was the consequence. Danny reflected that he himself had come 'some of the way' of Gerry Logan and concluded, 'He has given him a dangerous pass, a hospital pass, and scuttled up to the press-box to hide.' Unfair, I thought, but very nicely phrased.

The book was translated into various languages, but had its greatest success in West Germany, where it may have been taken more seriously than it deserved. Huge reviews appeared in serious publications. When for the first time I met Franz Beckenbauer, at an airport – he had just scored in Germany's first-ever win against

England, in Hanover – I was introduced by Horst Dassler as the correspondent of the *Sunday Times*. 'No, no,' said Beckenbauer, '*Der Profi* (the German title), the best book on football I have ever read.'

In 1974, in a TV studio in Wiesbaden, immediately after ZDF had shown Franz Beckenbauer leading West Germany to victory over Sweden beneath a deluge, Otto Friedreichs, who was interviewing me, held up a paperback of the book and said it was Beckenbauer's favourite. It was out of print. I was reminded of an expression dear to Domenico Biti and Prince Borghese: '*Se faceva capelli, nascono senza teste.*' (If he were making hats, they'd be born without heads.)

Early in 1964, I was sent to Miami Beach to cover the first heavyweight championship fight between Cassius Clay, as he was then, and Sonny Liston. I had already, somewhat alarmingly, met Liston, when I was in New York in 1962. The BBC had commissioned me to interview him for television, but it was easier said than done. John, the relaxed and engaging head of their New York office, roamed round and round Philadelphia with me, looking for him. He had broken training camp, we knew – he was preparing to demolish poor Floyd Patterson – but he wasn't at home, where his pretty wife received us graciously, and where the chairs and sofas were covered with transparent plastic. We ran him to earth at last in the office of his lawyer, an abrasive little man with wiry hair called Morton Witkin. 'You can talk to him,' he said, 'but no questions about his past. Otherwise I stop the interview. I stopped one right here in this office, the other day.' To my protests, he replied, 'You said you wanted to talk to him about Father Stevenson. And as soon as you talk to him about Father Stevenson, it comes out. This man learned boxing in the penitentiary. No. I will not permit it! This man has been exposed to calumny. No!' There was no stopping Mr Witkin, who said that for his money, Sonny, who impassively chewed gum, was as nice a guy as you would want to meet. 'He's got a good heart. He loves kids.'

Interviewing Liston, when eventually I was allowed to, wasn't easy. He sat there with his massive forearms resting on the arms of his chair. His answers were laconic. Patterson? 'I feel that I punch harder.' Patterson's combination punches? 'They bounce off me, like a B-B gun.'

With a punch like his, I asked, was he afraid that he might kill a man?

'How did you come here?' he asked.

'I flew.'

'What was that plane that crashed the other day? A hundred people killed. After that plane, another plane took right off.'

Mr Witkin, who had told us that a lot of people thought he was a son of a bitch, but that was just the way he talked, accompanied us to the door. 'I apologise for my attitude,' he said, 'but not for my action.'

The interview, in that dark office, was useless for TV but, on returning to London, I offered it to Pat Murphy as a sports feature. He turned it down, on the grounds that it had 'been done'. When Liston duly demolished Patterson, he wanted it without delay. Pat was an unpredictable fellow. Once, in the upstairs room of a Soho restaurant, he presided over a so-called sports lunch, where I sat at his left hand. 'We asked JB Priestley to do another *English Journey* for us,' he told me. 'He said he was too old; why didn't we ask one of the younger writers, like Brian Glanville.' My hopes rose. 'Well, we're not giving it to you,' said Pat. 'Our list reads: John Braine, Brian Glanville, Alan Sillitoe – in that order.' But in the end it was never done at all.

Priestley, meanwhile, generously endorsed *Gerry Logan*: 'I enjoyed this highly original novel.' One of Peter Shaffer's most diverting party pieces was of a meeting with Priestley in the smoking-room of a liner bound for New York, when Peter had hoped, in vain, to occupy a guest-room where Priestley went each year. 'I'll not waive my claim. You can go round looking for a room, then you can write an article about it and sell it: "How I looked for a room in New York!"'

It was a dialogue that concluded with Priestley saying, 'There comes a time in the career of every writer, and Shakespeare knew it, when you have to turn from realism to fantasy, as in *The Tempest*.'

An astounded Peter protested that *The Tempest* was among the most astonishingly realised works in all literature.

'You'll see!' Priestley said.

Floyd Patterson I found much more endearing than Sonny Liston; more sensitive, more vulnerable, immeasurably more approachable, qualities which hardly helped him when they met in the ring. We had first met in London, shortly after I began my sports column. 'Hallo!' said a harsh New York voice on the telephone from the Mayfair Hotel. 'This is Mr November.'

I answered that I hoped to see Floyd Patterson before he went away.

'*He* isn't going anywhere,' Mr November said. He turned out to be Floyd Patterson's lawyer: a large, bald, downright man of middle age. Patterson talked with such fluency. Had he had a good education? No, he said, he had left school at fifteen. Then did he read a lot?

'I don't like to read books,' said Patterson, 'because my manager, he reads books, and my sparring partner, *he* reads his books, and to me it seemed to be a sort of disease or something. They used to read until they fell asleep, and then wake up and read again. Well, if reading makes you that way, I'm not interested.'

We met again in that New York summer of 1962. He had come down from training camp for a television interview, and I caught up with him as he entered the studios. Before he could do so, a stubble-cheeked man in a candy-striped shirt came running across the road and demanded to know whether a certain doctor was any good; he was to have an operation. Patterson assured him, 'He's a good doctor,' and the man went off happy. Patterson said he had never seen him before.

Who should join us in the little dressing-room but Mr November wearing a straw hat. Patterson alluded to his celebrated *Face-to-Face* television interview with John Freeman: 'Over all the interviews I've had, I've never been so impressed. What was the name of the guy who interviewed me? Lew Friedman? Is that it?'

He wasn't trying to prove anything in meeting Liston, he said; the papers had got it wrong. It was his responsibility as a champion, and a man, to give Liston his chance. Besides, he was a Catholic: 'We have confession of sins ... This man certainly had a bad start, the same as I, but why keep pushing him back into the gutter? ... If society hadn't accepted me back, I might have gone the same way ... I would run away from home, play hookey and steal fruit. Now, they were minor crimes, but that was a start, and who knows, as my mind got mature, I might do bigger things; rob a bank, or something.'

'Steal melons,' Mr November said.

Cassius Clay, alias Muhammad Ali, who would cruelly demolish Patterson in his turn, was a very different kettle of fish. Arriving in Miami Beach at a second- or third-rate hotel, the Capri, pronounced Ca-pree, charging the then sizeable price of $18 a day, no one offered to carry my bag as I came in. Instead, a man behind the reception desk, who looked much like Groucho Marx, glanced up and said, 'Don't tell me! I know who it is. This is going to be Mr Glanville from London, England. My name is Mike Mitnick, I'm the manager.'

The deathless words of Hyman Kaplan, protagonist of Leonard Q Ross's celebrated book about an immigrant learning English in New York, returned to me: 'Crit-sising Mitnick is a picnic.' But I did not speak them. When I came down each morning, Mr Mitnick invariably greeted me, 'How are you, young man?' To which I would reply, 'Very well, thank you, Mr Mitnick. How are you?'

'Can't kick,' he would say.

Clay was training in the seedy environs of the Fifth Street Gym. He would erupt each day with his faithful sidekick, a former ship's cook, Budini Brown, and they would chorus:

Float like a butterfly, sting like a bee!
Yeah! Rumble, young man, rumble!

'I'm the greatest!'

'You were born the greatest in yo' crib!'

One day the Beatles turned up, scruffy and sullen, and stood briefly in the boxing ring. 'We're meant to do the photograph; let's do the photograph and go.'

Next day, Clay boasted, 'I'm so great, the Beatles came to get *my* autograph.' Budini told a sympathetic journalist, plaintively, 'I'm giving everything and getting nothing.'

Down the sea front, Sonny Liston, the incumbent champion and white-hot favourite, was training in far more salubrious quarters: The Surfside Auditorium. Clay, still trying hard, picketed it noisily, wearing a tunic inscribed BEAR HUNTING. Inside, Liston, solemn and minatory in a white-hooded dressing-gown, chewed gum and answered silly questions.

'Hey, Sonny! Is he the fastest guy you ever fought?'

'Is he fast? He didn't catch no bullet did he? If he's that fast, I don't want to fight him!'

At the weigh-in, Clay put on his extraordinary charade, yelling in Liston's impassive face, 'You a chump! You a chump!' Jim Manning bought it, whether or not Liston did, writing a front-page story for the *Daily Mail* in which he said that Clay was off his head; the bout should be postponed. It wasn't, as we know. After only six rounds, in which Clay had boxed with superb skill (despite having liniment rubbed in his eyes from Liston's gloves), Liston quit on his stool, pleading an injured shoulder.

Now the Black Muslims would move in, and for all his talent, all his ebullient courage, Clay, or Muhammad Ali, as he would now become, was ultimately doomed. Meanwhile, leaving the sunshine of Florida for the snow of New York, I seemed to meet him wherever I went. In the BBC offices on Fifth Avenue, for a start. I was there because I was making a documentary about boxing with Stephen Hearst called *The World of Billy Walker*, Billy being a blond, handsome young heavyweight who was being canvassed as the new 'Great White Hope', though the one who would ultimately emerge best from it all would be his elder brother George, a former cruiserweight boxer who had done time for armed robbery, repented, become Billy's manager, and parlayed financial success into a huge conglomerate. I liked them both. They had engaged Sugar Ray Robinson's former trainer, Harry Wiley, to look after Billy, which was why we were in New York.

Clay strode into the BBC's offices surrounded by an entourage almost as noisy as himself, including a well-known singer, Sam Fox, who would later be shot dead by the manageress of a motel. Clay sat down behind a table and demanded his cheque before he said a word. The cheque had been discreetly slipped between a row of books behind him. He grabbed it. Halfway through the interview, he stopped, demanding another payment; Harry Carpenter was interviewing him from London. His demand was granted, and the interview went on. It was a study in arrogance and greed.

A few days later, I went up to Harlem – you could still do that, then – to interview the Black Muslim leader Malcolm X, who had reputedly 'turned' Clay. It had been arranged for me by my friend Dick Schaap, then City editor of the old, sadly now defunct, *Herald Tribune*, who also arranged for me to meet Lennie Bruce.

Malcolm was staying at the Hotel Teresa where Joe Louis had always stayed in his years as world champion. On the steps, haranguing an admiring crowd was . . . Cassius Clay. We exchanged a weary glance. We had to stop meeting like this. Malcolm, a reformed criminal who had seen the Muslim light, was coherent, fluent and courteous. He still wanted ten per cent of the area of the USA as a black enclave. Afterwards, I told an American journalist how friendly I had found him.

'Oh, he doesn't have any problem with *white* people,' was the reply, 'only *black* people.' This was prescient indeed. It was not long afterwards that rival Black Muslims shot Malcolm dead. It was dangerous, even fatal, to cross the leader Elijah Muhammad.

We worked, on the film, with the Maysles brothers, Al and David, who had had great success with a documentary about the Beatles. Al said something I have long remembered. 'They wait and they wait and they wait. Then, when nothing happens, that's when they start to interview.' The film we made was the BBC's entry for the annual Academy award, but it didn't get it. *Goal!* would win it two years later.

I caught Lennie Bruce's act twice, first at the large Vanguard Theatre. When at one point the microphones failed, someone shouted up, 'There's enough of you up there!' which, Bruce admitted when I saw him again in Greenwich Village, he had at first misinterpreted as an anti-Semitic jibe.

In the Village, where Dick Schaap took me to see him, he was pulling in the then huge sum of $3,000 a week in a café without a drinks' licence. In the interval, he, Dick and I, and Lennie's private detective, an Irish-American who looked as if he shaved with a blowlamp, and a Catholic Irish couple called Carroll, repaired to a much smaller café, nearby. Carroll was then a young writer assigned to write about Bruce, which the omniscient Dick could have done with his eyes shut. Carroll's wife stared at Bruce, brooding in a Nehru jacket, as if he were the anti-Christ.

'What do you need it for, Lennie?' asked Carroll, 'this "fuck" and all that.' He wasn't entirely wrong.

Lennie busied himself, for a time, drawing on his newspaper. I watched him, fascinated. There was an advertisement for Kensington cigarettes, showing a plump, bald, genial man sitting in a chair with his hands on either arm. Over one side of the man's head, Lennie drew an electrode. Over his wrist on the same side, Lennie drew another. On the opposite side, emitting from the man's mouth, in a balloon, were the words, 'I like to know how the other half lives.'

Eventually, he answered. 'In the Latin Quarter, before the war,' he said, 'there was a notice up backstage, THE USE OF THE WORDS HELL AND DAMN WILL RESULT IN IMMEDIATE DISMISSAL. And they said to him, "What do you need it for?" And he said, "Like it's the way I talk." ' As we left the café, Bruce said to me, 'Did you hear the hostility? "What do you need it for?" ' His detective, who had felt the guns of a couple of snooping agents as they went into the show, told me, 'You seem like a pretty sympathetic person.' Bruce seemed wonderfully original to me.

I wrote a piece about him for the *Spectator*, assuming he would dislike it, as he seemed to dislike most such articles. Instead he sent me a cheque to put an advertisement for his new book in the *Spectator*.

Years later, in Los Angeles, Robert Mundy, an English film writer and aspirant producer, urged me to read Alfred Goldman's *Ladies and Gentlemen, Lenny Bruce*. I duly did so on a Dorset beach, to find myself called 'the most perceptive English critic of Lennie Bruce'. Then it quoted me. I've no idea what I meant.

Stephen Hearst and I roamed Harlem with the delightful Harry Wiley, who showed us photos of himself on military service in England and Europe. 'She worked in a night club,' wrote Harry in one caption. 'I was her day club.'

He spoke of coming under fire in France.

' "We going to die, Sergeant Wiley?" I said, "What will be, will be." '

It was in New York, in 1964, that I heard what had happened to John Moynihan. I was interviewing Joseph Heller, author of *Catch 22*. We had been back to Stanley Moss's apartment, now on Central Park West, and I had picked up my post. Crossing Central Park in a taxi, I suddenly gave out a cry of distress. 'What happened?' Heller asked.

'John Moynihan's broken his leg!' I said.

'Jesus, I thought one of your children had died!'

It was a letter from my wife. John had double-fractured on the Royal Hospital pitch where he and I had played so often, where he himself had originally arranged for us to play; just as, in his shy, persistent way, he had arranged so much for us in our delicate early stages. Never a natural footballer or athlete, but a consistent goalscorer with an amazing record of still more consistent appearances – it was so hard to envisage Chelsea Casuals without him; but his career with us was ended.

He had written a delightful book, *The Soccer Syndrome*, which in its own way has surely never been bettered. Its genesis came with a letter he wrote to me when I was on assignment in Catania. I read it one breakfast time in a large dining-room where I was the only customer, and where a posse of waiters looked at me with astonishment as I laughed aloud. It was a marvellous evocation of the Royal Hospital, Chelsea, on a wet Sunday afternoon, when the inimical groundsman had put games off on the two pitches, and when one of the hard nuts with a local team – 'pulling his cap down over his shiny red nose and bouncing on the ground the largest yellow football I have ever seen' – assailed the groundsman with an increasingly exaggerated barrage of abuse. That letter later modulated into the chapter 'It's Hoff!', which I used to read when asked to speak at football-club dinners.

There were many others, including a superb evocation of post-war-austerity London, when Chelsea fans queued along the Fulham Road for tickets for the FA Cup semi-final against Arsenal, one of them swearing he would gas himself – he was known thereafter as 'The Gasman' – if Arsenal won; which they duly did. Another, charmingly imaginative speculation, *We'll Never Know*, took its inspiration from a report in a local London newspaper, 'Apex 5 Rawlplug Reserves 6 (Shadbolt 5)'. The best of these *jeux d'esprit* were highly original and observant. They emerged in their own time, like pearls from an oyster. John was a perfectly competent journalist, but it was futile to ask him to produce such pieces to order, and indeed, he never quite did so again. In the latter fifties, when I knew him, he was very much a figure on the Chelsea scene. When he married his first wife, Diana, the reception took place by the river, in the studio once occupied by John Minton, the gifted painter, who had not long ago committed suicide.

Reg Drury arrived, his tie coruscating gently in the lamplight, to remark, 'I was told I was going to meet the Chelsea Set tonight. I came here expecting to be introduced to Jimmy Greaves.' Looking up to see a stuffed parrot hanging from the ceiling, he remarked, 'That's the best-looking bird I've seen here tonight.'

Towards the end of the party, John, who had imbibed a good deal, was trying to tell me that the original painting of the jacket for my novel, *Along the Arno*, which Minton had painted, was hanging in the lavatory. But each time he urged me to look at it, with encouraging gesture, a girl would sweep into the lavatory and bang the door.

Chelsea Casuals were a tribute to him; they would never have been born without him. He and I would often go training together, sometimes by the barracks in Hyde Park, subsequently in Battersea Park where we met 'The Man Behind the Goal', whom I put into the short story of that name. It began, 'He had brought his own football with him,' and so he had.

He would scamper about behind the goal that John and I sporadically shot into, like a busy retriever. His own football was a battered, half-inflated thing. He was a Geordie, who told us he had been in the Army, but got out when hostilities began, 'Because I hadn't joined the Army in wartime, I'd joined it in peacetime.' Sometimes when we arrived we would find him lying on the bench there, under a tree, talking to himself, then telling us he was listening to the finest sound in the world: his own voice. Or he might be looking up at the leaves and meditating on the mysteries of photosynthesis. Now and again I brought him food. The short story had a dismal ending, but it was quite invented; the little man eventually just disappeared.

In the ensuing years, I had seen a good deal more of Muhammad Ali, as he was now known, and grew to like him better as he became less frenetic, sometimes parodying himself, as he once did in his dressing-room at the White City gym: 'Let's go back to the *old* days; for just *five* minutes. If he give me jive, he fall in five! Let me *go*, Angelo, I want him *now*!' Angelo Dundee being his devoted trainer, who was appointed, initially, by the group of Louisville businessmen who had sponsored Ali's professional career. It was one day in that White City dressing-room, as he lay on the massage table, that I realised how irredeemably far things had gone.

'Other people have their advisers,' mused Ali. 'Presidents. There's my brains; right there.' I looked round, assuming that he meant Angelo Dundee, but instead he gestured towards a small, plump man standing in a corner of the room: 'Herbert Muhammad!' Elijah Muhammad's son.

That autumn, I covered the Olympic Games in Tokyo. The athletics were fascinating; the moment when, defying orders boomed over the loudspeakers at the closing ceremony, the competitors broke ranks and joyfully fraternised, most moving. It would not be allowed to happen again. Lucky enough to have Japanese friends in the cinema world, I was able to see and enjoy much more than the Olympics, though with Peter Snell challenging successfully for a superb double – the 800 and 1500 metres – and Robbie Brightwell inciting his British team to greater and greater achievements, there was much to enjoy there, as well.

In the mornings I would sit by a stagnant swimming pool by my hotel, working on a new novel, *A Second Home*, narrated by a neurotic Jewish actress. The Kossoff case was looming, though I still hoped it could be settled. Time after time I put myself through the most vicious cross-examinations, but I still could not see what kind of case the opposition had; which was worrying in itself. Surely there must be *something* I had not bargained for, something they knew that I didn't.

The football tournament in Tokyo was a diverting one, which culminated in an excellent Final between the Hungarians, inspired by Ferenc Bene, and the Czechs. Two years away from the next World Cup Finals, the Hungarians were clearly becoming a force again.

And so to the High Court. Almost to the brink, I had hopes that the case could be settled. William Frankel, the editor of the *Jewish Chronicle*, tried to bring it about, but Kossoff's lawyers were adamant. He did, however, make the worst possible start; and I, as I realised only long afterwards, proved to be immensely lucky that the case had dragged on so long. For Colin Duncan, the accomplished QC who had originally been briefed for the defence, had fallen ill, his place being taken by the far less formidable Peter Bristow, who, as it transpired, had had insufficient time to be fully familiar with the case. Colin Duncan, I am sure, would have given me a far, far harder ride.

My own lawyers were excellent: David Hirst, a humorous, talented QC who would himself become a distinguished judge, and his junior, Leon Brittan, of whom so much would be heard in future years, not in the law, but in politics.

Before the case began, Bristow asked Mr Justice Hinchcliffe whether, since Kossoff was appearing in a one-man show in Edinburgh, he might give his evidence out of turn. It seemed a ludicrous, self-destructive move; judges are God in their own courts. 'I have an alternative suggestion,' said the judge icily, 'that Mr Kossoff procure himself an understudy.' When I was under cross-examination, he frequently and genially intervened on my side.

On that first afternoon, David Hirst majestically made my case. Just as I expected, the episode of the wiped tape was salient. BBC ACCUSED OF SHAMEFUL COVER UP, thundered the *Daily Mail*, next morning. The jury, a member of whom winked at my wife as he left the box, were given a couple of days to read *The Bankrupts* and my second novel, *Diamond*, then we were off again.

David Hirst examined me. Peter Bristow stood up to cross-examine me. He was a tall, high-complexioned, middle-aged man, with a slight defect in his speech. 'Mr Glanville,' he began, 'you say you were very upset when you heard this broadcast. Are you still in the same emotional condition now as you were then?'

'Would you mind defining your terms?' I replied. He flung his papers on the desk in mock disgust, and we were away. It was a tense experience; rather, I said afterwards, like an infantry war, taking one wretched little objective after another. But as the cross-examination wore on, I realised that it was not going to be remotely as astringent as I had feared. I had put myself through far more rigorous questioning. 'Were you asked not to come to any of your clubs?' he asked, at one point.

'The only club I belong to,' I said, 'is a football club.'

At another point, he read out a series of hostile observations made by readers of the *Jewish Chronicle*. 'Does that not make an impression on you, Mr Glanville?' he asked.

'Yes, Mr Bristow,' I replied, 'and it would make a still greater impression if you'd read the rest of it.' Which in fact was favourable to me.

'Yes!' cried Mr Justice Hinchcliffe. 'You haven't read the rest of it.'

When I came back from El Vino's, where I had had lunch, in the early afternoon, Mr Connett met me. We had won. He had told me that morning, to my huge relief, 'They're nibbling at a settlement.' Apologies, £500 damages, and costs. I gave all but £50 to the Jewish Blind and kept the rest to buy lunches for those who had helped me. I would never go to court again.

'All's well that ends well,' said a smiling Judge Hinchcliffe.

6

CHELSEA CASUALS CONTINUED TO FLOURISH, but at the expense of my sanity. Players disappeared and opponents dropped out. Only an obsessional commitment to the cause could keep one going. My wife concocted an imaginary Sunday-morning phone call: 'Brian, I don't think I can play. I've broken my leg.'

'Fuck.'

Hugh McIlvanney joined us. He had come to the *Observer* from Scotland, the son of a Kilmarnock miner, one of two talented sons, the other being the novelist, William. At his peak, Hugh was probably the best all-round sports journalist this country has ever produced. The pity of it was that, when in due course he went to the *Daily Express*, they hadn't the wit to see that he was the perfect person to put an end to the ludicrous dichotomy between 'posh', and popular, writing, which exists in the realm of sports journalism, only in *this* country, and which I have always deplored. Instead the *Express* put him on to general features, and he eventually returned to the *Observer*, who were relieved to have him back.

As a footballer, an inside forward, Hugh was a hard, skilful, and sometimes abrasive player who scored some spectacular goals with his right foot. When Reg Drury retired, he was the ideal new captain. We acquired another talented Scottish player in Joe McGrath, the television and film director, who had played for Queens Park. But the pick of our team was Harry Clark.

Harry came to us through our Royal College of Art connection; he had studied television design and moved successfully into that field. In earlier days he had been a professional on Sunderland's books, understudying the legendary Clown Prince of Soccer, Len Shackleton. Indeed, he had played five times in the First Division. He had delightful ball control, was almost impossible to tackle with the ball at his feet, and passed with flair and judgement.

It was his predecessor, Keith Bell, however, who took part in a memorable game, years earlier, at the Slough Greyhound Stadium, where we met the TV All-Stars. They had a few ex-professionals, including Malcolm Allison, that idiosyncratic and flamboyant coach, and a former West Ham winger, Ken Tucker. They decided we were not strong enough to play them and insisted we use the former Fulham and England centre half, Jim Taylor. They even wanted us to use Tom Finney, one of the finest wingers ever to play for England but, perhaps fortunately, he wasn't able to turn out.

The inclusion of Taylor meant we had to use Mike Pinner in his correct position of goalkeeper; he was still, then, playing regular First Division football. In consequence, the All-Stars hardly had a kick throughout the first half, and we went a couple of goals up. Tiny Ronnie Corbett, the comedian, was playing outside right against me and at one point, in the words of the popular prints, appeared to aim a kick at me. It didn't bother me. Intentional or not, I had hardly felt it, but in the dressing-room at half-time, Jim Taylor, good old pro that he was, was up in arms. 'He kicked you, didn't he?' he said. 'You know what you want to say, if he does it again? You want to tell him: *"I'm* on this field, the same as you are!"'

Early in the second half, clearly by pre-arranged plan, Ken Tucker pushed one of our players in the penalty box, yelled, flung himself to the ground, and was given a penalty by the referee, Jimmy Hill, who was, then, Fulham's inside right, in the First Division. They scored, but we were still leading 3–1 near the end when Hill took off the referee's top, played for them, scored twice, and got them a 3–3 draw.

At the *Sunday Times*, Denis Hamilton succeeded HV Hodson as editor. I grew to like him, but I nicknamed him Major Major Major, after the character in Joe Heller's *Catch 22*. 'You can go in now, Major Major isn't in his office.' Or, 'You can't go in, now. Major Major's there.'

Denis, behind his moustache and the DSO that had nearly been a VC, was a terribly shy man. Once, when I wanted to see him, I was told to 'write in'. Yet if you met him on the stone of a Saturday night, when the paper was being printed, he would talk amiably to you ad lib. If you wanted to know why he still walked with a slight limp, you had only to ask Harold Shepherdson, the former Middlesbrough centre half who became his club's, and England's, trainer. Denis had fallen off Harold's shoulders in a pig-a-back race at elementary school, in Middlesbrough. He was in fact the son of a humble steelworker who had come up through the ranks of the Scouts and the Territorial Army. His accent now was impeccably up-market. The disguise was perfect. I used to fantasise that, after his bravery, he was promoted on a safe area of the field of battle, by Lord Kemsley, to 'Personal Assistant'. When Kemsley sold his papers to Roy Thomson for millions, his parting present to Hamilton was a photo of the cheque. Denis hung it in his lavatory.

We had our clashes and our disagreements but in the end I could not help but like him. There seemed to me to be a residual decency there; with the masquerade went a certain sense of *noblesse oblige*. I was sorry when, clearly to his great relief, Thomson bought *The Times*, enabling Denis to move upstairs again, and far above the fray. His successor was Harry Evans.

Harry, too, was and is a likeable fellow, but, though himself a Northerner, he is of a very different breed, eschewing social camouflage. The first time I met him was at the Lansdowne Club near Piccadilly, where my agent, George Greenfield, had invited us. Till recently the editor of the *Northern Echo*, he seemed, then, a wide-eyed provincial, fascinated and excited by the ways of the metropolis. What he inherited from Hamilton was a highly successful newspaper, staffed by extremely competent and gifted executives. All he really had to do was to let them get on with it; and this he did. He had a flair for layout and a lively appreciation of photographs, but he was never a decisive editor, as I discovered to my cost.

With Denis Hamilton moving upstairs and William Rees Mogg, who had been head of the school when I was at Charterhouse – and another amiable figure on the stone – taking over *The Times*, Harry found himself as the *Sunday Times* editor.

After years of toiling under Compston, I suggested to Harry that John Lovesey, then working for *Sports Illustrated* magazine in London, would make a good sports editor. He hired him as sports features editor, a job which, it had been agreed in the past when it was tried, was not a job at all.

Early in 1966, I walked into the *Sunday Times* office on a Saturday evening after reporting a London match, got an early copy of the next day's paper, and found that my sports column was gone. In its place was a column by Michael Parkinson. It was a shock. No one had had the guts or the decency to tell me about it. Not Compston, and not Harry Evans, whose friend Parkinson was. The irony of it was that, while at Bodley Head, I had in a sense 'discovered' Parkinson and tried to persuade him to write a book.

More accurately, I had discovered Jack Braithwaite, under whose name the weekly *Time and Tide* published a series of delightfully fresh and well-observed vignettes of Yorkshire League cricket. I wrote to Jack Braithwaite and had an answer, on *Daily Express* notepaper, from Michael Parkinson, whose pseudonym this was. Barney Blackley, the general manager of Bodley Head, and I took Michael out to lunch at Kettners, the Soho restaurant where Bodley Head had an account. It all went very pleasantly, but I did not succeed in getting a book out of him. Years later, however, when, before the publication of a book of his, he was given a Foyles literary luncheon in Park Lane, I was invited on the strength, it transpired, of having asked him all those years ago to write a book.

John Lovesey eventually succeeded Compston as sports editor in 1970, and almost at once, we fell out. The *casus belli* was my report of the 1970 Cup Final, in which, helped by some 'bum steers' from well-meaning colleagues, I had made a number of minor mistakes. As it happened, I had a new novel out the following Monday, and when I came into the paper on the Saturday evening, found that I had been given the two top reviews for the book, *A Cry of Crickets*, set in Florence, in the *Sunday Times* and the *Observer*, both highly favourable. So when, a few days later, I received from John a long letter of reproach, I sent an angry letter back. This was the beginning of a year of bitter contention.

In an ideal world, John would have expressed his dissatisfaction in a phone call or in person, I would have had my own say, and the thing no doubt would have blown over, as so many such Fleet Street quarrels do. It was the epistolary nature of it that had poisoned the wells and, for the next year or so, John did his best to replace me. Harry Evans knew all about it. A single word would have put a stop to it, but it was not forthcoming. Harry simply would not come down on either side. Indeed, he went to the most unusual shifts and stratagems to avoid doing so.

Eventually, he decided to bring in a so-called football editor, a job that had never before existed, in the shape of his former colleague Peter Roberts. This in itself was an excellent choice. Peter was a calm, emollient, professional figure, who would go on to become a notable managing editor first of the *Sunday Times* then of *The Times*. But the problem was not solved.

It was springtime when I met Geoffrey Greene, the patrician and much respected football correspondent of *The Times*, in the press room at West Ham United. 'What's all this about?' he demanded, in bewilderment. 'Your editor, Harry Evans, phoned me yesterday night when I was in Quaglino's. He said, "Brian Glanville has been spreading calumny about one of our executives. If you hear anything about it, would you pour oil on troubled waters?" '

This at once astonished and infuriated me. I rang Harry at the paper immediately and got straight through to him. 'No, no,' he said, evasively. 'I know now it was something that started at the *Observer*.'

John and I eventually resolved our differences and became good friends again. We had, in the meantime, shared a chilling experience in Mexico, of which I shall write later. But the idea that, having worked so hard, admittedly out of enlightened self-interest, to see that John became sports editor, I should then be any kind of threat to him was simply ludicrous.

Geoffrey Greene was a complex person. 'At his best,' I used to say, in the 1950s, 'he *is* the best.' There is no doubt that we young football writers of that era learned from him. He had a particular gift for the vivid simile or metaphor, perhaps the most famous of all being his glorious description of Billy Wright, in that fateful England versus Hungary match of 1953, going past Puskas, who had pulled the ball back with his foot, 'like a fire engine going to the wrong fire'. Another of his more felicitous phrases, though he used it more than once, was 'like trying to catch a sunbeam in a match box'.

He had a handsome if ravaged face; his drinking was prodigious and notorious, his stamina, in the circumstances, amazing. His voice, which worked splendidly on radio, was beautifully modulated if slightly roughened like, I once wrote, a scratched medallion. Insouciance was his watchword, the pose that kept the world at bay, but there was a deep bitterness within him. This was caused partly, perhaps, by the fact that his gentlemanly instincts – he was one of his generation brought up in India then shipped, like Kipling, to the cold indifference of England – were at odds with his resentment of his comparative poverty. He wanted better terms from his paper, but it was not *comme il faut* to fight for it. Reading, in due course, his autobiography, *Pardon Me for Living*, one gained an insight into the torment of his childhood and adolescence, living, as he did, with a coolly indifferent mother. Jerry Weinstein, who knew him pretty well, and worked for him during the 1954 World Cup when Geoffrey was sports editor of *The Times*, believed that there were unconscious sexual problems, too; demons that caused his drinking.

'Hitler was right!' I once heard him say on a train coming back from the north. He was talking about the little dark men he saw in nightclubs: 'They're the ones with the girls, they're the ones with the money.' Once we clashed violently at a manager of the year lunch at the Café Royal.

He had been a fine amateur footballer, an attacking centre half for Cambridge University and the Corinthians, who might have gone on to signal honours had a serious injury not truncated his career. In his heyday he understood the game as well as he wrote about it. He was an idealist and a moralist. The only pity was that, given his immense prestige, he did not, by and large, take up positions or give the lead he might have done.

There was nothing snobbish about him. When, at the start of a World Cup, a disdainful Swede suggested that he, Geoffrey, and other 'quality-paper' journalists should keep away from those of the popular press, Geoffrey replied that 'we're all colleagues, and we stay together because we like each other'. His comparative reticence in print may have been caused by a certain need to be liked, perpetually attending, as he did, football dinners given by this club or that. He had a string of familiar phrases: 'Over the rainbow.' 'Younger than springtime.' 'My old commander.' Usually they went down well, but at one dinner, given during an England tour, in central Europe, he turned to the British Ambassador seated beside him and asked, 'Am I boring you, Ambassador?' to which the Ambassador – who later regretted it – replied, 'Mr Greene, I don't remember ever having been so bored in my life.'

But Geoffrey could still be refreshingly funny. Once, after a major operation on his hip, he limped into the Queens Park Rangers press room on a stick. 'You look like Long John Silver, Geoffrey,' said a journalist, at which Geoffrey opened his bag, took out a stuffed parrot, and put it on his shoulder.

In his prime, he could ad lib a match report effortlessly over the telephone, the ultimate contrast with another good football writer of his epoch, Don Davies, who died in the 1958 Munich air crash. Where Geoffrey's silvered prose flowed straight into the phone, HD Davies's, alias 'Old International's', Saturday reports in the *Manchester Guardian* would take him three cloistered hours on a Sunday morning, and woe betide any member of his family who intruded.

In his final years, Geoffrey's once lambent metaphors were sometimes mixed. 'They danced like dervishes who have reached harbour.' 'But now the ball has been put firmly in their court by the stormy petrel.' 'But there was no will o' the wisp, so to speak, to take the game by the scruff of the neck.'

John Moynihan recorded his famous 'tired and emotional' radio broadcast after the FA Cup Final of 1957, when Aston Villa beat the ten men of Manchester United. 'They fought like nuts but the Cup was not theirs. And so the score is . . . *Manch*ester Un . . . *As* . . . ton Villa two, Manchester United one.'

We listened to it time and again.

Winterbottom's long reign as England's manager at last came to an end, and he was replaced by the very different figure of Alf Ramsey. A highly influential right back with Tottenham Hotspur, where he was nicknamed 'The General', Ramsey had never had much pace and was very vulnerable to a left winger who would take him on – Billy Liddell, Bobby Mitchell, Don Roper – but his authority and tactical sense made him a significant figure, often capped for England, for whom he would score from important penalties. Born in the East End overspill town of Dagenham, he in due course found himself managing Ipswich Town, owned by the very patrician Cobbold family. Perhaps it was this that induced him to take elocution lessons – the day of the cockney photographer and the fashionable hairdresser, not to say the plebeian actor, had yet to arrive – and to acquire a curious, Sarnt Major Posh, delivery. 'No thank you, I don't want no dinner,' he was reputed to have told a restaurant-car steward, in those aspirational tones. But he was no joke to his players, who often venerated him. 'You did it, Alf!' Nobby Stiles, England's tough little right half, would cry, immediately after England had won the World Cup at Wembley. 'We'd have been nothing without you!'

Under Ramsey, the selection committee disappeared. Instead it became the so-called senior international committee, whose motto might well have been, 'They Also Serve Who Only Eat and Drink'. Once, on a South American tour, Ramsey brusquely told them that if he had his way he would rather have the extra players than themselves, but at least they saved him from attending functions.

When he was appointed, in 1962, Ramsey announced that England would win the 1966 World Cup. The day before the Final against West Germany, out at Roehampton, at the Bank of England sports ground, he was asked whether he still believed it. After a long pause, he replied with a strangulated, 'Yes!'

While we were filming *European Centre Forward* in Turin, Ramsey's Ipswich Town were up against Milan, in the European Cup. Gerry Hitchens was anxious to see the game and, as a recent England centre forward, to remind Ramsey of his existence. 'Must say hallo to Alf! Wish good luck to the lads!'

Down the dressing-room corridor we went, before the kickoff. 'Hallo, Alf,' cried Gerry.

'Oh, yes,' said Ramsey. 'You're playin' in these parts.'

Gerry couldn't get over it. He sat beside me during the match in which, under teeming rain, Ipswich were thrashed 4–0, muttering, 'Prat! Prat! "You're playin' in these parts."' He never played for England again.

There were times when Ramsey could be humorous, almost playful. I recall sitting in a railway compartment with him and several other reporters. 'I don't know why you telephone me,' he said, and went round the carriage. 'I never telephone you. I never telephone you. I never telephone you –' till it came to myself '– you never telephone *me*!'

His famous, or notorious, categorisaton of the Argentine team beaten 1–0 in the World Cup quarter-final at Wembley was really an example of his being caught on the wrong foot. Alan Bass, the big, bluff, popular England team doctor (in Rous's day, incredibly, England never had one on their travels), told me that not only had the Argentine players tried to attack Herr Kreitlein, the German referee who had sent off their captain, Antonio Rattin, but they had urinated in the dressing-room corridor and tried to smash down the door of the England dressing-room. Interviewed hard on the heels of all this, Ramsey simply said that he thought England would play their best against a team interested in playing football, 'and not acting as animals'.

Words that would come back to haunt him. When England went on a tour in South America and Mexico in 1969 prior to the World Cup, Alf called the journalists together and emphasised the importance of creating a benign climate and of making friends. Alas, his own xenophobia was a kind of cloven hoof, which could not help but show.

England's first game was against Mexico in Mexico City at the old Azteca Stadium, which would be rebuilt for the World Cup of 1970. The players had had hopelessly insufficient time to cope with the oxygen debt at 7,200 feet above sea level, and did well to get a goalless draw. At the end, Hugh McIlvanney and I embarked on a kind of 'countaineering' expedition, at last succeeding in getting to the spot where Alf was giving his press conference.

Asked whether he would like to say something to the Mexican public, he replied, 'Yes. There was a band outside our hotel, playin', at five o'clock in the mornin'. We were promised a motor cycle escort to the ground. It never arrived. When our players went out to inspect the pitch, they were abused and jeered by the crowd. I would have thought that they'd be delighted to welcome England, then when the game began, they could cheer their own team as much as they liked.' A pause. An afterthought. 'But . . . we are delighted to be in Mexico, and the Mexican people are a wonderful people.'

In Guadalajara, things became worse. This was a 'B' international that England won with ease. Afterwards, again in a stadium shortly to be rebuilt, Alf chased the Mexican journalists down the tunnel to the dressing-rooms like Christ chasing the money-changers from the temple. 'Get out! You have no business here!'

'What do you expect from a man who called the Argentines animals?' a local paper asked, next day.

Despite the controversial arrest and brief 'domestic' imprisonment of their captain, Bobby Moore, on a trumped-up charge of stealing a bracelet from a jewellery shop in the team's hotel, England performed nobly in this World Cup. They would probably have gone beyond the quarter-finals had their outstanding goalkeeper, Gordon Banks, who had made an amazing one-handed save from Pele's bouncing header in Guadalajara ('He got up like a salmon out of bright water'), not been poisoned by 'The Fatal Glass of Beer'. So he missed the game against West Germany in the searing noon heat of Leon, where Ramsey, never really happy with substitution (this was the first World Cup to permit them), took off Bobby Charlton when he shouldn't have done and kept on his exhausted full backs when they should have gone off; and England threw away a 2–0 lead. Afterwards, the players stretched out like wartime casualties on the lawns of their motel.

Bobby Moore, rightly chosen as best player of the 1966 World Cup, perhaps had a still better, more commanding tournament in 1970. Grace under pressure was the essence of his game; though for him, composed and taciturn, pressure seemed hardly to exist. The night before the quarter-final, I sat with him at the bar of the motel where, oblivious to the coming game, his one concern was to see that his two London friends, Phil Isaacs, once of Chelsea Casuals, and Morrie Keston, Tottenham's most prominent supporter, would have somewhere to stay the night.

A few weeks after returning from Mexico, I received an unexpected letter from Colombia. '*Muy estimado Señor*,' it began. 'You may not remember me, but I am the policeman you sat next to at the matches between Colombia and England in Bogotá. You congratulated me when I caught one of the footballs that were kicked into the crowd. Little did I realise until I saw your photograph in the paper next day whom I was sitting next to.'

The photo had been arranged by a genial Colombian diplomat

who had apparently read some of my novels. It portrayed the Earl of Harewood, then a director of Leeds United, who accompanied the England team, Geoffrey Greene of *The Times* and myself.

The letter duly came to the point. 'I have a nervous disease which causes my hands to shake. This is especially bad in the winter when I have to go on traffic duty. What I would really like is a pair of good English gloves. Even if these were your own gloves, the mere contact with your hands would be a privilege for me.'

It was worth a pair of gloves, I thought, and I bought them for him and sent them to Bogotá. Some weeks later I got another letter. '*Muy estimado Señor*. When I had no answer from you to my previous letter, I was really disappointed. But now, I have received this magnificent pair of gloves. I thank you, my wife thanks you, my children thank you.'

The moral, I suppose, must be: never be photographed with the Earl of Harewood.

Most managers, at any level, have a finite usefulness, and Ramsey was no exception. By 1972, he was not the same man. It became quite clear when England met West Germany at Wembley in the first leg quarter-final of the Nations Cup, or European Championship, in that year. To my amazement, he had picked a team without a single tackler in midfield. In consequence, the big-booted, long-haired Gunter Netzer ran riot, and England lost, 3–1.

This meant of course that they must win by at least two goals in the return game in Berlin, if they were to qualify. But Ramsey, throwing in the towel, picked a team which had no hope of doing that; essentially, a team of hard men. There was Peter Storey of Arsenal, Nobby Stiles, Norman Hunter of Leeds United and Mike Summerbee of Manchester City. It was a deadly, goalless draw which did nothing for England. Gunter Netzer came off the field to say, 'The whole England team has autographed my leg.'

This was plainly the time for Ramsey, who had achieved so much, to go. Instead the international committee couldn't find the courage to replace him, and he lingered on for two more years. When he did go, it was in controversial circumstances, with Harold Thompson the villain of the piece. In fact, Thompson was surely right, but probably right for the wrong reasons. He was not a man who easily forgave, and Ramsey, once, had asked him to put out his cigar, as he was blowing smoke in the faces of Alf's young players.

It was Kaiser Bill and Bismarck all over again, in diminuendo. The pilot had been dropped. Thompson was deplored. Don Revie of Leeds United would, eventually, and disastrously, take over.

Meanwhile there was a beguiling interregnum in which Joe Mercer, a famous left half for Everton, Arsenal and England, and former manager of Aston Villa, Sheffield United and Manchester City, took over.

Under his genial tutelage, the tour of Leipzig, Sofia and Belgrade had a holiday atmosphere about it. No one could have been more relaxed than Joe, who liked nothing better than to preside, with a rich sequence of anecdotes, over little groups of journalists. If there was an element of the *flâneur* about it, who cared? Managerially, Joe had tended to go with the prevailing trend, but there was no doubt about his excellence as a player, an attacking wing half with Everton before the war ('You'd have liked me then, Brian'), a member of England's celebrated Britton–Cullis–Mercer half-back line during it and an inspiring and canny captain of Arsenal, when it was over.

Ted Croker, the new FA Secretary, who had once been on the books of Charlton, put on an England track-suit top and trained with the players, while Mercer, whose leg had been broken in his last Arsenal game and who now walked with a limp, wore suit and tie. This caused the *Guardian*'s witty football correspondent, David Lacey, to observe, 'We've got a track-suit secretary and a lounge-suit manager.'

Some time after his appointment to Lancaster Gate, Ted Croker, though he had never done as much as his brother Peter, who was the right back when the club won the 1947 FA Cup Final, visited the Valley for a match. Afterwards, one of the Charlton directors told him, 'It's surprising to see the Secretary of the FA at a Second Division game.'

'Well, I do like to see my old clubs when I can,' replied Croker.

'In that case,' said Charlton's large, red-headed young chairman, Michael Gliksten, 'you should really be watching Charlton Athletic Reserves.'

The only blemish on the tour came when poor Kevin Keegan was beaten up at Belgrade Airport. This would never have happened had the travel agent with the England party only absorbed the fact that there was a one-hour difference between Sofia, where England had played Bulgaria, and Belgrade. So it was that when the England players, all dressed in casual clothes and looking like a bunch of young tourists, arrived at Belgrade Airport, there was no one from the Yugoslav Federation or the British Embassy to meet them.

One or two of them started fooling about on the luggage carousel. Keegan, then a star forward with Liverpool, didn't. He looked slightly unwell after the flight and simply sat down, clutching a brown paper bag full of gifts and the like. A scruffy little man in a brown suit suddenly came up and tried to wrench the bag out of his hands. Keegan angrily resisted. At which point a huge policeman in peaked cap, grey uniform and jackboots strode in, grabbed hold of Keegan at one end, while the man in the brown suit lifted the other, and to the horror and consternation of the rest of the party, marched him out of the hall.

When he later returned, he was in tears. He had been beaten up. His resilience was shown when, in the eventual game, which was drawn, he capped an excellent performance with a goal. As the British Ambassador later remarked, such a distressing incident could have happened only at Belgrade Airport. Behind the Iron Curtain, the forbidden areas would have been rigidly cordoned off. In a genuinely democratic country, such supposed trespasses would not have mattered.

Soon after the 1966 World Cup, I was introduced to a new experience of park football: the Bill Naughton game, in Hyde Park. It was played, not where Chelsea Casuals had begun, but behind the police station in a more central area. Bill was its founder and its inspiration. A former lorry driver from Bolton, he had made his name with appealing short stories, most of them published in the much-mourned *Lilliput* magazine. From there he had gone to radio plays, plays and films, the most successful of which, *Alfie*, had made him rich and made a star of Michael Caine.

Bill was 57 at the time. Grey-haired, bare-chested, clad in a pair of white tennis shorts, he had an astonishing gift for cajoling passers-by to play. Postmen were among the regulars. They would park their Royal Mail vans on the path, while other players complained, 'No wonder we never get any fucking letters.' There were several waiters, the most voluble of them being Mario, a little Italian. And there was Mike.

I had already come across him in summer Sunday-morning games, heavily populated and alarmingly serious, played in front of the Knightsbridge barracks. But, as he reminded me, it wasn't the first time. That had been far back in 1952, shortly before I took off for Italy. Reg Drury had brought him along to Highbury before an Arsenal game to be given, from the shallows of my experience, advice. By some strange chance, he, a Hackney Marshes player, had been spotted by the French club Bordeaux, and offered a contract as an amateur; all found.

Should he go? It all sounded quite chimerical to me, and I don't know what I told him. Suffice it to say that he did go, and stayed several years in France, first at Bordeaux, then with the Paris University team. He had had a bike that day at Highbury and had a bike now – a big, black, heavy one, a kind of symbol of integrity. He was extremely dignified, often censorious, dressed invariably in black jacket and black trousers, secured by bicycle clips.

'The boys liked the short stories, Brian,' he told me, one Sunday morning, 'but *The Rise of Gerry Logan*. No.'

The first time I found Bill Naughton's game, Mike appeared, wheeling his bicycle. 'Want to play, Mike?' Bill asked him. He nodded, and went in what passed for goal: two deck-chairs, a few yards apart. A shot sailed in. Mike raised his hands in a kind of paraplegic gesture, but a goal it was.

'Bloody, fucking hell, Mike!' screamed Mario.

'That's quite enough from you, Mario,' said Mike. 'We don't want that kind of language here. If you can't control yourself, you'd better take yourself and your bad temper somewhere else.'

The game resumed. Another shot at goal. Again Mike raised his arms. Another goal. This time Bill Naughton trotted up to him. 'Don't play if you don't want to play, Mike.'

'All right,' Mike said, turning away and walking towards me. 'Tell Reg when you see him,' he said. 'Tell him what I've come down to. Being told how to play – by a fucking writer!'

Freddie Raphael played, too. I persuaded him to come. We were almost exactly the same age and had been contemporaries at Charterhouse, though we had never met each other. Our friendship would begin years later. Freddie, novelist and television playwright, had just won an Oscar for his screenplay of *Darling*, the film which made a star of Julie Christie. He hadn't played football for years, but, long and lean and committed, he soon settled down in defence. Vic, the postman, who had no idea who he was, conceived an admiration for him. 'Well done, Fred,' he would cry. 'He's come on a ton.'

Freddie was amused by Bill's subtle gamesmanship. 'He's not really interested in anybody else, is he? "Hallo, Fred, how are you?" "I've just broken my leg, Bill." "Marvellous!" '

Once, I had to break up a fight between Bill and an irritating young Swiss waiter, a blond boy who played, bare-chested as Bill did, in red track-suit trousers, and whom you could always kick if he annoyed you. Bill was more straightforward. Bending the rules, such as they were, one afternoon, he was incensed when the Swiss boy responded, 'Oh, let him. He will only cry.'

'What!' said an infuriated Bill. 'What? We let them come over here!' Whereupon he grabbed the boy in a headlock and dragged him to the ground. I pulled them apart.

Sadly, Bill made so much money from his plays and films that he decided to go into tax exile, in the Isle of Man. The game collapsed and I reinitiated it near my own home, in Holland Park. It took a very long time to get into motion. The first attempt was graced by John Cleese and Eric Idle, of *Monty Python*, and an American ski girl called Bunny. None of whom ever came again. But gradually it grew, till now when it has for many years been a popular Thursday occasion involving players from all over the world: from Colombia to Syria, from France to Brazil, from Argentina to Somalia.

Piero wasn't playing any more, but we did not lose touch. His life had taken an unexpected turn. Then a convinced Marxist – though in time he would emerge – he enrolled himself in a university course and intensively studied philosophy, spending summers in London while paying his way as a hospital porter. It took tremendous application and assiduity, but it would ultimately have its rich reward. In 1997, he would be taken on as assistant by one of the foremost Oxonian philosophers at All Souls.

That he should follow such a path, coming from the background he did, was remarkable. When I visited Florence with my wife, we were invited to lunch with Piero's family. His father had a flat above his grocery store, near the stadium. We arrived before Piero, and his parents, looking at Pam and me as though we were a strange new breed of animal, shut us in a sitting-room out of harm's way, until he arrived, ebullient and affectionate as ever.

Our meeting with Mauro was not a success. He drove us, hectically and alarmingly, up into the hills, and would hardly speak a word to Pam. 'Where on earth did you find that marvellous girl?' asked David, with whom we stayed.

I would see little or nothing of Mauro after this visit, but my friends in Florence, especially those on *La Nazione*, often told me about him. Rich now, he had bought his farm near Pisa, sailed in his boat, and he had married. Married a Pole, in fact, who was always referred to as *la polacca*; and married her in the strangest circumstances. An Italian youth football team was going to play in Poland. Mauro asked the coach, who was a friend of his, 'Find me a wife.' The coach obliged. He found *la polacca*. Over the years, things deteriorated. Till suddenly, shockingly, Mauro disappeared.

He vanished from his car, found by the banks of the Arno, its doors wide open, his passport still in its glove compartment. No one could find him. No one ever did. I had only once met *la polacca*, when she came to London and visited us, together with the English wife of a Polish immigrant. She was stupendously coarse, a mannerless vulgarian, a middle-aged woman who complained that, when she had gone dancing the night before, the English men would not respond to her advances. My Florentine friends told me she had been very good-looking before she had had a car crash. There would be another. When Mauro disappeared, she rang me in apparent despair to ask me if I knew whether he was in England. But one heard alarming stories.

The sports editor of *La Nazione* told me that Mauro had rung him once in tears. He had been beaten up, he said, by a bunch of young Poles, at the instigation of his wife. And his eyesight was failing.

Still no sign or trace of him. 'They gave him to the pigs,' a porter at *La Nazione* told me, bitterly. Every now and then one heard news of *la polacca*, though none of Mauro. Driving me to Genoa, after a match, a sports writer on *L'Unita*, the communist paper, told me that a woman he knew, invited to the farm, had had to flee from lesbian advances. '*La voleva leccare la fica.*'

La polacca had only to sit tight, wait for the statutory ten years to elapse from Mauro's disappearance, and the farm would legally be hers. But after ten years, almost to the day, she was involved in another car crash, and was killed.

The summer of 1967 I spent mostly in New York. For tax reasons, I had to write the screenplay of *A Roman Marriage* abroad. Needing something else to do while I was in the States, I wrote to ask Jack Kent-Cooke if he could find me any work with television or a newspaper in Los Angeles. He never replied.

Jack Kent-Cooke was a former band musician, a Canadian, who had grown rich with the proprietor of the *Sunday Times*, Roy Thomson. The word was that he had then cut Thomson out of a deal, and relations had been broken off for many years. Now, however, they had been re-established, which was why the voice of Kent-Cooke suddenly came out of a telephone at me quite early one morning. Roy Thomson had recommended me, he said. Professional soccer had been restarted in the States, the official League (there had been an unofficial one) would be importing teams from abroad to represent the various franchises. Could I get him one from England? What I didn't know at the time was that he had already contracted the America club from Mexico City, but then decided that he didn't want them.

Thinking about it, I decided that Wolverhampton Wanderers might be a good bet, and I spoke to their manager Ronnie Allen, once a West Bromwich and England centre forward. He was very interested. Wolves, then, were in pole position in Division Two and would eventually be promoted. He spoke to his directors, who agreed to go.

Some weeks later, on an Easter Monday, before a match at Craven Cottage (Fulham's ground), I heard heavy footsteps behind me as I walked the long corridor beneath the stand. It was Kenneth ('They think it's all over') Wolstenholme, the BBC television commentator, who at that time was running a company with a Spaniard called Jorge Sturrup, one of whose tasks was to find teams for the American tournament. '*What's* all this about Wolves going to America?' he demanded. '*They* won't go! I was with the directors on Saturday. Can you imagine them going, when they've been fighting for promotion all season?'

I mildly replied that Ronnie Allen had assured me they would go, but that I saw his point. Some time later, an anxious Ronnie Allen rang me. He had been telephoned by a still more anxious Bill Ridding, manager of Bolton Wanderers – Kenneth's home town – who was alarmed by the news that Wolves, not Bolton, would be playing for Los Angeles. 'He says they've bought new shirts and flags and everything.' But it was Wolves who went; and Wolves who won the tournament.

Hearing nothing from Kent-Cooke, I chose instead to go to New York, which was at least a city I knew well, and where I had many friends. Subsequently, I heard about Kent-Cooke from his fellow Canadian, the entertainer Bernard Braden. Once, he said, he had been visiting Kent-Cooke in Los Angeles. Kent-Cooke spoke about an old friend, who, in desperate financial trouble, had called him that day and asked for a loan. Kent-Cooke had bluntly refused him telling him to stand on his own two feet. At this, Kent-Cooke's wife observed that she remembered when he himself was out of work, and had appealed to his friend to help him. 'He got you a job, and made it possible for you to take *his* job, which you did.'

Kent-Cooke started to protest, but his wife answered, 'Stand away from me!' and left the room.

'I don't know why she said that,' he complained. 'We have this butler, and he has bad breath. When he gets too near me, I tell him, "Stand away from me!" '

Working for Jim Roach, the sports editor of the *New York Times*, was a perpetual joy, after those gloomy years of Compston. He was a tall rangy man in late middle age, the son of a Mancunian immigrant, always humorous, never perturbed. Our greetings were always the same. 'Good morning, coach.' 'How *are* you, coach?' It was hard to cope with such geniality.

Not one, but two, pro teams competed at the Yankee Stadium, where the sandy infield was a hazard of the pitch. For the Skyliners, alias Madison Square Gardens, Cerro of Montevideo, very much a distant third behind Nacional and Penarol, competed. This renewed my acquaintance with two old friends. Ondino Viera, manager of Uruguay's 1966 World Cup team, and his assistant, Omar Borras, who would manage Uruguay's turbulent team in the World Cup of 1986.

Cagliari came to town to play them, on behalf of Chicago. Their manager was an ironic Roman, Manlio Scopigno, known as 'Il Filosofo' because he had very briefly attended a course at Rome University. '*Ci arriverano, ci arriverano,*' he said, wearily, in the bowels of a functional hotel on Sixth Avenue, on a steaming hot day. 'They'll get there.'

The game, played at Yankee Stadium on a humid evening, turned out to be a deplorable one. A Cerro player whacked a Cagliari player across the back of the head. The referee, Leo Goldstein, who had mercifully survived a concentration camp, did nothing. An Italian fan stood up in the stand and shouted, '*Bestia, brutta bestia!*' (Animal, ugly animal!) There was a hiatus, then a little fat Italian fan climbed over the low fence around the ground and aimed a kick at a perfectly harmless linesman. In no time at all, a whole posse of Italian supporters was on the field, chasing the hapless Leo Goldstein. He fell on the sandy infield, kicked out at his pursuers, got up again, and escaped.

'Those Italian fans behaved like animals,' said the Italian-American head of the stadium police, whose coppers had done nothing.

Could I ever have believed that my first visit to Los Angeles would be with a Uruguayan soccer team, due to play Wolves? 'Don't go making this look bad,' I was warned, in flight, by the massive, genial former ice-hockey star who accompanied the team. 'We've got too much money on it!'

After arriving in Los Angeles, I was asked to give a team talk in Spanish to the Cerro players. Meanwhile the Six Days War had broken out in the Middle East, and newspaper headlines proclaimed it. '*Guerra?*' said the puzzled Cerro directors. Cerro lost. I didn't see Kent-Cooke. I did, though, see Floyd Patterson.

To my surprise, I found that he was staying at the same hotel as we were, out near the airport at El Segundo: the Hacienda, proprietor Al Widgeon. Your host on the coast!

Patterson came trotting out of the hotel, extremely cheerful, though no longer Champion. Sonny Liston had beaten him badly.

Muhammad Ali would beat him more badly and more cruelly still. But, at this point, he was a happy man, free, he said, from past encumbrances. 'I didn't have that octopus on my back, sucking my blood. I didn't have that seaweed round my legs.'

In 1998, he followed Ali into the shadows, incapacitated for ever by all those terrible blows to the head. It was poignant to remember him as he was.

New York Generals were the other team that played at Yankee Stadium, a member of the 'outlaw' League that had sprung up without FIFA permission. In due course, the two clubs would amalgamate. John Pinto, the Generals' President, a tall man with a stentorian voice, would honk from the directors' box at every home game: 'Come on, Generals!' but it was hard work for Freddie Goodwin, the manager, a former Manchester United wing half. One would see him in the dressing-room, in the bowels of the stadium, standing at the blackboard, trying to teach tactics to a couple of bemused West Indian wingers.

Scopigno, who had done so much for Cagliari, was sacked as a result of what happened on the disillusioning tour. He had apparently urinated in public. Later, in Rome, Biti and I would run into him and have a coffee in the Galleria Colonna. 'I'm a tourist,' he would say. Scopigno – a handsome man with a noble face, a thinker, if not a philosopher.

Virgil to my Dante, in New York, was the English expatriate, Paul Gardner, a well-read man who once had written to me at the *Sunday Times*. He showed me the reply; I had, thank God, on that occasion written back at length, politely. Paul adored football, wrote about it with succinct intelligence, and was thus anathema to those trying to get pro soccer off the ground, who wanted nothing but boosters. Once perfectly described to me as 'Her Majesty's Loyal Opposition', Paul should have been employed by one of the major newspapers or television outlets; though he would, in time, become the colour commentator for the ABC Network, when it had a contract to show games in the North American Soccer League. He lived on the West Side with his two huge apartment cats, standing out sternly against hyperbole.

Originally a trained pharmacist with a degree from Nottingham University, he had come to New York to be assistant editor of a pharmaceutical journal. From there, he had branched out into football journalism, writing a couple of well-founded books, *The Simplest Game* and *Nice Guys Finish Last*. He was a generous host and friend beneath a misleading abrasive exterior. But he frightened people.

Dany Blanchflower was in New York at the same time, providing commentary for CBS television. He found it hard to conform with their Panglossian approach to things. 'Don't you think there's a positive truth and a negative truth, Danny?' they asked. 'Instead of saying it was a poor shot, can't you say it was a good save?' He couldn't. One lunchtime in Toots Shoors, the restaurant patronised by sports people, which had once been a speakeasy, I was introduced to two of the CBS executives. 'How'd you like to take Danny Blanchflower's job?' one of them asked.

I replied that I didn't take people's jobs, and he laughed it off. After lunch I went to the NBC offices to see a writer friend, Morton Hochstein, who had worked on a London TV programme in which I had appeared, the previous year. I told him what had happened at Toots Shoors. He grabbed his telephone. 'Call them, call them! Tell them you didn't mean it!'

'I did mean it,' I said.

That London programme had been a curious experience. I had been interviewed under a drizzle one Sunday morning at Hyde Park's Speaker's Corner, the interview lasting much longer than was scheduled, since Geraldine Chaplin failed to turn up. The presenter, Hugh Downs, was a kindly, modest, somewhat puzzled man, obliged at one point to hold a tray of toothpaste tubes up to a camera, and extol them. We spoke first about *Goal!*, the 1966 World Cup film I had written. Then it came to the turn of Barbara Walters, who had yet to ascend to the political stratosphere, when she would, on his behalf, offer Henry Kissinger to speak to foreign rulers.

'I read your novel, *Second Home*,' she said. 'It was on the *New York Times* book review list for weeks and weeks. It was all about women; these are our problems, and you write about football?'

'I must have been going through one of my transvestite periods,' I said.

'It's a novel about an actress,' she told Hugh Downs. 'She isn't married, but can we say she has people living with her?'

'You've already said it,' he replied. After a little while, he clearly felt he should come into the conversation. 'Mr Glanville,' he said, 'do you think the kind of life you've been describing represents a threat to the existence of the family, which has always been the basis of Western civilisation?'

'*Goal!*,' said Michael Samuelson, of the celebrated film-equipment firm, a main mover in almost every area of the documentary – producer, financier, cameraman – 'wasn't a film, it was a happening.' I could well see his point. By the time I was brought in, they were at rough-cut stage, and in a state of some desperation. The footage, or much of it, was splendid, but it was nowhere near to being a coherent film. I was approached by pure chance, since a girl who had worked in London for Granada, when I interviewed sports stars for a programme in the north of which the host was Michael Parkinson, suggested that I might be helpful. 'Make your voice heard,' advised David, the production manager.

There was a babel of voices. Octavio Señuret, the Chilean head of a firm called Frigo Establishment, was the immaculately dressed, silvery-haired producer. One director was a young, then inexperienced, South African, Ross Devenish. The other was a Turkish painter, the charming Abedine Dino, who claimed to have worked in Moscow with Eisenstein. A claim which, in the strangest way, would be confirmed. Johnny Hawkesworth, an accomplished jazz musician, had written the score. Abedine told me he knew he must be the right man when, with great assiduity, he had accompanied him and his wife all the way down the escalators at a tube station, and put them on the wrong train.

The original writer had been BS (Brian) Johnson, who always described himself as an experimental novelist, and would ultimately kill himself most cruelly, at an early age. Things had not worked out well, and he had left. Several of the highly accomplished cameramen were French. Avoiding any kind of cliché, they would provide the material for sequences that would have a profound influence on football's television coverage for years to come.

David said he thought he could persuade the well-known actor, Nigel Patrick, to provide the commentary. This seemed exciting. My father, in fact, had known Patrick and his wife, the actress Beatrice Campbell, very well; they had both been patients of his. My fee was nominal and non-negotiable; a few hundred pounds; all that was left in the pot. I wanted to do it, anyway; after all the joy and the drama, the euphoria of England's success, I fervently wanted the film to be a success, as well. The heartaches and the thousand natural shocks of the Final were still very much with me. Ray Wilson's misplaced header, enabling Helmut Haller to put West Germany so traumatically ahead. The body blow of the Germans' late, fortuitous equaliser. The free kick that should have gone England's way. The way it bounced off Karl-Heinz Schnellinger's back, creating a *trompe-l'oeil* that made me, from the press gallery, believe he had handled it.

The dynamic running in extra time of little, red-haired, Alan Ball, whom Bolton had once rejected, telling him, 'You'd make a good little jockey.' The pregnant hiatus after Geoff Hurst had driven Ball's cross against the underside of the bar, while Dienst, the Swiss referee, consulted Bakhramov, the long-haired Soviet linesman; till Bakhramov pointed his flag towards the middle. Was it a goal? Did the ball cross the line? Time and again I looked at the incident on the moviola while we were finishing the film, in Cricklewood. I couldn't tell. I never have been able to, on any other evidence, though a few years ago a German laboratory produced 'evidence' that it was not a goal.

Gradually, we pulled the film into shape. Some of the sequences were extraordinary; and nothing to do with me. Especially the prolonged retreat of the huge Argentine captain Rattin after he had been sent off in the quarter-final, as he made his way around the pitch, pausing to wipe his hand on a Union Jack corner flag, his accompanying trainer exchanging insults with the fans. All this accompanied by John Hawkesworth's evocative music.

And yes, Abedine Dino had indeed worked with Eisenstein, who himself might have been proud of that sequence. At a party given by the writer Angus Wilson, near Primrose Hill, in honour of the Russian translator Rita Rait, who had known Eisenstein well, I mentioned Abedine. 'Abi!' she cried. 'He was madly in love with my girlfriend. I would lend him the keys of my flat.'

Nigel Patrick arrived and crisply gave the commentary. At a time when the Finneys and Courtenays, with their unreconstructed accents, were changing the face of English acting, Patrick was one of the older school. His anecdotes were of the war, of times when actors were anxious to be seen as gentlemen. He himself had been an officer, and had served in Italy. There was an anecdote that involved the Duke of Edinburgh: 'Suh!' Why, when I was sitting right next to him in the recording studio, did I let him keep calling the Final's referee Dee-enst, instead of Deenst? But, overall, his patrician voice worked well.

Our crew, it transpired, had very nearly failed to film the Final at all. Harold Mayes, whom I had known so well in his *Empire News* days, and who seemed to have accumulated bile in the years since he had lost his role in journalism, had been made chief press officer for the tournament. As such, he was Draconian. 'The first man to be shot in this tournament,' said an aggrieved German journalist, 'should be Harold Mayes.' He even succeeded in making the ultra-gentlemanly Tony Pawson, who in his light-armoured vehicle had faced shells and bullets in North Africa, lose his temper. Forced to go all the way back from Kensington to Kent to fetch a ticket. Tony was told by Mayes on his return that he still could not get into the game.

At Wembley, shortly before the Final, Mayes felt our camera team had somehow infringed the rules, whatever they may have been. 'Right!' he said. 'All Frigo Establishment passes confiscated.' Denis Follows, the FA Secretary, had to be dragged out of a banquet to overrule him.

I saw the completed film for the first time in an Odeon cinema; a private viewing, in Northwest London. When it was over, I walked up and down outside in a seething fury. Every line of commentary had been cut from the sequence that showed film of one of the finest, most dramatic games of the tournament: Hungary's victory over Brazil on Everton's ground, which included a sensationally volleyed goal by the Hungarian right winger, Farkas. It would have mattered less had the team not been given wretched camera positions that evening, so that the action was not well shown. Octavio came out and tried to calm me. He had been responsible for the cut. I am still not sure why he did it, but the documentary had an excellent reception both here and in the States, where it ran for months in both Los Angeles and New York, and was praised in the *New Yorker*. It still gets shown, can still be seen on video, and clips cost a fortune. None of which finds its way to me.

Slow motion was skilfully used. There was a glorious sequence of three England players dancing joyfully in line, like the three Graces. It was indeed a happening, to which almost everybody involved had contributed. I don't think there will ever be a World Cup film quite like it.

7

N SEPTEMBER 1968, I flew out to Buenos Aires, where Manchester United were due to play Estudiantes de la Plata in the first leg of the ill-starred, so-called, Intercontinental Cup. It was the first time I had been to Buenos Aires, and I liked it from the outset. It seemed to me like an agreeable time warp, an Italian provincial city of the 1950s, where no liaison could be consummated before a six-month courtship.

Visiting a press party, I was delighted to be greeted by journalists who for years had been familiar names to me in the Italian press, colleagues on *Corriere dello Sport* and *Calcio Illustrato*: big, mournful Oreste Bomben, and little, lively Romolo Babusci. Afterwards we all went to one of those *al fresco* steak houses for dinner. The day before the match, I joined Manchester United's players to watch a polo game. Kenneth Wolstenholme strolled past in bright-red trousers, which elicited tart comments from the team.

The match itself, played in Boca Juniors' Bombanera stadium, with its steep terraces built so close to the pitch, was a nightmare, at least for United. Estudiantes came out from the very first kick to kick and intimidate. George Best told me afterwards that he had simply stopped playing after a quarter of an hour; it was pointless to try. Bobby Charlton had his shin cut open with a kick from the midfielder Pachamé. Carlos Bilardo, who would later win a World Cup as Argentina's manager, with Pachamé his right-hand man, split Nobby Stiles's eyebrow with a back header. United lost by the only goal.

Then I flew off to Mexico City to cover my third Olympics. I had already finished writing my novel, *The Olympian*, which appeared in New York and London the following year. It was essentially an allegory, in which I used the figure of an English miler – as a kind of

Faust – driven to greater and greater illusory efforts. Those were the days when drugs in athletics were still relatively uncommon, in contrast to today, when athletes will take them, not to make sure that they will win, but to ensure they do not lose. It was also a time of shamateurism, a time when the top performers could make a good deal of money, but always secretly, whereas today, vast sums are paid to overt professionals.

The *Sunday Times*, as one of their time-serving executives took delight in telling me, had not wanted to send me to Mexico; a clause in my contract ensured that they did. In the event, it proved just as well, though for the most gruesome of reasons. Arriving in Mexico City, I found a state of tension. The students had reportedly been 'rioting' against the Government; that Partido Revolucionario Institucional which, by hook, crook, force and corruption, had been in power for the past forty years. The previous day, the blue-helmeted riot police, the brutal Granaderos, had smashed down the door of a barricaded polytechnic. That evening, in the huge Plaza de las Tres Cultures, there would be what was known as a *mitin* of the students, where violence was expected. I was ordered to attend it.

Rain poured down on the vast Plaza de las Tres Culturas at the end of the long Paseo de la Reforme. A huge crowd had gathered to listen to student speakers. The Granaderos lurked on the edges of it. The three cultures were represented by Aztec ruins, a Spanish Colonial church, and a colossal, yellow-walled block of apartments that dominated the square and, from one of whose balconies, the student leaders addressed their audience. I had no idea what might happen, though I knew the tanks had been out the day before. In the event, nothing did. I managed to find some students, and dodged around corners with them, in another apartment block, asking them about what was happening. Speaking Spanish was no problem but nor, as it transpired, was it any help. From a purely journalistic point of view, I would have been better off without it.

I divided my time between the Villa Olimpica (the Olympic Village), a kind of nirvana twenty miles outside the city, and the city itself, where I attempted to keep up with developments. Thus I attended a protest march by silent women from the Monument of the Mother. But I was generally assured that the violence had died down. Nothing would imminently happen. How wrong.

The following Wednesday, I came up from the Villa Olimpica on a press bus with John Roddha, the pleasant, modest, athletics correspondent of the *Guardian*. He asked me if I would be going to the *mitin* that night. 'No,' I said, flippantly, 'first because it's

Wednesday and it wouldn't keep; secondly, because I don't think anything is going to happen.'

John would have good cause to disagree. That night he would find himself face down on the balcony from which the students had been speaking, a secret policeman's gun pressed into his head, while bullets pinged off the wall behind him. Oriana Fallacci, a famous Italian journalist, was dragged down the steps from the balcony by her hair. When he heard about it, the dreadful old President of the Olympic Committee, Avery Brundage, an apologist for Hitler at the time of the 1936 Games, asked, 'What was she doing there?'

The following morning, I was meant to be going to Acapulco, for the solitary free day I would have. I never got there. John Lovesey phoned me early in the morning at my hotel. 'All hell's broken loose.' He and other journalists had been summoned from their beds in the middle of the night and driven to a Government briefing; a Government whitewash. There had been a 'riot' in the square, and a few deaths.

Together, we visited the square that morning. Tanks were dotted about it. A huge scar from a bazooka shell ran down the yellow wall of the flats. Bit by bit, we pieced together an appalling story.

At a certain moment of the *mitin*, a helicopter had buzzed overhead, and dropped two flares. This was the signal for secret-service agents, wearing white gloves, to draw their guns and shoot into the air. That in turn prompted an invasion of the square by troops who had surrounded it. They came in shooting and bayoneting the defenceless crowd. At least 300 died. Their bodies had been taken to Camp Militar Numero Uno, and burnt. A brutal President, Diaz Ordaz, and his brutal generals, believed that they had acted with impunity; believed that a mere bunch of sports journalists would never give them trouble.

Had they been thinking only of the older Americans, stuck in their perpetual adolescence, they might have been right. I remember, still shaken, walking down the Reforma, some days later, and coming across the chief sports columnist of *New York Times*, the large and lumbering Arthur Daley (Jim Roach would much have preferred the talented Red Smith). I tried to tell Daley what had happened. 'But that was just in one area of the city,' he replied.

Later, I imagined meeting him in Jerusalem, immediately after the crucifixion. 'But that was just in one area of the city . . .'

But the German, the Italian and several of the English journalists tirelessly pursued the truth of the atrocities, and to the fury of the Mexican Government, the truth duly appeared. It also appeared –

though not in the castrated Mexican press – in a magazine called *Por Que*. It was to *Por Que*'s offices in the Colonia Roma that frustrated photographers repaired, knowing there was no chance of getting their horrific pictures into their own newspapers. In those devastating photographs, dead bodies sprawled on the ground. A grinning Army officer held a student by his hair. John and I wrote about it all, and our article appeared in the *Sunday Times* that weekend.

Above all, we were helped by the young editors of *Por Que*, Mario and Roger Menendez Rodriguez. Mario was a large, cheerful, hefty figure; Roger, his younger brother, handsome and more aesthetic. They came from a well-known crusading journalistic family in Yucatan. Mario pulled open the drawer of his desk to show us a revolver. One attempt had already been made to kill him. A bus had been driven straight at him, but he had jumped on to the bonnet of a stationary car. The man standing next to him had been knocked down and killed.

These horrors left one in a state of shock, but out at the Villa Olimpica, it was as though nothing had happened. With the exception of a few concerned athletes such as the admirable Mary Peters, from Belfast, destined to win an Olympic gold medal for the pentathlon, none wanted to know about it. I sat next to the pretty English 800-metre runner, Lillian Board, on the steep grass bank above the training track. 'I know it sounds terrible,' she said, 'but I'm more interested in that girl down there. You see, I'm running against her.'

I really had no right to be surprised. One of the themes of *The Olympian* was the narcissistic self-involvement of the athlete. In a series called 'Apocryphal Interviews', in the *Sunday Times*, I had invented Ron Trudge, Britain's hope for the obstacle race, who said, 'I reckon if I could only get the right religion, I could do the most fantastic times.' But I vowed I would never cover another Olympic Games; and I never have.

The football tournament was some small consolation, though its final was ruined by bossy refereeing and the excessive use of the red and yellow cards that had just been introduced to the game. The all-professional Mexican team was beaten by France, and humiliated by a surprisingly effective Japanese side, led by the powerful, broad-chested, centre forward, Kamamoto. The Japanese, under the shrewd guidance of the tiny German coach, Dettmar Cramer, took a well-merited third place, but it would be many years yet before Japanese football truly took wing.

When I returned to Mexico City the following year, accompanying the England football team, Mario was in solitary confinement. It had not prevented him from writing a scathing attack on Diaz Ordaz: YOU ARE A LIAR MR PRESIDENT! cried the headline on the front cover of *Por Que*. The magazine had been hounded out of its offices in fashionable Colonia Roma and was now on the other side of the Reforma in the drab Calle Xochimilco. Roger was in charge, and kept his gun on his desk. He told me that lorries carrying copies of the magazine were frequently hijacked. Secret police would roam around Mexico City and confiscate copies of it found on the bookstalls.

After the 1970 World Cup, I lost touch with Mario and Roger for years. But in 1986, when the World Cup was held in Mexico again, I chanced to see, as I wandered through the streets, a familiar cover on a sidestreet bookstall. It was a magazine called *Por Este*, but the resemblance was plain. I bought it, and opened it; it was simply *Por Que* under another name.

I telephoned their offices. Mario himself answered the phone. 'Of course I remember you,' he said casually, as though it had been a matter of months, not years. With Paul Gardner, who was in Mexico commentating for an American TV network, I went down to *Por Este*'s offices.

Mario and Roger were there, so very little had changed; but their adventure had been extraordinary. They told me how Mario had been 'sprung' from prison when a guerrilla leader kidnapped the rector elect of the University of the State of Guerrero, and demanded the release of several political prisoners, Mario among them, in return for setting the rector free. Mario went to Cuba, to be welcomed by Castro, and spent the next few years working on a Ph.D.

Roger was less fortunate. He was tortured, imprisoned in his turn, and *Por Que*'s printing plant was smashed up by thugs. It was only when Portillo was elected president, and wanted to improve relations with Cuba, that Mario was amnestied and returned to Mexico. Compensation was paid to the brothers for the destruction of their plant, and they were allowed to start their magazine again, with the peculiar proviso that it should not be called *Por Que*. So they called it *Por Este*.

Late in 1969, I made a film for the BBC 2 television series, *One Pair of Eyes*. Its *donnée* was supposed to be my novel, *The Olympian*, published that year, but as is always the case in such endeavours, television has its own way with such ambitions, and the documentary, as it turned out, was far more the director's concept than mine. But it did allow me, for the first time, to meet my old hero, Eddie Hapgood, and to nail a wretched lie about him.

I had spoken to him once on the telephone; a saddening conversation. There was a bitterness, even a latent paranoia, about him. I mentioned a letter he had written to the paper, criticising something I had written, and saying I had not been sure it was *the* Hapgood. 'Oh, you didn't think I could write a letter like that?' I told him how much I had admired him as a player. 'Yes, but look at you, now, a successful journalist; and look at me.'

His managerial career having long since foundered – Blackburn Rovers, Watford, Bath City – he had been running a hostel for apprentices of the Atomic Energy Authority, at Weymouth.

I agreed with the director of the documentary, the able and likeable Michael Houldey, that we should interview Hapgood in Weymouth. Meanwhile a book had appeared called *Arsenal from the Heart* by Arsenal's chief executive, and grey eminence, Bob Wall. This was a man who had begun as Herbert Chapman's office boy and slowly, gradually, worked his way up into power. He had not fought in the war, which enabled him to consolidate his position at Highbury.

In his dull, self-serving book, Wall wrote about an episode allegedly involving Hapgood and another dedicated Arsenal player, a future manager, 'Gentleman' Jack Crayston. At the end of the war, these two were supposed to have demanded benefit payments from Arsenal, who refused, since at that time the club was in financial trouble. Hapgood and Crayston were then supposed to have appealed, in vain, to the Football League. Eventually, Arsenal, in better economic condition, offered the benefits to Hapgood and Crayston: who, in turn, refused.

The story seemed strange to me, not least because I knew that in that era benefits were optional, a grace and favour bonus that clubs, after a certain period, could pay if they wished. The amount was, I recall, £650.

Visiting Hapgood – much diminished by recent heart trouble – in his little house in Weymouth, I put the story to him. He was appalled, and instantly sought out a file of letters. Never, he said, had he made any such demands on Arsenal; a club that, clearly, had commanded his affection through the years. The file contained a devastating exchange of letters. Hapgood had just lost his job at Bath City and was on his beam-ends. He wrote to Arsenal asking for help, and pointed out that he had not had the benefit due to him. The response was a letter offering him £30. This to the left back who had helped the club win five Championships and two FA Cups, and who had captained them superbly.

I put it to Bob Wall and heard to my surprise that he had been told the story by none other than Tom Whittaker – a man who, as club trainer, Hapgood had almost idolised. If this were so, could it have been that Whittaker, never the most confident of men when he emerged upstairs from the treatment room, had feared Hapgood as a future rival? Hapgood, it was clear to me when I interviewed him, would have liked to have spent the rest of his working life at Arsenal; though in the event, he showed scant talent as a manager. But his popularity and prestige as an Arsenal and England captain were immense at the end of the war. Could this have moved Whittaker to concoct the legend?

I telephoned the Football League; they could find no evidence of such an appeal being made by Hapgood and Crayston. I asked Wall to let me examine Arsenal's minutes. The Spenlow and Jorkins reply – *vide David Copperfield* and the classic excuse of 'the man upstairs' – was that the chairman would not permit it. 'You can,' said Wall, heavily and defensively, 'write whatever you like, but Arsenal will not answer.' How, indeed, could they?

Indeed I wrote what I liked, or what I thought was the abysmal truth, in the *Sunday Times*, and indeed Arsenal did not reply. I nailed the lie; I deplored the mean, miserly way Hapgood had been treated. I even introduced him to a solicitor, an Arsenal fan, who initially was prepared to take the case to court on the grounds of manifest libel. Ultimately, however, the solicitor decided that the *Sunday Times* article was recompense enough.

Perhaps. But my memory of a sick and tearful Hapgood was not easily erased. As a sympathetic Danny Blanchflower said to me, when I spoke to him about it, 'Arsenal isn't Bob Wall. Arsenal isn't the chairman. It's the players like Hapgood.'

Poor Danny's own life would end wretchedly. I first had intimations of his plight when he and I, and Ken Jones, footballer, football journalist, and a member of the illustrious Jones family that included Bryn and Cliff, flew up to Glasgow for a TV pilot. Ken and I were convinced that, with Danny in full flow, we would be little more than supporting cast. Instead, Danny, on camera, was so hesitant and rambling that we had to keep prompting him. Now and again, quite uncharacteristically, he would use obscenities. Afterwards he told me miserably that a piece of wood had fallen on his head, and that he had been confused ever since.

Alas, it turned out to be Alzheimer's disease, and he would never recover. All that fine fluency, that bright originality, that love of paradox and controversy, dimmed for ever. He had not long to live.

8

'**G**O AWAY, YOU HAVE NO POWER HERE,' says Glenda, the Good Witch of the North, to the Wicked Witch of the West, in *The Wizard of Oz*. She might just as well have been talking to journalists. However much some may delude themselves, they can at best be only secondary figures. So much became clearer than ever when Keith Botsford and I, in 1974, embarked on an investigation into corruption that he later termed 'The Years of the Golden Fix': the years in which rich Italian clubs corrupted or tried to corrupt the referees of European games in which they were involved. To get the mighty Juventus of Turin 'bang to rights', as we unquestionably did, was one thing; to bring about any kind of condign punishment was totally another. The *Sunday Times* was powerful, up to a point. But Gianni Agnelli, the patron and Croesus of Juventus, then still head of Fiat, was one of the most powerful men in Europe. Juve slid effortlessly off the hook. Journalists have power only to move the powerful; and even then it becomes a case of where the ultimate power lies.

Gigi Peronace, meanwhile, had taken up residence in England, and did all he could to promote the Anglo-Italian football tournament, towards the end of each season. Alas, it seemed doomed from the start, even when it was contested by major rather than by lesser clubs. Somehow the meeting of British and Italian football seemed a recipe for combustion. Game after game was spoilt by violence and controversy. '*Bisogna far qualcosa, Brian, bisogna far qualcosa!*' Gigi would cry (one's got to do something), but the Anglo-Italian tournament could stagger on only so far, and its decease went unmourned by all but Gigi.

He still did all he could to cut a dash; a *bella figura*, accepted in England, lampooned in Italy. On one occasion, when England played in Rome, he gave a dinner there, bringing over, in addition to those of us covering the game, Geoffrey Greene and the jaunty, shameless Desmond Hackett, of the *Express*. An unkind writer on a Roman paper described the restaurant, not without cause, as one 'of exquisite vulgarity'. *Bisogna far qualcosa!* But a new chance would come.

My elder son, Mark, made his debut for Chelsea Casuals at the age of thirteen, oddly enough at Cambridge, where the club had begun. He had honed his ball control in our back garden, endlessly juggling a tennis ball, and when he went to Pimlico Comprehensive, he was so adept at evading tackles that he became unpopular with the resident toughs; and there were plenty of them. He, and my other children, went to Pimlico *faute de mieux*, because they were all so unhappy in private education. Suffice it to say that at Mark and Toby's North London prep school, the pressure, then, was such that the chief psychiatrist at the Tavistock Clinic removed both his boys; one without notice.

But where to go next? Mark had already been accepted as a day pupil at Westminster School; against whom, in the future, he would score a number of flashy goals for Casuals, inducing their gamesmaster to ask anxiously, 'He *is* coming here, isn't he?' He wasn't, as it transpired.

Mark was a promising clarinetist at the time (he would eventually turn into an opera singer), so it seemed that Yehudi Menuhin's Hampstead school for gifted young musicians might be the answer. But, for sport and recreation, all it had was a swing in the garden. Pimlico, then just about to start, in its glass house – as I write, there is controversy over whether it should be pulled down – seemed a logical answer. They intended to create a special section for musicians. But, in the event, Mark did not join it; he had come to Pimlico too soon and, in any case, the section turned out to be a kind of middle-class ghetto.

Pimlico may have been a comprehensive, but football was very much an elitist sport. Either you got into your year's team, or you didn't get a game. Mark at eleven years old got in at once, but, then, the louts who dominated the team tired of being turned inside out in the yard, threatened to beat him up if he came to training, and that was that.

He would play just one more game for the school – for its first team, in his final year – scoring both goals for a ten-man side in a 2–1 win against Rutherford, otherwise unbeaten all season. But that was that. 'I can't stand the dialogue in the dressing-room. "Fuckin' 'ad 'er in the fuckin' boiler room." ' And that was it.

He played at Cambridge, against Trinity Hall, because Phil Jacobson, a tough half back, did not get there till well into the game. Mark did well enough and was not afraid to hold the ball and take on defenders. He even beat the goalkeeper, only to be frustrated, mortifyingly, on the line, when a defender deliberately handled. To add insult to injury, our talented but eccentric Glaswegian, Davie Reid, missed the penalty kick. The defender turned out to be Steve Tongue, later to become a journalist colleague who even shared a room with me in Montreal, on the way to the 1986 World Cup.

For poor Mark, worse was to follow. When Jacobson arrived, he was substituted and came off the field in a fury. Then, after the game, which we lost by the odd goal, he was violently ill as we drove back to London.

Toby, our younger boy, would play in the Pimlico team that won the Inner London Cup two years in a row; yet he did not get into the team in his first year, playing basketball instead. It was Peter Purves, a presenter on the children's BBC TV programme, *Blue Peter*, who brought him back to football in a game he organised on a Sunday morning, in Holland Park, in which his own son was involved. Alas, Toby ran straight into a tree on one of those mornings, concussed himself, and had to be taken to St Charles Hospital in Ladbroke Grove, a place to which both he and I have cause to be grateful. But once he recovered, he resumed his football with enthusiasm, got into his second year's team, and there remained.

He made a memorable debut for Chelsea Casuals at Lancing, at the age of fourteen. For a long time, he had been badgering me for a chance to play, and on that occasion, let down, as so often happened, by one of our key men, I had no choice.

It was an appalling, foggy Sunday, and driving down to Sussex, where we were to play the school first eleven, was a hazard. We got, creaking, out of our cars, went almost straight out on to the field, and were a couple of goals down in no time, one going through our goalkeeper's legs.

Eventually, we got a right-wing corner. As the ball approached the near post, a figure emerged from the fog, met it with a perfect header, only for a Lancing defender to nod the ball, in turn, off the line. Who could it have been? I had seen the number twelve on his shirt. Number twelve? It was Toby!

Soon afterwards, Toby had the ball just outside their penalty box. 'Toby!' shouted Norman, our painter-captain, and began to run through. Toby chipped the ball precisely into his stride. He scored. We eventually won by one goal. My other salient memory of the game was of Davie Reid, by then our centre half, not our centre forward, with boot poised, and finger placed on the head of the recumbent opposing centre forward – a provocative young man whose father had been a well-known professional footballer.

One summer, Toby, then fifteen, asked me if I would manage a five-a-side team, to enter a tournament in Memorial Park, Notting Dale. I was none too keen having just emerged from yet another gruelling season running Chelsea Casuals. Once, Toby had come into my study and seen me sitting, in baffled gloom, by the telephone, devoid of players. 'I don't know why you do it,' he said. 'All you ever get out of it is misery.'

In the end, I agreed to run his Holland Parkers team, which turned out to be just as fraught and delicate a job as running Chelsea Casuals. By and large, till two of Toby's Pimlico team friends, Mivvy Smith and Stephen Griffiths, joined them, they were essentially a local, middle-class team who did not even have similar shirts; they wore whatever white shirt or jersey they could lay hands on. By contrast, the opposition was kitted out to the nines, wearing up-to-the-minute apparel, whether it be in green-and-white Celtic stripes or in the colours of some other club.

Toby, however, was a lion, spurring his team on to some remarkable results. The strength of the opposition may be gauged by the fact that the eventual winners included two boys who would become full professionals: Wally Downes, with Wimbledon, and Mark Lovell, with Fulham. But when the five-a-side representative team was picked, Toby was in it.

He and his twin, Elizabeth, were both studying Italian at Pimlico at the time. Lizzie, indeed, would eventually go to live in Rome, where, at the time of writing, she has been teaching English successfully for the best part of fourteen years, and making a life for herself in a city where I signally failed to do so. I took them both on a CIT tour, starting in Rome, then going on to Venice and Florence. When we had a spare afternoon, I arranged for Toby to go training with my old friend Domenico Biti, who by then was managing a D division team called Velletri. Next morning, Biti rang me.

'I've got all these fathers coming to me saying, "My boy can kick like this, can head like this, can run like that." And I tell them, "*Aoh! Ma tu non credi che esageri?*" [Don't you think you're exaggerating?] You didn't tell me anything about your boy, but he can really play.'

I answered that I was hardly going to tell a coach like him anything about Toby. But the upshot of it was that, for a year, Biti kept ringing us, asking if Toby could come to play for him. By that time there was a great deal more of Toby; a skinny five foot four and a half right back had developed into a six foot one inch midfielder.

'Every time I see Toby,' said Norman Ackroyd, when he visited us, 'it looks as if you've been stretching him at both ends!'

Even when he was small and thin, there was no intimidating him. Not least in a game against the Army Crusaders at Longmoor Camp when he was fifteen, the same age as several other players in our team. It had poured with rain all day and I had hoped the game would be off with so many of our players being absent. But no, on it went, and we put out a side full of teenagers. 'How do you think we'll do?' I asked our burly left half Bobby Norfolk, before we kicked off in the Longmoor Camp stadium. 'They'll probably walk all over us,' he said; but they didn't.

For twenty minutes or so, Crusaders (officers and gentlemen), but not always, in our long acquaintance with them, Corinthian, hardly had a kick at the ball. We scored. We would have surely scored another had not one of their defenders pulled little Stephen Griffiths back by holding him round the midriff, as he cut in on goal. Their equaliser was a freakish in-off goal which beat our sixteen-year-old keeper.

Late in the game Toby, who had won every tackle ('Wasn't Toby smashing?' said Norman Ackroyd, at the end), won yet another on their centre forward, a well-spoken fellow whom one would meet, dressed in a three-piece suit, at Wembley internationals. The centre forward put his studs into Toby's ankle. Toby stood up and kicked him. A great cry rang out over Longmoor Camp: '*Don't* you retaliate on *me*!'

Giorgio Chinaglia played for us. Just one game. He had been the Lazio and Italy centre forward, but by then was President of, and centre forward for, the New York Cosmos. In his office at the Rockefeller Centre, I had watched him drinking glasses of Chivas Regal, and reproached him. '*Son' nervoso!*' he explained. (I'm edgy.) Now he was in London to commentate for television on England's World Cup qualifying match against Italy.

He and others turned up at Pimlico School for a somewhat abortive television programme; then we adjourned for lunch to a restaurant nearby. Someone asked me whether Chelsea Casuals were playing next Sunday, and I said that we were. 'Is there a game for *me*?' asked Giorgio, in his Italo-Welsh accent. An immigrant, brought up in Cardiff, he had once been with Swansea Town and fined so often that he had to steal milk bottles from doorsteps for his breakfast. He was wealthy now.

'Well,' I said, in mock seriousness, 'Toby's visiting his friends in Seaford. I think we can fit you in.'

'How much?' he asked.

'It will cost you twenty pence,' I said.

The game was on the big pitch at Chelsea's Royal Hospital. We picked up Giorgio and his amanuensis, Peppe Pinton, a former classics teacher, on the way. They were sitting at the bar of the Basil Street Hotel. Giorgio was smoking a cigarette, drinking a whisky, and eyeing an American blonde. He played in midfield, in an exemplary way. Shooting in, before the kickoff, he bounced a tremendous shot off the chest of our sixteen-year-old goalkeeper, Ben Cannon. The opposition was Academicals, alumni of University College, London, who had a good young team. It was a close game, which Giorgio enjoyed.

The following afternoon, I drove him and a *Corriere dello Sport* colleague to Wembley, to meet the *azzurri* on their arrival at a hotel near the stadium. I had reluctantly agreed a match, on the Bank of England ground, between Chelsea Casuals and an Italian press team. Reluctantly, because, as a midweek game, it took a great deal of arranging; while the Italians, contrary to what they had told me, hadn't even brought their shirts; this meant borrowing huge, heavy, white rugby jerseys from the bank, and taking them home to be washed.

'They're so sure they're going to beat *you*,' said Giorgio, as we drove away.

'Well, they might,' I said, thinking he was referring to the international. 'This isn't a very good England team.'

'No, no, the journalists!' he said. 'I didn't say I'd played for you. I told them, "They've got a lot of young kids. They run and run." They said, "Class will tell!" ' After the match, Mark said, 'It did.'

He scored three of our goals; we won 11–2. Mark was eighteen at the time, and told me seriously of the old Juventus and Italy half back, 'Dad, I don't think I treated Umberto Colombo with sufficient respect.' Umberto, whom I had known well for years and once visited in Bergamo, had, two years earlier, looked invincibly good when the English press played the Italian press on the same ground. A close friend of John Charles, he had once opened a restaurant with him in Turin, but alas it had been on an upper floor, and it did not succeed.

Toby, sixteen then, was in the team, as was another lively sixteen-year-old, our little blond winger Piers Douglas, who had played for West London Schools, and was the son of two well-known actors. Ours was a very young team indeed then, and a joy to play in. Three other goals had gone to our centre forward, Philip Hook, a large, handsome, patrician figure who had won three blues for Cambridge and who had scored against Oxford at Wembley. His father was the Bishop of Bradford. He played loyally for us for many years, headed many a fine goal, and had extraordinary self-control, however badly fouled or injured. An expert on nineteenth-century painting, he became a director of Christie's and, later on, of Sotheby's.

Once, when we were playing RAF West Drayton, a favourite fixture against hospitable airmen, we were winning quite easily when Neville Cheetham, Philip's fellow-striker, an ardent goalscorer, and the man who bravely succeeded me in running the club, worked his way to the left-hand goal-line, drawing the keeper. Philip waited patiently in the middle for the inevitable cross and easy tap-in. Neville shot into the side-netting. With a massive shrug of resignation, Philip dropped back to play in midfield.

One did not shout at Philip. There were ways, and ways, of approaching each player. 'Philip,' I called, 'would you mind going farther upfield?'

'Not under present circumstances,' he said.

Had I but known it, I was given a kind of precursor to our Golden Fix investigation in Turin, when Derby County played Juventus in the first leg of the semi-final of the European Cup. At half-time, there had been an angry scuffle in the dressing-room corridor when Derby's assistant manager, Peter Taylor, tried to stop Helmut Haller, Juve's German international inside right, from talking to the German referee, Herr Schulenberg. Derby lost 3–1; there seemed to be nothing wrong with any of the Italian goals, the veteran Brazilian José Altafini being in rapier form, but Schulenberg had booked two Derby players, centre half Roy McFarland and inside forward Archie Gemmill, both key men, who would thus be out of the return.

After the game, Brian Clough, Derby's outspoken manager, opened the door of the dressing-room on the crowd of Italian journalists and said, 'No cheating bastards will I talk to. I will not talk to any cheating bastards.' Then he shut the door. The journalists clamoured to me to tell them what he had said; I affected ignorance. Then Clough opened the door, again. 'Tell them what I said, Brian.' I did, and the headlines next morning were combustible: BASTARDI TRUFFATORI!

The return game, at the Baseball Ground, was drawn, and refereed impeccably by Francisco Marques Lobo of Portugal. Little did we know ...

Early the following year, I had a phone call from a colleague on the *Sunday Times*, Stan Levinson, who had formerly been sports editor of the *Daily Worker*, alias the *Morning Star*. He hinted at an extraordinary tale of bribery, confirmed that I was interested, and put me in touch with the remarkable Charlie Coutts, in Budapest. Charlie was a Scot from Aberdeen. During the war, he had been imprisoned by the Japanese, and, apparently, was so disgusted by the behaviour of the English officers that it turned him into a communist for life. He worked in the English section of Radio Budapest. And the story he told was appalling.

When Derby were drawn against Juventus, he said that Italo Allodi, then the general manager of the club, sent Dezso Solti (the Hungarian refugee whom he had 'run' when he was Secretary of Internazionale) to Lisbon to bribe Lobo. Certainly it had worked at Inter in the past. It had been virtually an open secret that the Yugoslav referee Tesanic had been 'fixed' for the return European Cup semi-final leg of 1964 against Borussia Dortmund at San Siro. When Luis Suarez, Inter's Spanish inside forward, brutally kicked the opposing half back and put him out of the game, Suarez went unpenalised and Inter won. Later, on a seaside holiday on the Adriatic at Inter's expense, Tesanic met a Yugoslav tourist and unwisely told him all. The Germans protested, but UEFA, the European body, characteristically did nothing.

The following year it was Liverpool who were the victims. They had beaten Inter 3–1 at Anfield in the first leg semi-final of the European Cup. At San Siro they could do little against the refereeing of the Spaniard, Ortiz de Mendibil, who gave Inter two highly contentious goals in a 3–0 victory. The first came when Peirò, another Spaniard, kicked the ball out of the hands of the Liverpool keeper Tommy Lawrence, and shot home; the other came from a free kick by Mariolino Corso, which had first been given as indirect. At the end of the game, an incensed Tommy Smith, Liverpool's tough, locally-born midfielder, literally kicked de Mendibil all the way back to the dressing-room. The word was that the referee had a sick child and badly needed money to pay for treatment.

Of the 1966 semi-final return leg, and an abortive attempt to buy a third referee, we shall hear later. But Lobo was himself unbribable. Approached by Solti, who had once run dance troupes from Vienna, and had been apprehended trying to smuggle a valuable religious book out of Hungary, he temporised, then told his referees' association what had happened. They, in turn, informed the Portuguese Football Federation. Lobo had sensibly made a tape of a phone conversation with Dezso Solti.

The upshot of it was a farcical meeting of the UEFA disciplinary sub-committee at the Atlantis Hotel in Zurich. The head of that committee was Denis Follows, Secretary of the Football Association, but, since an English club was involved, he stood down. Stood down, and apparently, inexplicably, banished the whole thing from his mind, since he never rendered the affair public and, when I phoned him the following year, went affably up to his attic, to see what papers he could find. Certain elements in UEFA believed he must have been part of the plot, but I am personally convinced that he was simply naive and inadequate.

Both Lobo and Solti were summoned to the disciplinary hearing but, amazingly, they were not confronted with one another. When the hearing had finished, Hans Bangerter, the Secretary of UEFA, a Swiss, sent a letter to Juventus, thanking them for their cooperation and exonerating them! Later I would be told by Artemio Franchi, then the President of UEFA, that this had been done wholly without his knowledge.

To crack the case, someone had to talk to Lobo, but I knew no Portuguese. Keith Botsford did. A fine linguist whose articles in *Commentary* magazine of New York on Latin American politics I had long admired, I had first met him when he turned up one summer Sunday afternoon on my doorstep, accompanying Jorge Elliott. Jorge, a polymath, had shown me great hospitality in Chile. Serious or playful as the occasion decreed, he was perfectly bilingual in Spanish and English and a notable translator, not least of Harold Pinter. Now he was visiting England, and Keith had chauffeured him. I invited them in for tea.

Keith, with his wolfish good looks, his abundance of handsome, gifted children scattered around the world ('It's the quality that counts'), had an American father who was a gifted tennis player, and an Italian mother – a Rangoni-Macchiavelli which, as the Americans say, figured. He spoke flawless French, excellent Spanish, Italian and Portuguese and decent German. He had worked as a secret agent in Hungary at the end of the war where, he told me, he had been arrested by the Russians. He presented himself as a kind of latter-day Renaissance man: infinitely versatile as novelist, critic, musician and linguist. For years, he had known and worked with the famous American novelist Saul Bellow, and when some thought Bellow had included a cruel caricature of him in *Humboldt's Gift*, as Pierre Thaxter, he blandly observed, 'Oh, I put Saul in *my* novels, he puts me in his.'

When he heard that Mark played the clarinet, he remarked, 'Oh,

I wish you'd told me that. I've just written a clarinet concerto for one of my friends.' We let him live, one summer when we were in the country, in our house with pretty young Sally, whom he had met while both were working for the PEN literary organisation. She would become his common-law wife and present him with yet two more children, of whom Matthew went on to captain a tank in the Gulf War, and Polly went on to Oxford.

Not only was I delighted to have him aboard our investigation, rightly convinced that he could get Lobo to talk, but also I canvassed his claims as a foreign correspondent with Harry Evans. Alas, not for the first or last time, he overreached himself. Assuring the foreign department that he was an old friend of General Spinola, head and hero of the Portuguese revolution, and that he could surely get to him, he failed to do so, and they wouldn't forgive him.

But his visit to Lobo was crucially important. The whole story of Solti's abortive bribe – just $5,000, a car, and a trip to Turin, but riches for a Lisbon telephone engineer – emerged. Since standing up for decency and honesty, Lobo had virtually been excluded from international refereeing.

We prepared to launch the story. John Lovesey, fascinated, even, one sometimes thought, hypnotised by Keith, thought that before we published I should first go to Turin, confront Giampiero Boniperti, now President of Juventus, with the facts, and give him the opportunity to answer. This I did, visiting 'Boni' in his presidential office in the centre of Turin.

Above him hung photos of himself shaking hands with royalty, before the FIFA versus England celebratory game, at Wembley in October 1953, and scoring one of the two goals he got that day. As he heard the story, his blue eyes were expressionless. At the end of it he said, '*Brian, se ci sono questi pazzi in giro!*' (Brian, if there are these madmen going about!) And then, 'What's happening in English football?'

So publish we did, on an April Sunday when, I remember, the *Sunday Times* was selling over 1.5 million copies a week. To give Harry (as well as John) his due, he was wholly beside us. We had a news item on the front page, a double-page spread on the sports pages. The reaction in Italy could scarcely have been more hypocritical, dishonest and indicative.

SCANDALOUS ACCUSATIONS AGAINST JUVENTUS! ran the headline. The *Corriere dello Sport* at least had the honesty to publish our article in its entirety, though they continually attacked us in their leaders. Mario Gismondi, the southerner who edited *Corriere* at the time, told me earnestly that he had to do that, otherwise people would have thought he was playing Lazio's game against Juventus! Ezio De Cesari came to London in May to report a match between England and Argentina and, at a reception at the Argentine Embassy, told Keith and me, 'I'd have given a year of my life for a scoop like that.'

Gianni Brera, I was sure, would be horrified. Gianni Brera, I was sure, would support us. How naive of me! Brera was a short, sturdy Milanese who prided himself not on being Italian but on being *lombardo*, a Lombard. He had infinite contempt for the struggling south and at a moment in the Juventus versus Derby game when Juve did not seem to be doing well, he told me he would explain why and, with a smug smile, handed me a list of the southerners playing for Juventus.

In Munich, for the World Cup, I greeted and embraced him as I always did. He had seemed a friend. I had worked for him. In Italy he and his ideas were venerated, though they sometimes seemed defeatist to me, above all his fervent belief that Latins were physically inferior to Nordics, ergo Italians had to play with a *catenaccio* defence.

It was in Germany that I was told he had abused me in a magazine called *Guerin Sportivo*, then a newsprint weekly rather than the glossy magazine it became. My informant was Massimo Della Pergola, an elder statesman of Italian journalism who had invented Totocalcio, the Italian form of football pools, which subsidised their sport and their Olympic movement. In due course he sent me the paper. In the middle of an article, Brera had referred disparagingly to our revelations and wondered whether it was something I had been told 'by my brother in Jehovah'.

I sent him a letter: GIANNI: TU SEI PUTTANA! (Gianni, you're a whore!) A small magazine in Milan publicised the fact. There were inevitable, vicious responses in print and on television. A leading radio and television commentator with whom I had previously been friendly, Sandro Ciotti, a gravel-voiced Roman, would never speak to me again, cutting me dead by a chestnut barrow outside Rome's Olympic Stadium, a lift in Mexico City and in an airport lounge in Munich. Yet not a word of our investigation was disproved, with the possible exception of our statement that Franchi had been present at the disciplinary committee meeting. We were told he had. He assured us that he hadn't. But Keith had obtained his statement from Lobo, and I, getting lucky, had walked into the telephone exchange in Milan and traced evidence of Solti's call to Lobo.

Just before Christmas, John Lovesey sent Keith and me across Europe for further investigations. We flew first to Vienna, where Solti had lived so long, and where a little knot of Hungarian-Jewish refugees could be found each day at a café table in the open; most of them people concerned with football. We stayed – Keith always liked to do things the grand way when he could – at the Sacher Hotel. In his room on our first morning, he brayed to Sally down the telephone, 'He brought *shoe*-cleaning material to the Sacher,' which I had. Looking outside his door, where he had optimistically left his shoes, we found that they had not been touched.

With much ingenuity, Keith tracked down a press photograph agency where he could examine photographs of the European Cup Final which had taken place in Vienna in May 1964, when Inter had beaten Real Madrid. Sure enough, he eventually tracked down pictures of Solti, a man of whom Inter professed no knowledge, celebrating around the Cup with Helenio Herrera, Italo Allodi and the club President, *il gran petrolifero* (the great oil magnate), Angelo Moratti.

At the World Cup the previous summer, Allodi and I had missed each other when I visited the Italian training camp at their hotel in Ludwigshafen. Next morning, in the *Corriere della Sera*, an Italian correspondent wrote that I had been up there and was greeted by the Italian players like Father Christmas, but that Allodi had done a slalom to avoid me.

An infuriated Allodi held forth to a group of journalists. He hadn't avoided me, I had avoided him. And he would bring an action against me, yes, why not in London? General manager of this Italian World Cup team, on no basis anyone could fathom, he ranted on while, said a report, foreign reporters looked on in astonishment.

Next, we drove to Budapest. After crossing the border, Keith, filling out forms for visas, put his occupation down as 'poet'. Once, in the café of the Intercontinental Hotel, where we were staying, we sighted Solti but decided not to speak to him. Later, Keith thought we should have done so, and he was no doubt right. We interviewed one of the referees, clearly an honest man, who had been innocently involved in one of Inter's tricks. The well-known referee Istwan Zsolt, who 'happened' to be attending a European Cup game in Belgium, offered to fill the referee's report in for him and somehow 'forgot' to mention that an Italian half back had been booked.

We saw a lot of Charlie Coutts, who took us through the labyrinth of Hungarian football, where there were as many good guys as bad guys, and where everything and everyone, in football terms, seemed to centre round Radio Budapest, a hive of gossip, rumour and intrigue. Charlie, elderly now, and married to a Hungarian, was a good companion, though we could not share his politics. Keith and I felt it would be heretical to come to Budapest and not see a football game, though the Championship was suspended.

We found out that there was a match, just one, in the mining town of Tatabanya, and there we drove, singing *en route*, to the tune of the 'Hallelujah Chorus', '*Ta*-ta-banya, Ta-ta-*ban*-ya, Ta-*ta*-ban-*ya*.' When we got there, the mine manager and his wife asked us to lunch. Drawing a bow at a venture, I asked him if he had ever known my friend Peter De Hosszufalussy and his family. Amazingly, he had.

He and his wife were Jews. In the war, Peter's father had protected them. After the war, he had given Peter's father a job on the staff of the mine. So it was, that evening, that I found myself visiting Peter's father and his second wife – as discreet as Peter's mother had been flamboyant – in their Budapest flat. It was a moving experience, though, with no common language but a smattering of German, we could hardly communicate with one another.

Keith and I drove on. We drove into Switzerland, visiting Berne, where UEFA had their headquarters. At UEFA's recent meeting in Budapest, we heard from our spies that Harold Thompson, a new vice-president, whom we had diligently briefed at every stage of our investigation, had stood up to make a bitter attack on us. When the Solti question was to be discussed, Artemio Franchi suggested it might be better if he left the room. Not at all, said Thompson. He knew these journalists. He knew their distortions. It had lately happened to himself.

This was pure paranoia. Thompson was referring to criticism of himself over the sacking of Alf Ramsey. Yet Keith and I had never written a word about that; I was even in agreement that Ramsey had to go; and this I had publicly made clear.

On into Italy, and to Milan, where, still high on the hog, we stayed at the Parco di Principe. Back in London, we produced another huge, documented article, 'The Years of the Golden Fix', with abundant chapter and verse on a string of fixed referees or, in Lobo's case, referees who would not be fixed. Inter were the most constant offenders. Juventus had sinned after Allodi joined them. Milan had bought the Greek referee Michas of the 1973 Cup-Winners' Cup Final in Salonika against Leeds United, who lost after a series of outrageous decisions by Michas, who was later suspended.

UEFA had suspended Solti *sine die*, an easy thing to do, but with the crazy implication still being that he had acted on his own. They set up a farce of a two-man committee, Lucien Schmidlin, a Swiss lawyer, and the Frenchman Jacques Georges, who would be an unimpressive successor to Franchi. They had no investigative arm and, as Keith wrote, could do little more than shuffle papers to and fro across a desk. Later, they summoned me to Berne. I refused to go. They huffily responded that they withdrew all cooperation from us. Franchi laughed. 'I told them you'd never go,' he said.

Perpetually evading and escaping us was the experience of another Hungarian referee, Gyorgy Vadas. Our information was that in 1966, he had refused to 'bend' yet another semi-final at San Siro, between Inter and Real Madrid, and had suffered in consequence. Keith and I went out to Budapest to talk to him. It was a nightmare. Keith, in one hotel, fell ill. I, in another, waited endlessly for a telephone call that didn't come. At last it did; Charlie arranged for us to speak to Vadas – inevitably, at Radio Budapest.

He would say very little, though he did not deny the story. Eventually he agreed that if we brought him to London, he would talk. We did try, but he never came.

It took a lively young Hungarian journalist, Peter Borenich, employed, again, inevitably, at Radio Budapest, to crack the story open. He told it in a devastating book about corruption in Hungarian football called *Only the Ball has a Skin*.

Solti had greeted Vadas and his linesmen when they arrived in Milan for the game. In due course, he took them up to the villa where Angelo Moratti lived; he offered them the kingdoms of this earth. Money: the equivalent of five Mercedes cars – so much more generous than Juventus – more still if Inter won in extra time, even more if they should do so on a penalty. He proferred electrical goods that were not even known then, in Hungary. Vadas did not accept. He refereed the game with total objectivity. Real drew, and went on to win the Final. Solti came into Vadas's dressing-room and screamed at him; he had lost a fortune. In the small hours of the morning, Vadas had a phone call from the Secretary of the Hungarian Federation; part of the plot. Did he know what people were saying about him? He would never get another international game. Nor did he.

When Liverpool reached the European Cup Final in Rome in May 1977, I was standing in the foyer of the Excelsior hotel on Via Veneto when Italo Allodi came up to me, grasped my hand and said, 'We've never met, but I'm Italo Allodi. I would like to talk to you.' We had, in fact, met, before the European Cup Final of 1973 between Juve and Ajax, in Belgrade. I had sat beside Allodi, watching him gamble on roulette in the Hotel Belgrade. Every now and then he pushed me a chip, which I promptly lost.

That evening, outside the Olympic Stadium, I met Enzo Bearzot, Italy's team manager, ever at daggers drawn with Allodi. A large, intense, yet humorous man from Fruili in the northeast, with a face of slightly Red Indian cast, he grinned and said, 'You don't know what gifts are about to descend upon you, from the sky.' Allodi, once a moderate professional footballer, who worked his way up from being secretary of the Mantova club, had always been renowned for gifts. But we have never met again.

In a subsequent article in a Milanese newspaper, he was asked whether it distressed him that I kept up my campaign against him. Yes, he said, especially because, when I had been ill in Florence, he had been among those who sent money so that I could stay in Italy! It was a fiction so shameless and outrageous that it was hard to credit. I had indeed been taken ill in Florence, nineteen years before I ever met Allodi. But as we know, far from staying in Florence, I came home to London.

I published a letter in the newspaper saying that Allodi was a better novelist than I was, and set out the truth. He replied that perhaps I had forgotten my friend, the football coach Mauro Franceschini. It was through him that he and others had sent me money! So far as it went, this was ingenious. He knew that Mauro was almost certainly dead and could hardly contradict him. I realised what must have happened. Appointed, for no good reason, to run the official coaching centre at Coverciano, just outside Florence, he had met there a number of friends of Mauro who had known me when I had lived in Florence and had told him that Mauro was a friend of mine, and had mentioned that I had been ill. He had grasped what he could of it and distorted it into a bizarre self-serving story. Yet knowing him, perhaps he even persuaded himself to believe it.

That he should be appointed to Coverciano showed Franchi at his least effective. He knew I had criticised the hiring of Allodi for the job of drawing up a plan for Coverciano, and, in the foyer of the Crillon Hotel in Paris on the occasion of a European Cup Final between Leeds United and Bayern Munich in 1975, he told me with a smile that, while indeed Allodi was to draw up such a plan, who could say that it would ever be adopted? Cunning old Franchi, I thought. Then the smoke cleared and not only had the plan been adopted, but Allodi was in charge!

His feud with Enzo Bearzot became increasingly bitter. Bearzot, an honest, decent man, who had read classics at school and whose father hoped he would be a doctor, but then became what Enzo called 'a silent fan', was playing for Torino at the time Stephen Hearst and I were filming *European Centre Forward*. When Italy were drawn in England's qualifying group for the 1978 World Cup, it was Gigi's chance. He would become guide, philosopher and friend to Enzo on his many visits to England. He even persuaded the Italian Federation to dignify him with the grandiose title of general manager of the *azzurri*.

Never, when Enzo came to London, would Gigi let him out of his sight. He clung to him like grim death to a knobstick. Never, well though I knew him, did I manage to invite Enzo to my house, on his many visits to London.

'*Non mollare, non mollare!*' (don't soften), Enzo would apostrophise me, when he came. He wanted me to take the Lobo–Solti investigation to the end, knowing how deeply Allodi was involved.

Escorting Enzo, Gigi became puffed up with the importance of his role. Once, I needed to interview Enzo for a German television documentary I was making. 'No!' said Gigi. 'I've let you talk to him once!' At this I assumed the persona of William Bendix talking to Kirk Douglas in the film *Detective Story*. 'This is *me* talking to you, Gigi.' Gigi backed down, and the interview took place.

In Rome, rigid man-marking by the Italian defence and the opportunism of Roberto Bettega helped Italy to beat England 2–0. By the time it came to the return match at Wembley, Italy were home and dry. England's victory was pleasing but irrelevant. And so to Argentina.

There, Gigi made an excellent job of what he termed 'pooblic relations'. Out at the Hindu Club, some twenty miles from Buenos Aires, the Italians generously gave a press conference every day. Enzo would speak. All the players were available. He had them in good psychological fettle, after a period of what he called 'disintoxication', assuaging the poisons and pressures of the Campionato.

But the Italian journalists were still not satisfied. 'They're *giornalisti di assalto*' (attack journalists). One of them, especially petulant, noisily protested when the players, one morning, had not yet emerged. 'I can't drag them down by the neck,' said Bearzot, unhappily.

The following day, when the journalists arrived at the Hindu Club, it was to find no one there to meet them. Occasionally, as in some Antonioni film, an official or a player would appear behind a glass partition and wordlessly address them; that was all. The lesson would be learned.

Now Gigi had Enzo with him every day. Once, in Barcelona, Rob Hughes, my colleague in Buenos Aires, had taken Enzo off for a coffee while Gigi went elsewhere. When we returned to the hotel, Gigi was beside himself. Where was Enzo? Where was his meal ticket? He was like an anxious mother, separated from her child.

Italy made good progress. They even beat Argentina. Paolo Rossi, the boyish centre forward of Lanerossi Vicenza, a very late arrival in the team, proved a revelation. Quickly a goal behind against France in Mar del Plata, Italy revived, in their opening match, to win.

Though an idealist in many ways, Enzo had a curious, ambivalent approach to violent players. He was very upset when, in their losing game against Holland in the River Plate stadium, Renato Zaccarelli, who had done no harm to anyone, was kicked hard by Aarie Haan. What he ignored was the fact that Haan, proceeding up the left-hand touchline, had just been kicked by Romeo Benetti, a notorious hard man.

Harder still was Claudio Gentile, the defender Bearzot put on Maradona when Italy played Argentina in Barcelona in the next World Cup. To say that Gentile close-marked Maradona would be giving him all the best of it. He maltreated him throughout the game. True, nothing that he did came into the category of the brutal assault by Germany's keeper Toni Schumacher on the Frenchman Patrick Battiston in the semi-final in Seville, a forearm smash that could have killed him. But these beyond doubt were double standards.

This, in Argentina, was the era of the notorious junta; given the endemic violence, there had been some doubts whether the World Cup could take place there at all. A general was blown up by a bomb planted by a friend of his daughter. A naval building *en route* to the River Plate stadium was known to be a torture centre. *Los desaparecidos* (the disappeared or vanished ones), sometimes dropped out of helicopters by the military, were legion. Once a week, there was a small, infinitely sad protest march of the mothers of vanished children, in the square outside the Presidential palace. There was no doubt the junta hoped that the World Cup would bring them sympathy and prestige, and the reckless overreaction by left-wing sources in Europe, not least England, undoubtedly helped them.

The left-wing-dominated National Union of Journalists was one of the worst offenders. Executives such as Denis McShane, who seems now to have matured into some kind of Labour moderate, but was, then, a pestilential gadfly, was one of the most shrill. Dropped by the BBC after he had phoned a programme under an assumed name and libelled a politician, he was involved in an NUJ campaign that plumbed the depths by trying to issue journalists with a phrase book in Spanish, including the likes of, 'Stop torturing me.'

There was an appalling case for the junta to answer, but they cunningly used such excesses for their own purposes, presenting them as an insult to Argentina. And as the team, grossly favoured by referees in the first couple of games, made progress, so nationalism and euphoria grew, so the crowds in the streets got larger and larger after every victory.

Criticising the abysmally one-sided refereeing in Argentina's opening game against Hungary, I found myself hysterically abused on the radio by the fat commentator Munoz, and attacked in *El Grafico*, a magazine with which I had long had friendly relations. Its leading writer, Juvenal, who had taken Rob Hughes and myself out for lunch when we arrived in Buenos Aires, now refused to speak to me.

Rafaello Paloscia, an old friend and colleague from Florence's *La Nazione*, wrote in his paper, 'Brian Glanville, the most hated journalist in world football, is in trouble again in Argentina. But their second game showed that he was absolutely right!'

A bonus of being in Buenos Aires was that I was able to visit Jorge Luis Borges, that remarkable artificer of fables and literary conceits. I had first interviewed him in his very modest apartment the year before and been fascinated by his conversation. All but blind, speaking flawless English ('You can't say that in Spanish,' he would say, 'in fact you can't say anything in Spanish!') he spoke of his overwhelming reception in London by an ecstatic young audience. 'I thought they'd think I was just an old gaucho!'

Beyond doubt, he was a monumental egotist. The novelist Francis King – whom I had first met when he was working for the British Council in Athens in 1955 – was outraged at the old man's solipsism, and wrote as much. I could see what he meant. I had, for example, gone to some trouble to send him a number of books for which he had asked; they had never been acknowledged. Had he received them. 'Yes!' And on to the next thing that interested him. But my earlier visits had proved delightful.

Rob and I shared a room in a hotel in the middle of town. I liked the place as much as ever. There was air conditioning in our bedroom, but what I failed to realise was that it was suddenly switched off at night, leaving one at the mercy of the cold night air. I found myself walking around bent double like Sycorax in *The Tempest*, and eventually had to resort to tablets with a cortisone basis.

On the morning of the Final, I managed, going back into a hotel to greet an English club's manager, to walk hard into a plate glass window, and split open my nose. The excellent medical room at the press centre took care of that, too. It was, though, hardly a way to approach the Final, after which both Rob and I were due to get on the tour bus that had brought us to the stadium, and drive straight to the airport at Eziza. Each of us, however, had an extra piece to do: mine was for the *Washington Post*, his for the *Herald Tribune*. In consequence, the bus left without us.

We took a press bus back into town, and found Reconquista, the central square whence airport buses were meant to depart, a seething antheap in which it was difficult even to move. Someone told us buses went to the airport from another square. We went down into the underground railway. One kindly fan gave me a token and Rob was waved through by a guard. But when we emerged at the other end, the chaos was as bad as it had been in Reconquista. Not a bus in sight. Time was ebbing fast away. If we did not catch that plane, there were no rebates.

In desperation, I began asking people in their cars if they could help us. At last, miraculously, a group of Argentines said they would. They drove us, out of the great kindness of their hearts, all the way to Eziza, some twenty miles distant. They consisted of a man and wife, a daughter and her fiancé, whom she was soon to marry. At one point, going through a military zone, we were stopped by a young soldier. The mother gave him a sharp burst of rebuke then, as we drove on, told us, 'Don't think this is normal. He's a man alone. He has to work tonight, while everyone else is going mad.'

So we flew home. We wanted to send a wedding present, and had taken the mother's address. We wrote to her, but we never received a reply.

Poor Gigi did not have long to live. He and his family – a charming and resourceful wife, and five engaging children – lived in some luxury in Twickenham. He had had a marble staircase built into the house. But there was still the same, lurking desperation. The Italian Federation were not paying him enough, he said. He had had an idea. He would like to become general manager of Manchester United. Would I write a letter for him in English? Of course I would, but it produced no result.

In December, 1980, he was in Rome with the *azzurri*, preparing to fly to Montevideo for a tournament called the Gold Cup. Enzo Bearzot was with him when, in his hotel room, he was suddenly afflicted by a tremendous, lacerating heart attack. He died, in agony, in Bearzot's arms.

Huge debts had been left behind. A bank manager, it was said, received the equivalent of the Molotov Siberian power-station exile. It was Alvaro Marchini who apparently came to the rescue. A millionaire, although a communist, he had previously been president of Roma, writing an autobiography, *Io Presidente*, that contained a devastating critique of Helenio Herrera and his heartless treatment of a player who died in the dressing-room at Cagliari, when Herrera was in charge of Roma. Signora Peronace took the family off to Latina, the town between Rome and Naples that Mussolini had drained the swamps to build. All the children have done well. Gigi, for all his attitudinising, his frenetic endeavours, his slightly comic persona, was at heart a decent, generous man. Not easy to forget.

9

N 1978, MARK WENT TO OXFORD and Toby went to Formia. Mark got straight into Oxford from Pimlico, which, I remarked at the time, was rather like crossing the Pacific on a balsawood raft. In those days, the older universities had more freedom of action. They could assess an applicant on the grounds of his perceived promise, rather than on his A levels, and Mark almost certainly got into Pembroke College on his general paper. At his original prep school, well known for its Latin teaching, this had been perhaps his strongest subject. 'But when I left Pimlico at seventeen,' he later remarked with some bitterness, 'I'd just about got back to where I was when I arrived there, at eleven.'

Liz and Jo, the girls, were lucky enough to leave after their O levels, for two years at Camden Girls School, renowned for its teaching, and not yet – quite – a comprehensive. When Jo opted, like Mark, to study classics, she was taught by the remarkable Terry Buckley, a red-headed football-loving Londoner from an Irish working-class family, whose success was such that Oxford's great New College asked to be associated with Camden. He eventually taught at Roedean. Liz would study modern languages at Durham University, with a happy year off in France. Jo would go to Worcester College, Oxford, get first-class honours and a classical scholarship in Honour Mods, walk out, return to university at 28, and get another First, this time at the School of Oriental and Arabic Studies, with a fascinating middle year living in the Christian–Arab quarter of Jerusalem.

Domenico Biti had been ringing us for the best part of a year to persuade us to let Toby come and play for him; he was by then in charge of Formia, a club down the coast from Rome that he had taken up to division C2. Toby played in the final of the Lewis, Inner

London, trophy when Pimlico beat the formidable Holloway School even though, no professional pitch being available, the game had been played on Holloway's home ground in Finchley.

Alan Wright, who had transmogrified into an idealistic games master, was in charge of Holloway's football. Toby and I had met him in the Wembley press-box some time before, at a schoolboy international. In some ways, he hadn't changed. Whatever happened on the field seemed no more than a trampoline for self-projection. Toby listened seriously, silently and intently. When Pimlico eventually reached the final against Holloway, he said, 'I don't think we've got much chance, Dad. That man we met at Wembley, Alan Wright. They've got all those six-foot black players on Arsenal's books.'

I told him not to worry; Alan was known for his hyperbole. 'And if those black players were any good, they'd be in Arsenal's first team.'

There was in fact a bizarre moment when one of these players, the centre forward, was sent off the field, and yelled at by another, the centre half, whereupon he turned round and shouted, 'You black bastard.'

Holloway seemed to have a pro footballer as coach every ten yards down the touchline, but Pimlico won after extra time, and Alan was both gracious and generous in defeat.

After O levels, Toby said he had no intention of taking As unless we allowed him to leave Pimlico. This we did. He studied at home for As in French and Italian, going, eventually, to a tutor for the first and working with myself on the second. We agreed that he might go to Formia for a few months, living with Biti and the team.

Shortly before he was due to leave, there was a phone call from Biti to say that he had a problem. Though Toby would be playing only for the youth/reserve team, the rules of the Italian Federation at that time decreed that no player coming from a foreign federation could play in Italy at any level. 'He can train with us,' said Biti, 'and on Sundays he can play for Gaeta, the nearby medieval town.'

Toby was appalled. 'It's going to be hard enough fitting in with them anyway,' he said, presciently as it turned out. '*You* say you know people. Why don't you do something?'

I decided he was right and phoned Artemio Franchi, then president both of UEFA and of the Italian Federation. '*Ci penso io,*' he said. (I'll see to it.) He was as good as his word. Toby was registered in Florence, the practice at that time, as Tobia Glanville, born Florence, father English, mother Italian. And off to Formia he went for four months.

I visited him there. Formia is a pleasant seaside town with a fine beach; though this was winter. There is also a remarkable *montagna spaccata* (a split mountain), with its caves. Toby, Biti and the team were living in a huge mausoleum of a hotel on the sea front. The players themselves were a lively bunch, divided between a number of veterans, for whom this was probably the end of the line, and several young players of promise. Biti was famous for launching them. At that time, he had no fewer than fourteen playing either in Serie A or Serie B. Tall and elegant in a pristine white cricket jersey, Toby strolled at ease about the hotel, casually making *cappuccini*. 'This is luxury,' he said, when he saw me.

Biti was as amiable and anecdotal as ever; full of the old sly humour. 'This man,' he would say, of a player, 'disguised as a centre half!' I stayed in the hotel and ate with the team. Before a somewhat acerbic landlady, Toby had to maintain the fiction that he was half Italian. In the dressing-room before a game, he was told to keep his mouth shut when the referee came in. At this stage, he told me with enthusiasm how much time there was to read and study. But by the time he came home for Christmas, he had been sucked into the pro footballer's routine. Training, meals, a stroll into town, back for a meal again, bed.

Training took place up in the mountains on a 'beaten earth' pitch; the club's training ground was being rebuilt. Pietro Mennea, the famous Olympic gold medallist in the 200 metres, trained on the track in town, the headquarters of Italian athletics. We would meet him: the quintessential southerner by contrast with his predecessor, Livio Berruti, who had won the gold at the 1960 Roman Olympics, and whom I had come to know quite well. Relations between them were not good. Some time later, when Berruti visited Formia, Mennea led him across the track and into an ambush, where he was attacked by Mennea's friends. Mistakenly, Mennea thought Berruti had accused him of being a coward. The chasm between north and south was as wide and as deep as ever.

I watched Toby play in a reserve game in Latina. It wasn't easy. Biti was trying to wean his players away from *catenaccio* and man-to-man marking to a zonal game, but as often as not when Toby marked a man who came into his zone, he found one of his own team trying to mark him, too. Before the game, there was one of those strange eruptions that occur in Italian life. I have no idea what provoked it, but the manager of the Latina club, a young man running a game on a pitch beside the stadium, kept shouting, '*Bada ai cazzi tuoi!*' which might be politely translated as 'mind your own business', did it not include a reference to the male organ. The police arrived. An elderly man, perhaps a club official, appealed to the senior officer, 'We're both fathers of families!' He saw me watching him and gave me a resigned smile. It all blew over.

Picking up his camera, Toby ceased temporarily to be a footballer and reverted to what he had been for some time now, and seemed likely to be in the future: a photographer. We went gradually up the peninsula, working on photos and articles, visiting the Roma training ground and staying in Florence at the Hotel Berchielli on the Lungarno, which I had known well in my Florentine days. It being well out of season, they gave us no less than a suite, though Toby was less impressed than I. Since then the hotel has been hideously refurbished at immense cost. Lie in your room and you seem to hear herds of elephants thundering down the pretentious marble stairs.

In Padua, we looked at the churches and chapels. In Vicenza, we found Paolo Rossi in training in the stadium. Slightly reluctant at first – 'You've read *all* the interviews?' – he agreed to meet us for dinner that evening. We went to an *al fresco* restaurant above the city; he brought his pretty fiancée, and made us his guests. It was a most enjoyable evening. Paolo has great charm. He had come to Vicenza as a discard of Juventus, an outside right, who, one of the coaches told us, had to be cured of his *dribblomania*, his passion for dribbling. Reborn as a centre forward, he had become a prolific scorer, a success in the 1978 World Cup.

The seeds of disaster were sown when Giussy Farina, the volatile president of Lanerossi Vicenza, decided to go head to head with mighty Juventus, in an auction for the half-share in Rossi which each possessed. Juve could logically be expected to win, but this was a moment when the Italian economy was shaky, and Juventus were anxious, for all their wealth, not to be seen as spendthrifts. So Vicenza outbid them with an offer ludicrously higher than their own, one which virtually condemned them to bankruptcy.

This, in due course, forced them reluctantly to put Rossi on the market. But the price was so high that even the major clubs were not prepared to pay it. Rossi might have gone to Napoli, but the idea of playing in that turbulent city did not appeal to him, which in retrospect was a pity. For what happened was that he was shuffled off to Perugia, a beautiful university city, but a peripheral football club, with a shaky hold on its status in Serie A.

It seems probable that the profound sense of anticlimax and disappointment induced Rossi to do the stupid and uncharacteristic thing he did. At a time when two small-time Roman crooks, Trinca and Crociani, were running riot among Italian players in the so-called Totonero (black pools, scandal, fixing game after game), Rossi was down South at Avellino with the Perugia team. The story went that he was playing a game called tombola when asked if he would join in the fix and, scarcely bothering to turn round, he had replied, 'Yes, if I can score a couple of goals.' This he did. The game was drawn 2–2, Rossi was eventually implicated, and banned for three years. He made, it was said, a poor impression in front of the tribunal in Milan. All for two million lire.

Amnestied after two years, however, he was brought back into the squad for the 1982 World Cup Finals in Spain. Italy, and Rossi himself, looking understandably rusty, began badly in their qualifying group in Galicia. Back in Coverciano, Allodi made the most of it. One of his protégés, the young club manager, Eugenio Fascetti, made a vicious public attack there on Bearzot, claiming that his team and tactics were defiling Italian football.

'How can I work with a Brutus at my back?' demanded Bearzot.

'If I'm Brutus,' retorted Allodi, 'he must think he's Caesar.'

But Bearzot would emphatically have the last laugh.

In Formia, Toby played relatively seldom, even when promised he would do so. The explanation was a very Italian one. The coach of Formia's youth team, Purificato, was an employee of the mayor in the town hall. The mayor had fallen out with Biti, who discouraged him from interfering. So when Toby was picked, Purificato was told, 'That English boy is not to play.'

Meanwhile, the huge hotel in which he was living had fallen on hard times. The telephone was cut off: the ultimate nightmare for an Italian footballer. When I wanted to phone him, I arranged to do it in a local bar. Each time I called, the proprietor would shout to him, 'It's your mother!'

At Oxford, Mark continued to play. He was a devoted fan of Manchester United, whom, since he was an eight-year-old, he had supported, believing then that Manchester was a suburb of London.

To save money, he would travel to their away games with the then notorious Cockney Reds, their London fan club, a byword then for violence in a very violent era. That began when he was still in Pimlico, and went on when he was at Oxford. 'Dad,' he once said to me, 'I'm worried. They hate students, and if they ever find out I'm reading classics at Oxford, I don't know what will happen.'

They never did. At the end of a vacation, a strange dialogue would ensue.

'Well, cheerio lads, won't be seeing you for a while.'

'What, going on 'oliday?'

'No.'

'You're not?' Head bowed.

'They all think I'm going inside,' he said.

Toby and I went to the 1980 European Championship Finals together; I as journalist, he as photographer. We slogged our way up and down the peninsula, from Turin in the north to Naples in the south, where we saw a superb game between West Germany, who won, and Holland. England, beaten by Italy in Turin, where there was much trouble on the terraces with their fans during a previous game against Belgium, were mediocre. For forty years, they had had the Indian sign on Italy, had time and again beaten them or avoided defeat when they seemed doomed. But the sequence had been broken at last at Wembley when Giorgio Chinaglia, of all unlikely people, had gone round Bobby Moore on the line, presenting Fabio Capello with the simplest of tap-ins.

Ron Greenwood was now the England manager, having replaced Don Revie, who, in the middle of a South American tour, had defected to Arabia. He was brusquely kicked out by the FA, but even here Harold Thompson carelessly acted both as judge and jury, so that when the case was taken to court Revie won it, though the judge condemned him as 'greedy and dishonest'.

Greenwood was highly acceptable to Thompson, since he had coached at Oxford University. At West Ham he had established a kind of 'academy', where skill was pre-eminent. The club had contributed three essential players to England's World Cup team of 1966: Geoff Hurst, Bobby Moore, and the accomplished Martin Peters, described as being 'ten years ahead of his time', and successfully brought into the World Cup team in midstream, by Ramsey, as a left-sided midfielder. Not a winger. Ramsey had by then tried all those he had and found them wanting. His team would go down as 'The Wingless Wonders'.

Greenwood was one of the coaches who had been promoted under Walter Winterbottom, and had previously had a spell at Arsenal. But by the time he was appointed as England manager he had become deeply disillusioned with the game and had retired from his job at West Ham. Now, he would make some curious choices; even to the extent of dropping one of his most gifted West Ham protégés, the playmaker Trevor Brooking, in favour of the workaday Liverpool midfielder, Ian Callaghan, previously, as it happens, one of the wingers who had been dropped by Ramsey.

Later, when Tottenham's Glenn Hoddle made a coruscating debut for England at Wembley against Bulgaria ending with a spectacular goal, Greenwood promptly dropped him, too, with the significant words, 'Disappointment is part of football.'

Hoddle, who would eventually become an England World Cup coach himself, was obliged to get used to disappointment; like so many creative English players before him and like Paul Gascoigne, after him. Bobby Robson, who succeeded Greenwood as England's manager, had for long made no secret of the fact that he was not one of Hoddle's admirers, though no other English player had the same technique and the same flair for using the defence-splitting pass.

In 1985, when England were preparing for the 1986 World Cup, he grudgingly picked Hoddle for the game against Scotland, but both there, and in Mexico where the team went for a miniature tournament, tried to exile him, absurdly, to the right wing. In Mexico City, the other players entered a kind of tacit conspiracy to enable Hoddle to play and pass in the middle.

Yet by the time they reached training camp in the USA the following year, Robson had seen the light, praising Hoddle effusively, and saying that he had never thought he would see a player to compare with his old colleague at Fulham, Johnny Haynes. This moved me to write, at the time, that it was interesting to learn that the Road to Damascus passed through Colorado Springs.

It was in Mexico City on that tour that Robson told us at a press conference, 'Pressure? There isn't any pressure. You people provide the pressure. If it wasn't for you, my job would be twice as easy and twice as pleasurable.'

As for Greenwood, he did bring England close to the Final in Spain. It eventually depended on a group qualifying game against the Spaniards themselves, in Madrid. Against all expectations, Greenwood put on Kevin Keegan as a substitute. At his best, Keegan had been the epitome of the fine self-made player. Endowed with few natural gifts, he had worked on himself and his game until he matured from a quick and clever outside right, acquired by Liverpool from humble Scunthorpe United, into an attacker capable of playing right across the front line with verve, intelligence and opportunism. But his star had been on the wane for some time; he had recently been injured and, in fact, the England party had smuggled him out of Spain to have an operation in Germany.

When the easiest chance of that whole game fell to him, one that the old Keegan could have taken in his sleep, he headed wide and England were out, though no one had beaten them. Thus they did not reach the semi-final.

That game was a goalless draw. So was their previous game in Madrid, against West Germany. At his subsequent press conference, Greenwood said he was amazed nobody had asked him a certain question. When nobody did, he said at last, 'We didn't let Manny Kaltz get in any crosses.' Stunned silence. Kaltz had been the German right back!

John Lovesey was succeeded, as *Sunday Times* sports editor, by David Robson. By then I was very sorry to see him go as we were good friends again; but I also liked his successor. David was a very different breed of cat: the quintessential Jewish intellectual, an Oxonian, shrewd, humorous, ironic and perceptive, but not the greatest of organisers, occasionally obstinate to a degree, and not always at his best in a crisis.

Such as the one that so fearfully occurred at the Heysel Stadium in Brussels in 1985. Before the European Cup Final between Liverpool and Juventus, Liverpool's fans ran riot on the terracing at one end, forcing the Italian fans across it till a wall collapsed. Thirty-nine spectators died. England's clubs were banned from Europe for five bitter years.

That the disaster was utterly avoidable was no consolation. That it would never have occurred but for the aggression of the Liverpool fans, many of whom had been drunk long before the game, was equally true. And yet . . . And yet . . .

In the first place, the run-down old stadium was totally unfit for such a major game. One learnt that the UEFA delegation that was meant to inspect it, on a cold winter's day, had for the most part stayed indoors. The Italians were there because the Belgians, absurdly, had put tickets on sale, in Belgium, for those terraces, when they must surely have known that thousands of Italian immigrant workers would easily snap them up and either use them themselves, or send them home. This in turn meant that the Italian fans on those terraces, in proximity to Liverpool's, were not the regular ones who followed Juventus, among which, too, was a formidable hooligan element. They were passive, peaceful fans, many quite unused to the ways of the terraces, who came simply to enjoy an evening out, and were totally defenceless when attacked.

Next, there was the incompetence and cowardice of the Belgian police. They had done little or nothing to stop Liverpool fans slipping into the ground illegally, some ducking under the wire fence. When trouble began, then subsided, they had a good quarter of an hour to get on to those terraces and prevent it recurring. British police who, whatever criticisms may be levelled at them, are certainly brave, would have dealt with the problem in minutes. As it was, when another squad of police did arrive, their commander could think of nothing better to do than line them up in the middle of the pitch and inspect them.

Though, after the second attack, one side of the terraces looked ominously clear, though messages began to be broadcast one after another asking for the relatives of certain Italians to come forward, I had no idea of the extent of the horrors till the *Observer* photographer Eamonn McCabe, an old opponent from Sunday football, came to stand beneath the press-box, held up the fingers of both hands time and again, and drew a line with his forefinger across his throat.

Two days later, instead of flying to Mexico City with the England team, I found myself cycling to 10 Downing Street. With half a dozen other journalists also present, there was a meeting with the Prime Minister, Mrs Thatcher. 'I want to know what *you* think,' she told us; 'I want to know *your* opinions' – though it quickly became clear that her desire was not insatiable.

At one point she said, 'I think we want to get the *decent* fans to express their disapproval.'

I suggested that part of that very problem was that no one disapproved more of themselves than those most directly involved. They were alienated. She gave me her familiar smile and said, 'I *don't* think I'd use that word!' while a picture formed in my mind of 'decent' fans reproaching a hooligan: 'Here, mate; I don't think you should kick that old man.'

Liverpool's fans, I knew, from information from the battlefront – Mark's – had long been a byword for violence among supporters of other teams; just as Manchester United's had been, before them. The Liverpool journalists present disagreed with me, looking shocked and offended, but what did they see, what did any of us see, from the press-box?

'We're the best-behaved supporters in the land,' they used to sing in the 1960s, but it was at that time that I wrote a sketch that Tom Courtenay performed on Ned Sherrin's successor to TW3, 'Not So Much A Programme, More A Way Of Life', when he came on as a Liverpool supporter who never saw a game, because he had always been arrested before kickoff. Asked whether he didn't think he was missing something, he replied, 'No, because I'm the one supporter this season that's not seen Liverpool beat!'

In an increasingly technological age, an alienated underclass with little hope of any kind of fulfilment (their manual jobs constantly disappearing and with them their self-respect) was drawn to violence as a *raison d'être*. Not simply in England, but all over Europe. Drive such violence out of the stadia, as our police with their technological aids have largely been able to do, then it simply spills out into the streets. Italy, France, Germany, Holland and Spain have all been afflicted by it and will no doubt continue so to be. When England played Italy in a World Cup eliminator in Rome in the autumn of 1997, the violence of their hooligan fans before the match, and the reputation that had gone before them, brought, in its turn, a violent reaction from the police at the stadium in which, as always, the innocent suffered. There's no end to it; or none in sight. Football has paid heavily for its very popularity.

I followed England again in the 1986 World Cup, in which they began abysmally but ended honourably, sunk in the Azteca Stadium by Diego Maradona's notorious 'Hand of God' goal. That he followed it up at once with another, a stupendous solo, which has been acclaimed as the finest goal of all time, surely had something to do with the clandestine nature of the first, when he punched the ball past Peter Shilton, with no let or hindrance from an inept linesman and referee. Gianni Melidoni, the sports editor of Rome's *Il Messaggero*, remarked to me afterwards, 'The England team were still in a state of shock: like a man who's had his pocket picked.'

No such excuse, however, could be advanced in the next round, at the same stadium, by the Belgians, who conceded a goal of equal brilliance, with Maradona's stocky little figure slaloming past man after man.

Opening their programme in the agreeable city of Monterrey, England began abysmally, losing clumsily to Portugal, then being immensely lucky to survive against Morocco. But in that drawn game lay the seeds of their recovery. Bryan Robson, their captain, was obliged to leave the field with a dislocated shoulder. Ray Wilkins, usually the most impeccable of players, threw the ball at the referee, and was sent off. So both men dropped out of the team.

Why Bryan Robson was playing at all constituted a great mystery. His shoulder had constantly been going out, prompting, from Bobby Robson, the asinine statement – absurd when it came from so experienced a manager – that if the shoulder came out easily, then it would go back easily.

Of course it would, for God's sake, as no one knew better than I, who had dislocated a shoulder three times, playing for Chelsea Casuals. By the grace of God and specific exercises, I was able to avoid an operation and it ultimately stayed put. But when a shoulder goes in and out like Bryan Robson's, only an operation can put it right. It had gone out again in a World Cup preliminary in Los Angeles where England had beaten Mexico. Bobby Robson denied it, but admitted in his execrable diary, published after the World Cup, that this was a 'white lie'. Why did he tell it? Why was he so anxious for his namesake to play, though all logic was against it? We can but speculate.

As for Wilkins, he would not be missed. As a young inside forward of immense promise at Chelsea, he had been an exciting player; intelligent, prepared to beat his man and possessed of a powerful shot. But with the passing of the years, he had become increasingly predictable and cautious, noted for his constant use of the square ball and even the pass backwards. The team had virtually rebelled in the dressing-room at half-time in the game against Morocco. One player was said to have apostrophised the coach, Don Howe, 'You're always telling us what to do. What the fuck do we do, now?'

With Trevor Steven, Peter Reid and Steve Hodge giving new life to the midfield, Peter Beardsley dovetailing so unselfishly with the now rampant Gary Lineker, this was a revitalised England team. It swept Poland aside, and easily disposed of Paraguay in the Azteca Stadium. Lineker scored again, even though he had to go off the field for treatment after being brutally chopped across the throat by the Paraguayan centre back. 'It was an accident,' he said, so characteristically, afterwards. 'At least, I hope it was.' Lineker was the living proof that a great sportsman does not have to be 'aggressive', denying the conventional wisdom.

If Bobby Robson was a 'lucky' manager as, at international level, he so often seemed to be, his and England's luck ran out when Diego Maradona punched that goal. John Barnes came on for the last quarter of an hour to give a dazzling performance of left-wing play, severely exposing the limitations of Argentina's 3–5–2 formation, making a goal for Lineker and so nearly creating another. But the game remained just out of reach.

10

SE FACEVA CAPELLI, NASCONO SENZA TESTE. I had frequent cause, in the 1980s, to recall the adage. After so many years, I found at last that I *could* write a play. It was called *A Visit to the Villa*, was set in Tuscany, and concerned a fraudulent art dealer and grand old man of painting with a dubious past. I wrote it under the aegis of Toby Rowland, of the Stoll Moss organisation, an American, originally from Montana, who had long worked for 'Binkie' Beaumont and the HM Tennant organisation, which for years dominated the West End Theatre. I still believe that a play is the hardest literary form to master. Like patriotism, dialogue is not enough. It requires a special flair, a special kind of creative intelligence that has little or nothing to do with pure intellect. Toby and I had tried before, and it hadn't worked, despite all his encouragement and goodwill, though that play provided me with the basis for my novel, *A Cry of Crickets*.

This one, however, worked. Toby showed it to Patrick Garland, who was just about to take over the Chichester Memorial Theatre. Patrick wrote to him saying that it was the best new play he had read since *Forty Years On*, by Alan Bennett; a play that he himself had directed and that had had major success. It could, he said, go straight into the West End with the right star. Alas, we never found the right star, and though Patrick generously assured me there was 'nothing to stop it being an international success', stopped it emphatically was. Too many star actors turned down the part of the eighty-year-old art connoisseur, Levinson.

Among them was John Gielgud, though his agent, Laurie Evans, was keen for him to take it on. How different things might have been if he had! As it was, Gielgud would play the lead fourteen years later, on the BBC World Service.

But there were consolations. Sitting in Toby's office at Stoll Moss – which stood directly opposite my father's old surgery in Crabourne Street, where my uncle Gerry was still ensconced – Patrick spoke of how keen he was to put on a musical about the Crazy Gang.' He had already worked on a television programme with the one surviving member, Chesney Allen. This fascinated me. Bud Flanagan, the central figure of the group, had been a patient of my father in the very surgery opposite Stoll's windows, and I had interviewed him once at the Victoria Palace, in his dressing-room, while a devoted dresser cherished his every word.

A frustrated performer, I asked Toby and Patrick whether they had ever heard Bud's monologue, 'Our New MP'. They hadn't. I knew it thanks to my old schoolfriend, Clive Marks, who had a record of it, all those years ago. I imitated some of it: 'When the Japanese went into Manch . . . When the Japanese went into Manch . . . When the Japanese went into Manchester . . . *Oi!* . . . The Chancellor of the Excheck . . . The Chancellor of the Excheck . . . Neville Chambermaid! He says, "Take care of the pence and the pence will turn into shillin's! Take care of the shillin's and the shillin's'll turn into pounds." Take care of the pounds, and he'll take 'em off you! Oi!'

Patrick was so impressed by this that he asked me if I would write the show. This we did together, though in retrospect it was plainly a grave mistake not to involve its star, Roy Hudd, from the beginning. As it turned out, Patrick was so busy setting up the new season at Chichester that I was largely left to my own devices, and what did I know about writing a musical? My great good fortune was that I was able to spend time with Chesney, who had outlived the other members of The Gang even though, after the war, he had been the first to retire. He then became their agent. Moreover, he had been very much the straight man in their group, even referred to sometimes as 'Straighty'. This did not prevent his having a sly, delightful humour of his own. Indeed one of my most agreeable memories of the whole saga was seeing him and the star of the show, Roy Hudd, perform, just for me, a sketch about a stolen watch, in the stalls bar at the Prince of Wales, shortly before the London opening.

Patrick's initial idea was that the first act should be, so to speak, historical; the second, a variety show. The story of Bud and Chesney was itself a dramatic one. They had first met as soldiers behind the lines in the First World War in an *estaminet* at Poperinghe. Both, later, had been gassed. Bud, in the artillery, had an anti-Semitic sergeant whose name he took for the stage. Chesney was in the Royal

West Kents. They met again by chance in Piccadilly when Chesney had a small part in a West End show. Bud, who would walk all the way to Glasgow for an audition for the Florrie Forde company, met him once again when it transpired that Chesney was her manager.

At Chichester, where the show opened to immense enthusiasm – after a very grudging early response from the local community – Chesney appeared every night after the interval, stepping in for Christopher Timothy who was impersonating him. 'So you're . . . Bud . . . Flanagan,' the voice would say, over the loudspeakers. Then he would take the stage himself to tremendous applause. Over eighty years old, he still had presence and charm and could still sing duets with Roy.

Roy was the heart and soul of the show, reshaping it with his immense knowledge of show-business history and skilfully choosing a series of bright production numbers. He it was, too, who kept 'The Gang' in order, a group of small, adroit, experienced comedians who had been working for years in seaside resorts, at concert parties, had the heart of the matter in them, and bickered endlessly. When one of them, down at Chichester, Peter Glaze, put on his own one-man show in the studio theatre, not one of them came to see it. One of them, at the back of the stalls at the Prince of Wales, once told me that he wanted to hit him. But when poor Peter died from a sudden heart attack, they all lamented his passing in the most fulsome way.

Roy stayed in the show for only a year. He had already told us he would, but it still surprised me. It was the first major West End role he had 'created'. True, he had had a long run as Fagin in *Oliver!* but that was as successor to Ron Moody. 'In *Oliver!* I had the kids,' he told me. 'In *Arches*, I've got the Gang.' Bernie Winters and Leslie Crowther took over competently enough, though Bernie had none of the driving energy of Roy, none of his authority over the little men. The heart and discipline went out of the show; it did not once cover its costs with the new pair, and it eventually closed after fifteen months in the West End.

Billy Gray, impersonating his extraordinary brother 'Monsieur' Eddie, juggler and surrealist comic, had been a patient of my father, too; just a few hundred yards down the road. 'That man was the greatest man I ever knew,' he said. He brought off one of Eddie's monologues with great aplomb.

Working, again, under Toby Rowland's aegis, I turned my novel *The Comic*, published in 1976, into another play. This time it came closer still to the stage. Dave King, comedian turned accomplished actor, agreed to play the lead. Bill Bryden, then a leading director at the National Theatre, once captain of a Scottish boys' team that included the resplendent Charlie Cooke, would direct. Stoll Moss had the theatres. What could stop it? Answer: the sudden and surprising defenestration of Lew Grade from his own companies, at the instigation of an Australian entrepreneur. Grade, who got up earlier in the morning than any living impresario! *Se faceva capelli.*

The Comic has never been produced, though it seemed certain to be broadcast on BBC radio, with Roy Hudd, who had always liked the book, playing the lead. The Head of BBC Radio Light Entertainment wanted it. A talented young director was keen to do it. But these, alas, are the days of bureaucracy at the BBC. An extra echelon had been created; a head of department no longer saw his writ run. The extra echelon turned the play down.

The *Sunday Times*, meanwhile, moved to Wapping. It was the beginning of the end of the stranglehold that the greedy, disaffected, recalcitrant printers' unions had had on Fleet Street for so long. So often did they sabotage the paper that it came to be known as the *Sunday Sometimes*. Week after week, one's work went up in smoke. Having held out, Luddite style, for so long, pocketing so much, you might have thought that the print unions would have realised the time had come for an accommodation. One or two of their leaders saw as much, but they were dealing with a Gadarene syndrome. Like the old – but not the new – *mafiosi*, printers by and large did not educate their sons; why should they when they could go into 'the print' and gobble up a fortune? So when the writing was on the wall, there was no one bright enough to read it. The lotus-eating could go on for ever. There would always be someone like the eighty-year-old printer who, every Saturday night, got into a taxi, came down to the plant, collected his money and went home again. It would always be possible to sign 'Mickey Mouse' and pocket your pay, to drink heavily and sleep it off in a back room on the premises. To run your own business in your abundant free time.

How strange that journalists from *The Times* should be instrumental in bringing the whole fiasco to an end. But then, broadsheet journalists at that time were strangely deluded about their powers and potential. When the *Sunday Times*, like *The Times*, was taken off the streets for eleven long, sad, futile months, I remember a meeting of the *Sunday Times* journalists' chapel, or union, at which the possibility of a new proprietor was discussed, and the nature of the proprietor they might or might not want was bruited. It was astonishing to hear them. They would accept this, they would not stand for that. I thought of Mao Tse Tung's doctrine,

'Power Comes Out of the Barrel of a Gun'; in this instance, out of a proprietor's money. Another analogy might have been taken from Freud: the image of the clown who makes believe he is controlling the circus.

Jacob Ecclestone, a Yorkshire communist who had taught in China, was the unknowing catalyst of what would happen. He persuaded *The Times*' journalists to strike over an issue where they may have been morally in the right, but where they were legally out of order. That was enough for the proprietor, Ken Thomson. *Figlio di papa*, in Italian parlance, 'Daddy's son', he had none of the reverence of his father, Roy, the self-made barber's son, for the British Establishment and its symbols. To acquire the *Sunday Times* and then, *mirabile dictu*, *The Times*, had been the crown of Roy's career. But Kenneth had been brought up rich and, for him, the two newspapers merely constituted perpetual worry. The *Times* strike was the last straw. He put the papers on the market. Rupert Murdoch bought them. The unions at last had met their match.

The battle that followed was a harsh one. The unions had already served notice of how they would react to any challenge to their power and privileges when, in the north, they had literally laid siege to the printing plant of Eddie Shah, who boldly decided to bring out a new newspaper without them. Doing a deal with the electricians union, Murdoch secretly moved the *Times* operation to Wapping, and then used the new, Thatcherite, legislation to sack the printers.

Several of my most able colleagues refused to go to Wapping, and I respected their stand. For my part, I could not see that there had been any alternative to fighting fire with fire; even if it meant that some of the gentle herbivores, as opposed to the voracious carnivores, suffered in the process. When Brenda Dean took charge of the print union there did seem hope of a decent, reasonable settlement. Twice she seemed on the brink of attaining it, but each time the *sans culottes* of the union frustrated her. She should surely have resigned; but she didn't.

So I found myself cycling once a week to Wapping from Holland Park, and back, knowing that at least one cyclist – wholly unconnected with the plant and the papers – had been beaten up *en route*, knowing that each time I would have to face the five pickets who kept watch, abusively, opposite the narrow entrance. Did he think, I asked Mark, something of an expert on, though never a participant in, street violence, that my cycle hoop lock was a reasonable means of self defence? 'A padlock on a chain's better,' he said, which was what I took with me. The watching coppers obviously thought it was for the bike. I never had to use it.

When Hunter Davies wrote a profile of me for the *Independent*, he quoted me, quite fallaciously, as saying, 'The pickets tried to beat me up.' This was sheer nonsense, and I had to write to two broadsheets to nail the lie.

We did have some fairly ripe exchanges. The trick of it was to answer as pungently as possible while eschewing any kind of bad language, since the police would take it that this was to provoke the pickets. Once they even asked the editor, Andrew Neil, to tone down a drinks party that was being held on a terrace which overlooked the entrance (bidding a journalist farewell), since the pickets might be upset by the noise.

I lost patience with them after an evening when I had addressed the Harrow Referees Society at a pub in Pinner, a quid pro quo for one of their members who had refereed Chelsea Casuals' games. He picked me up in his car in Holland Park. 'There's something I have to tell you,' he said. 'You may not want to come. We've had a telephone warning that if you do speak, there'll be two hundred pickets outside.' We went.

I had scarcely begun speaking when two large louts, father and son as it turned out, stood up and started abusing me. 'You evil bastard!' A study in moral self-deception. 'You cunt!'

'It takes one to know one,' I said. They were thrown out, and the talk went on. Next time I emerged from the entrance and descended the few steps opposite the pickets at Wapping, a few days later, the same chorus went up: 'Scab, scabby! Scab!'

I looked at them. 'What are you getting out of this, anyway, lads?' I asked them. 'Yob satisfaction?' The response was one of satisfying outrage.

The 1990 World Cup was played in Italy, and I should have enjoyed it more than I did. Fear of the English fans induced the organisers to place England in Cagliari. Foolishly I took pot luck with hotels, though thanks to Toby, who had been taking photographs there, I had met two of the senior tourist officials in London. The consequence was that I was dumped in a motel on the ghastly outskirts of the city.

Press relations with the England team were all but non-existent. This because both Robsons, Bobby and Bryan, had had their alleged sexual proclivities attacked and exposed in the tabloid press. This had nothing whatsoever to do with the football journalists but, not for the first time, they paid the price for the colleagues who were known as 'the rotters'. In Tunis at a warm-up match before the tournament started, the England players looked as if they had taken a vow of *omertà*.

'Look at them,' said Mike Langley, sports columnist of the *People*, and a notable, adventurous traveller. 'Twenty of them sitting on a wall and not a smile among the lot of them.'

Access to England's hotel, outside Cagliari, was denied to journalists, but freely offered by Bobby Robson to a novelist called Pete Davies who was writing a book about the tournament that in the event would stitch up almost everyone in sight; Robson and his players included. Journalists who paid for Davies's meals paid again when they were lampooned. Bobby Robson, in his *naiveté*, gave Davies a free run of the England hotel, and lived to regret it. Reviewing the book in the *Sunday Times* I wrote that I strongly recommended it, 'with the strongest possible reservations'.

Paul Gascoigne was one of Davies's victims. In a passage no 'mere' tabloid football journalist would ever have written, he described being in a phone booth adjacent to Gazza at London Airport, where Gascoigne let out a torrent of abuse at a girlfriend who apparently hadn't been there when he wanted to talk to her.

Gascoigne was the new reality in the England team. Two years earlier, when England had played ineptly in the European Championship Finals in West Germany, and Bobby Robson had seemed in a state of strange confusion, my colleagues had derided me when I said I thought Gascoigne should have been chosen. By 1990 his claims were unanswerable, though Robson had given him a peculiarly hard time, banishing him to the left wing in 'B' internationals, blaming him publicly and harshly for once giving the ball away and announcing before a friendly against the Czechs at Wembley before the World Cup that this was virtually Gascoigne's last chance. This put enormous pressure on Gascoigne, who seemed in a frenzy in the tunnel before the teams took the field, but who proceeded to play superbly.

Emerging from what might not unkindly be described as a 'problem' family in the north-east – it was said that he preferred to sleep in Newcastle United's boys' hostel rather than go home for the night – his talent was nevertheless phenomenal. No English player of his generation had the supreme skills, the glorious playmaking ability, the sheer originality, of Gascoigne, a born inside forward in the classical sense. That he was immature, occasionally violent, kept doubtful company and was intensely self-destructive was undeniable. One remembered what André Gide said, when asked who was the greatest French poet: 'Victor Hugo, alas.'

Bobby Robson called Gascoigne 'daft as a brush' and that was giving him all the best of it. He came south to Spurs, and continued his remarkable career, until the second of two crazy challenges in the 1991 FA Cup Final at Wembley against Nottingham Forest put him out of the game for a year. Out he would later go again when, in a training match with Lazio, the Roman club he next joined, he suicidally tried to tackle a young reserve – as he was then – Nesta, as the boy shot; and he suffered a broken leg in consequence.

When Gazza decided to join Lazio, I observed, 'Wrong city, wrong player, wrong club,' and so it proved, though he didn't forgive me, greeting me when I visited Lazio's training ground with a mouthful of abuse. No rare event in his saga. But the Lazio fans adored him; his fellow players liked him; and though his spell in Rome ended in anticlimax, there was a period when he was the idol of the crowd.

His exceptional skills, his astonishing ability to 'photograph' the field and react with the unexpected pass as soon as the ball came to him, were paramount in England reaching the semi-final when, as we know, he broke down in tears after being booked, aware that he would miss the Final, if England reached it. Their path to the semi-finals was an odd one. They began in Cagliari with a draw so dull that an Italian paper headed its report, NO FOOTBALL PLEASE WE'RE BRITISH.

Bobby Robson had long been adamant that he would never play with a sweeper defence, which he thought alien to English players, and he unquestionably had a point. Yet when England met Holland in Cagliari, a sweeper was what they employed, and they managed to draw. In the quarter-final against Cameroon in Naples, Roger Milla, the 42-year-old Cameroon centre forward who had come on as substitute in the second half of games, a miracle of agelessness, was running the English defence ragged, and Cameroon seemed likely to win, till Robson gave up the sweeper formation and close-marked Milla with little Paul Parker. England won, and next day on a hotel terrace outside Salerno, bathed in brilliant sunshine, Robson told a press conference, 'A flat back four saved us.'

Distressed by the 'revelations' of the tabloids, he had already stated that he would leave the England managership after the World Cup. This made it all the more astonishing that the late Peter Swales, chairman of Manchester City, should say he was glad England had not won the World Cup: because if they had, then Robson would have stayed!

Swales, a self-made millionaire who had prospered in the field of electrical goods, sometimes seemed a living illustration of Bernard Shaw's dictum that intelligence had nothing to do with making money. When he sacked Mel Machin as manager of Manchester City, he said that Machin 'had no repartee with the fans'.

This was something too good to miss, and as luck had it the *Sunday Times* sent me to Manchester that very Saturday to cover a City game. I wrote that I assumed when the fans shouted, 'Machin out!' he simply sat in the dugout and said nothing. I added that a comedian's son (actually the son of Issy Bonn) had once explained to me the origins of repartee. It was when one caveman threw a club at another caveman and the other caveman picked up the same club and threw it back. But the club, I added, wasn't Manchester City.

Having lost Robson, the senior international committee made the abysmal mistake of appointing the manager of Watford, Graham Taylor. Taylor, whom I had first met and interviewed when he was successfully running Lincoln City, was a great believer in the long-ball game, which he practised with exceptional results with Watford, taking them from the Fourth Division to second place in the First Division. 'Direct route', long-ball football became a *casus belli* in England, the subject of violent disagreement.

Taylor and Charles Hughes, who had become Director of Coaching of the Football Association, were on the one side and had turned 'direct football' into what many of us regarded as a pseudo-science, a dangerous and destructive new orthodoxy. Well, new up to a point. The theories in fact were borrowed from Wing Commander Charles Reep, a retired RAF officer who in the 1950s had propounded something called 'Match Analysis'. This, through a plethora of diagrams, purported to show that the most effective form of football, the greatest number of goals, came from the use of the long pass. His prescriptions were enthusiastically embraced by Stanley Cullis, the former England centre half, then manager of his old club, Wolves, and for some years they worked very well. It was Bob Ferrier, in the *Sunday Dispatch*, who exposed the tactics and their limitations. But here they were again, not only enabling Watford to go shooting up the league, but being forced willy-nilly on the country's coaches and its coaching courses. Around him Hughes gathered a little band of believers and acolytes. Those who did not believe tended to be replaced. Phrases like 'Position of Maximum Opportunity' began to be heard. There was a ghastly period when it looked as if Hughes had Bobby Robson under his spell, and that the long ball heresy would be imposed not only on those international junior teams over which Hughes had domain, but right the way up to the senior England side.

A few of us, notably Jeff Powell of the *Daily Mail* and myself, constantly attacked this orthodoxy, convinced that it was doing terrible harm to the English game, substituting a crude form of football for subtlety and intricacy. My own mind went back to an anecdote told to me by Jimmy Hogan. When he and Hugo Meisl brought the Austrian Wunderteam to London in 1932 to play England at Stamford Bridge, he took the players, on the previous Saturday, to watch Chelsea meet Everton, at Stamford Bridge. Each side had a famous centre forward, Scotland's little Hughie Gallacher for Chelsea, big Dixie Dean of England, for Everton. And all that both sides did, said Hogan, to the wonder of his players, was bang the ball down the middle to one or other striker.

In other words, the long-ball option has always lurked menacingly in the English game. Charles Reep isolated it and tried to make it respectable. Graham Taylor, and who can blame him, used it for several years to remarkable effect with Watford, who even reached an FA Cup Final. Charles Hughes, with his computers and his fanatical credo, his bizarre belief that Brazil had 'got it wrong', appeared to be preaching a pseudo-religion.

Graham Taylor did not take kindly to criticism. At Watford after one game, he had heated exchanges with Jeff Powell. And at the beginning of a season, when he and Queens Park Rangers' Jim Smith came into the press room at Loftus Road after a game, he refused to shake hands with me. 'No, I can't, I can't,' he mumbled. Then, standing behind the little table where managers face the press, he assailed me: 'You're a liar, you write lies, you're a liar, you write lies.'

What on earth was he talking about? Gradually, as the smoke cleared and the words flew between us, I began to realise what it was. I had written, a good while ago as I recalled, in the magazine *World Soccer* rather than in the *Sunday Times*, about an England youth match in Israel. There, my colleague Rob Hughes had sat beside Taylor on the bench and told me afterwards that he had substituted a full back who had disagreed with his long-ball tactics. I had written this.

'Do you want to go on?' asked Taylor, eventually, and we went out on to the concourse to resume our quarrel. Why, I asked him, if he had felt as he did, had he not made a reply, which I would certainly have had published? No, he said, he hadn't wanted to. 'You didn't check with me,' he said. 'When you wrote something pleasant about me, at Lincoln, you checked with me!'

This made no sense at all. I had simply been to see him at Lincoln City then written up the interview. Next time I was at Queens Park Rangers Jim Smith, a straightforward and engaging Yorkshireman, shook his head in wonder and told me, 'I couldn't believe it. It was nothing to do with you.'

In fact, returning home, I had looked up *World Soccer* and found that the offending article had appeared . . . three and a half years ago. Taylor's outburst had clearly been an example of what Freudians call displacement. The Tel Aviv affair was no more than an excuse to vent his rage for my sustained criticism of his long-ball tactics.

As Henry IV dropped Falstaff, so Taylor, eventually, discarded Reep. Reep protested to Watford, but it was pointed out to him that it was not the club that had employed him.

Taylor's appointment to the England managership never made a shred of sense. He began clumsily, dropping Paul Gascoigne – how history repeats itself! – from the early game against Ireland in Dublin. The initial rationale was that Ireland's long-ball game would cut out the midfield. But then to replace Gazza with the still smaller Gordon Cowans made no sense at all. *Ex post facto*, Taylor hinted that Gascoigne's psychological condition made it unwise to play him, but that made scant sense, too.

Making a series of bizarre choices, Taylor eventually compromised England's hopes of qualifying for the 1994 World Cup when the team he put out against Norway in Oslo in June 1993 was the stuff of science fiction. Alarmed by the fact that Norway used their big striker Jostein Flo wide on the right, so he could race in for headers, Taylor decided to use Gary Pallister, the Manchester United centre half, as a left back and shuffle his defence in consequence. The England team never began to knit; bad defensive mistakes gave the Norwegians a couple of goals, and England's hopes of qualifying were hanging by a thread. This duly snapped in Holland where Taylor, unwisely allowing himself to be filmed on the touchline for a television documentary, came out with the unforgettable words, 'Do I not like that!'

By then, we had restored diplomatic relations. After a match at the old Den between Millwall and the club he was then managing, Aston Villa – where he did pretty well – he appeared in the press-box to give a radio interview. Extending his hand, he said, 'Shall we start again?' We shook hands, and we did.

At the *Sunday Times*, John Lovesey, whose expert knowledge of computers had played a crucial role in the move to Wapping, came back for a while to be sports editor of the *Sunday Times*, and I was happy to work with him again. When he moved on, there was a hiatus while management looked for a successor.

Rob Hughes and I, in our unwisdom, supported the claims of the deputy sports editor, Chris Nawrat. Peter Roberts, the managing editor at the time, was justifiably appalled. Nawrat did not cut a beguiling figure. Half-Lithuanian, half-Irish, large, pale, with pitted countenance and shaggy blond hair, his rise had been unusual. He had studied at Essex University when it had been a hotbed of the Left, and had himself been known there as an 'activist'. He had worked for the communist *Morning Star*, and had subsequently been employed by the *Sunday Times* to work on the 'Inside Track' column of sporting gossip and news. He wore a leather jacket almost as a guarantee of his left-wing *bona fides*, but as soon as he was elevated to the assistant sports editorship, the jacket went, to be replaced by a grey, pinstripe suit. In the prevailing fashion, however, he did nothing to modulate a strong London accent. And he drank a good deal.

The editor of the paper was Andrew Neil, a Scot who had been appointed by Rupert Murdoch to succeed the more patrician Frank Giles. Neil had great energy, drive and ambition, though when he was appointed, no experience with a national newspaper; his name had been made on *The Economist*, notably with his dispatches from America. Personally, I rather liked him and never exchanged a bad word with him, but under his regime, there is no doubt that sycophants and toadies flourished. He did not give the impression of having any huge, residual self-confidence, either in the way he ran the paper, or in his much-publicised romantic life, which occasionally led to some embarrassment.

The trouble was that, obsessed by politics, where he was beyond question an original and challenging mind, he had little interest in sport and seemed oblivious of the way the sports department was accelerating downhill. Rob Hughes and I quickly passed out of favour, and the climax came when Nawrat, attending a luncheon given by the England managers, Graham Taylor and Lawrie McMenemy, publicly abused me. The guests were the sports editors of Sunday newspapers, and one of them wrote to me:

> In short, the conduct of your sports editor, insofar as the conversation involved you, was quite unforgivable. He engaged England manager Graham Taylor in conversation about how he handled you, his soccer columnist, and what he thought of the copy you produced. No one was left in any doubt that he does not rate you highly.
>
> Graham Taylor hardly had to push the conversation. Mr Nawrat seemed intent on telling all his fellow sports editors and his FA hosts what he thought about you. He could, certainly, have realised his error in talking publicly about a member of his

own staff. But no, he worried at the topic and, quite frankly, his behaviour was the main talking point when I left the Royal Garden Hotel later that afternoon.

I would hate to think that I could ever give such a public display of disloyalty to a member of my staff, whatever private reservations I may hold. Your sports editor's behaviour displayed, at best, a flagrant lack of tact. At worst, it was utterly misplaced and reprehensible.

Had Peter Roberts still been managing editor, the consequences might well have been Draconian. In the event, Nawrat was obliged to write a grovelling letter of recantation to Taylor, who sent him a weasel letter back, alleging – no doubt he had much enjoyed the occasion – that he could not recall anything derogatory being said.

As for Rob Hughes, who – once a young Leicester City professional – had, over the years, made himself a formidable and influential expert on world football, he fared no better than myself. When I accepted a tempting invitation to join the *People* as sports columnist in 1992, Rob was seemingly the automatic favourite to take my place. Instead, Nawrat brought in a television commentator who inevitably found the job an ungrateful one. Rob, by contrast, was steadily marginalised until Peter Roberts had him very properly made football correspondent of *The Times*.

Nawrat's own days were numbered. What might politely be called confusion over moneys paid out of the sports account and moneys paid out of a special account designed to cover a *Sunday Times* book on sport led to his departure.

I was delighted to get away, and happy to join the *People* where an old friend, Bill Bradshaw, was sports editor. There was some surprise at the time; after all I had been *Sunday Times* football correspondent for 33 years. The paper kindly gave me what might be called a gangster's funeral at a fashionable restaurant at the top of Tower Bridge Road. I reflected that when my mother was born in 1905 at the other end of that road, she and her family – a widowed mother left to bring up seven children – could hardly have known what a restaurant was.

Andrew Neil gave a generous speech in which he said I would always be known as 'Brian Glanville of the *Sunday Times*'. David Robson recalled an incident in 1986 when I was in Mexico City covering the World Cup and Borges died. The paper had tried several academics – it was a Saturday, time was of the essence – but they all replied that they could indeed write the obituary, given a few days.

Then David remembered I had visited Borges in Buenos Aires, and he called me. By the grace of God, the meetings were just fresh enough in my mind for me to 'ad lib' an obituary. Certainly I could never have done that in later years.

Scarcely had David told the story than Nawrat cried: 'I could have done that! I read Latin American literature at Essex! I could have done that thing on Borgs [sic]!' There was a surprised silence.

Joining the *People* made perfect sense for me. For so many years I had insisted that sports journalism should be one seamless garment. In the magazine *Encounter* in 1965 I had published an article called 'Looking for an Idiom', emphasising the difference between British sportswriting, with its quality–popular dichotomy, and American, whose chief sportswriters wrote for everybody. I could just as well have adduced sports journalism in Italy and France, and did so some thirty years later in *Prospect* magazine.

My thesis was that both the 'quality' and the 'popular' writer were in some sense failures. The first because although he could largely write as he pleased, about mass-interest sports, he reached only a fraction of the public. The second, because although he reached the public at large, he was rigidly confined to a highly stylised, ultimately patronising, form of journalism, which treated the readership with implicit contempt.

I found it particularly frustrating that, writing for a paper like the *Sunday Times*, though it hugely increased its circulation over the years I was there, and though we did manage to attract more and more football fans, the players scarcely read it at all, and the managers and coaches all too seldom.

The *People* by contrast, though its circulation now was well below the massive five million it had once reached, had always prided itself on its football coverage, its football investigations and its football news. Not at all to my surprise, I had four very enjoyable years there, but all good things come to an end. My sports editors, first Bill Bradshaw, from the Northeast, a devoted Sunderland fan, then Ed Barry, a Londoner, and a follower of Arsenal as I had been myself, were easy and congenial to work with. 'You've been here four years,' said Ed, when I was about to leave, 'and I've never heard your voice raised.'

'You should have heard me at the *Sunday Times*,' I said.

It was many years ago that I framed Glanville's First Law of Fleet Street: Loyalty's What They Fuck You With. A 'law' that has received bitterly resigned endorsement by so many fellow journalists. When things go wrong, in what may now only generically and nostalgically be called Fleet Street, I tend not to be remotely surprised. But when I heard that a journalist who had just lost his job on the *Today* newspaper, which had collapsed, had been seen visiting the *People*'s deputy editor, once a sports editor on *Today* himself, I did begin to wonder.

My wife dismissed the vaguest possibility of my being supplanted; I was this, that and the other. 'You may think so,' I said, 'I may think so, and it may even be true; but I'm not interested in what you think, or what I think. I'm only interested in the irrationality of other people.'

And sure enough, in time, the rumours began to fly; even from as far away as South Africa, where journalists were covering a tour. I was going to retire and be replaced by the writer from *Today*. People asked me about it in football press-boxes. No one had told Ed Barry a thing. But it turned out to be perfectly true. Crocodile tears were wept in the editor, Bridget Rowe's, office, where I met her and the deputy editor, Len Gould. I was coming up to 65; retirement was mandatory. Of course they'd still want me to do this, that and the other.

Technically, this was unanswerable. The retiring age was indeed 65. But a few weeks later, it emerged that the new sports columnist of the *People*'s sister paper, the *Sunday Mirror*, would be ... Mike Langley, my predecessor at the *People*, who was now 72! Moreover, such was the anxiety to get rid of me that I was asked to go, though paid up till the end of the contract in September, as soon as the Euro 96 football tournament ended.

'There were promises made across this desk!' None of them was kept, but I was lucky enough to find a haven in *The Times*.

I stopped running Chelsea Casuals after thirty years; given time off, I put it, for good behaviour. It had never been an easy job. I used to joke that it was bad enough when it was a £20,000-a-year job, unpaid. When it became a £50,000-a-year job, still unpaid, it was too much. Things, beyond question, had got increasingly difficult. Not only your own players but opposing teams and even those who leased your grounds would constantly let you down. Compulsively, I had always tried to honour our fixtures, even when I knew it meant putting out a severely weakened team, and if a club due to play us pulled out on the Friday night, I would still try desperately, often with success, to get another fixture. The final straw came when, with a badly weakened team, we lost an evening match on Astroturf in darkest Southwark. I had tried several times to resign over the years, pass on the baton, but each time had had to come back when I saw the club was going to disintegrate. But this time, I meant it.

Neville Cheetham, who had scored so many goals for us, and who ran the Hertz cars operation in England, ably and self-sacrificingly took my place. His two sons, excellent players both, would figure in the team. Paul, a fine young goalkeeper, played for Loughborough University firsts, a formidable standard. Neil, who had come to our games as a tiny boy, and grew into a very tall one, looked an admirably rational player from the very beginning.

There was nothing particularly rational about David Cameron, the redheaded Scottish Highlander who had scored over ninety goals for us in one amazing season. I had found him, like so many Casuals players, in the pick-up game in Holland Park. He had a strong physique, fine ball control, and an urgent desire to score as many goals as possible, whatever the game in which he was playing. Holland Park was his world; if he were not playing football there, he would be at the cricket nets or, much less impressively, playing tennis.

He seemed to me far too good to stay in Sunday football, though we were grateful for his goals; even if passing was not his chief priority. I promised I would try to find him a club. He told me that he and his father had agreed there was this gap in the Arsenal midfield. I suggested it was a little early to think in those terms. How about a club like Orient? I arranged for him to have a trial but he never went. I heard he had told someone that he could be finished at thirty.

One day, there was appalling news. He had been arrested, and banged up in the notorious Ashford remand home, accused of demanding money with a gun. The charge seemed ludicrous to me; eccentric he might be, but there was nothing of the violent criminal about him. It appeared that he had been arrested in Holland Park and imprisoned in the Earl's Court police station, where he had become almost frenetic while locked in his cell.

Gradually, I uncovered the truth. In the park, he had met an Indonesian restaurateur who apparently hung about the tennis courts and cricket nets. The Indonesian had invited him to come to a sauna where he had made a pass at David that was angrily refused. Next day, he had come across the Indonesian again in the park and had fierce words with him. The Indonesian had run out of the park, straight into the arms of a police woman, whom he had told that there was someone there who had just threatened him with a gun, demanding money.

No one of course had done anything of the sort, but what the Indonesian knew, and I certainly did not, was that David, in his foolish innocence, his fear of London, had been carrying about an unloaded air pistol.

At Earl's Court police station, he was accused of being a Glaswegian who had come down to London to roll queers, charged, and eventually immured in Ashford. The problem was that the nature of the charge, however fatuous, created a momentum of its own. Because it was so 'serious', he could not at first be released, and prosecution in a Crown Court was going to follow. Eventually he was released on bail to go home to Scotland, but the case dragged on, even though in the meantime the Indonesian was convicted of shoplifting and showed no desire to pursue it. He was also found guilty on the substantially lesser charge of opening after hours.

To my astonishment, the case was eventually set down for Knightsbridge Crown Court, postponed – and transferred to the Old Bailey! I promised David I would appear as a character witness.

The Indonesian's accusations looked ridiculous in court. The judge gave a devastating summing up. David, he said, had a totally umblemished record. There were of course instances when those who had such a record could still be guilty of a crime. But he made his own feelings perfectly clear. A solid working-class jury found David not guilty. The fact that the case had gone all this way seemed scandalous.

I made another court appearance in May 1994, but the outcome was far less happy. A couple of seasons earlier, I had been at Anfield to report a match between Liverpool and Chelsea. In the first half, Paul Elliott, the Chelsea centre half, whom I had known many years, often visiting him when he played for Pisa, went into a tackle from behind on Dean Saunders, the Welsh international striker. Saunders jumped, and came down heavily on Elliott's knee. The referee, John Key, gave a foul against Elliott, who was carried off in agony.

Just before the game restarted, I stepped across from the press-box to the edge of the directors' box where Ken Bates, Chelsea's chairman, had just arrived, to ask him anxiously how Elliott was. 'Ligaments,' said Bates. 'The players want to lynch Saunders. They say he stamped on him.'

Elliott was only 28 at the time, one of the best centre backs in the League after a career begun at Charlton, carried on at Luton, Pisa – where he survived a previous severe knee injury – and Celtic, where he was player of the year, though often forced to put up with racial abuse. Now, he would never play again. It seemed to me he had a strong case for compensation, and I spoke to a very old friend, the veteran barrister, Edward Grayson. I had first met him through Jerry

Weinstein, who had helped him compile his *magnum opus*, *Corinthians and Cricketers*, in which he celebrated the achievements of the Corinthians and Pegasus, and chronicled his beguiling acquaintanceship with that heroic Corinthian, the former England centre forward, GO Smith. An embattled idealist, author of the treatise *Sport and the Law*, Edward would later found the eponymous society. He set the wheels in motion and the case dragged on, till finally it came to the High Court under the aegis of Mr Justice Maurice Drake.

Time and again I had watched the video of the incident, and had no doubts that Elliott had been the victim, even if the foul had been given against him. I was far from alone in this belief. I had not then, and did not later, blame the referee Mr Key for not having clearly seen what happened. Who could, at the time? It was over in a flash. But overall, I had deemed him an inept referee and given him the lowest possible mark (4) in the *People*. Not long after that, in fact, he was removed from the Championship list.

To be in the witness box in the High Court in a case that did not directly concern oneself was a far less unnerving affair than it had been in 1964, when I stood to lose so much. My cross-examination by opposing junior counsel, Mr Anthony Berisford, was hardly more exacting than had been Mr Peter Bristow's. 'You're enjoying this, aren't you, Mr Glanville?' he asked me at one point. 'But you're such a marvellous straight man, Mr Berisford,' I replied.

I wrote, in the *People*:

Mr Berisford is a strutting little man who clearly, if debatably, feels attack is the best form of defence.

He's much given to moments of mock exasperation, and he has a strong tendency to sneer. This was plain last Monday, the first day of the trial, when the former international referee Ken Aston was impressively giving evidence for Elliott. At 78, Aston has scarcely changed from the large, upright, mellow figure of his refereeing days.

There was no need for Mr Berisford to say, referring to the monochrome photos of the incident, 'that's in black and white', not least because that isn't even what monochrome means.

Aston resented it, but stood up well. The High Court can be a formidably intimidating place, if you aren't used to it.

Clearly anxious to subvert my report on referee Key, Berisford doggedly ploughed his way through a long, favourable report by the refereeing assessor on Key's performance that day. It sounded, I told him, like a private dialogue. Referee language. For me, Key had been too permissive throughout.

Could I give him instances, asked Berisford. No, I said, not after eighteen months. Didn't I keep notes on such things? 'Mr Berisford,' I said, 'I live in a very large house but if I kept all those notes, there wouldn't be room for me.'

He then harped on endlessly about Elliott's disciplinary record, which didn't seem uncommon for a modern centre back. Certainly it didn't, as Berisford maintained, suggest a 'dirty player'.

When I'd seen Elliott sent off for Pisa against Napoli, I recalled, it was because the notorious Bagni had flung himself at Elliott, then dived to the floor.

Mr Berisford then produced another rabbit from his hat – or wig. A report by the referee who'd booked Elliott just days before the incident at Anfield.

Unwise. The poor ref had written Chelsea v. Blackburn at the top but referred to Southampton throughout his report.

'Not on your intellectual level, Mr Glanville,' sneered Berisford.

'Not even on yours, Mr Berisford,' I replied.

Mr Berisford suggested it was cheap of me to emphasise the Blackburn–Southampton error. I rejoined that when a referee confused two cities hundreds of miles apart, you couldn't put much confidence in his judgement.

As it transpired, I achieved less than nothing through this cross-examination, since Mr Berisford disappeared from the case, which was pursued by Liverpool's QC, Mr Colin Mackay.

I should have been warned when Ken Bates went into the box. White-haired, famously abrasive, he cut a calm, quiet figure here, but it was plain that Judge Drake hadn't taken to him. Bates stood by what he had said to me at Anfield but, surprisingly, there wasn't a single Chelsea player to confirm what they had surely told him at half-time.

When judgement was finally given, I sat there with sinking spirits. Mr Drake quibbled with the evidence given by Aston and the Chelsea player Dennis Wise, which had differed, though hardly radically, from their original statements. Yet he commended the evidence of Vinnie Jones, who had had to be subpoenaed to appear, had strolled into the box in a striped shirt and jeans, and given evidence which was hard to reconcile with an original statement that surely favoured Elliott.

When it came to Bates, Drake's subjectivity was manifest. He suggested that in saying what he did, Bates had a bad memory. Yet what he had said, and said to me, a witness, had been spoken not two years after the event, but some three minutes after he had emerged from the dressing-room!

Mr Drake begged leave to disagree with me over the merits or demerits of the referee, Mr Key. Yet what right had he to do so? Some 40,000 people had that right; they had seen the match. Mr Drake had simply seen the video and as we all know, even the most convincing televised version of a match cannot, by definition, show the panoramic picture. So Paul Elliott lost, Dean Saunders winked at me across the court and Paul, his career in pieces, had a £500,000 bill to pay.

Soon afterwards, I was off to the World Cup in America. Based in New York, a city that had enthralled me for so many years; able to eat at my favourite restaurant the Tout Va Bien, over which the former Marseille inside right, the genial Carlo Migliaccio, still presided; watching games at Giants Stadium; comparing notes with Paul Gardner – how could one help but enjoy it?

Above all, I enjoyed the first game that I saw where, to general surprise, it was the Irish, not the Italians, who took over Giants Stadium *en masse*, and the Irish who won. In a stadium dominated by green and white, by those Irish supporters who, so unlike their boorish English counterparts, contrive to sing inoffensive songs and enjoy themselves at football games, Ray Houghton scored the only goal. Just as he had against England in Stuttgart in the European Championship six years earlier when the busybody British sports minister, Colin Moynihan, small but imperfectly informed, was buzzing around, an interview looking for somewhere to happen. Houghton headed the goal in Stuttgart, after monumental blunders in the English defence. After blunders in the Italians', when Baresi's and Costacurta's headers didn't get sufficient purchase on the ball, he sliced a shot with his weaker left foot over the head of the desperate Gianluca Pagliuca.

In Italy's next game, still further woe was to befall Pagliuca. He was sent off for a foul outside the box. Arrigo Sacchi, Italy's controversial little manager, who had never kicked a ball in anger – 'You don't need to have been a horse to be a jockey,' he proclaimed – pulled off the 'Divine Ponytail', Roberto Baggio, to make way for a substitute goalkeeper. As he left the field, Baggio's lips were read by millions of television viewers: '*Quello è matto!*' (That man is mad!) Sacchi was forced to restore him and that gifted player's goals got them to the World Cup Final in Pasadena. Well might Sacchi have echoed the reported words of Bobby Robson after England had reached the semi-final four years earlier: 'We've got here. I don't know how.'

It was a World Cup Final that ended in shame and fiasco; the final of the greatest competition in the game decided on penalty kicks. But under the ineffable regime of the ineffable João Havelange at FIFA, this was going to happen sooner or later. Neither manager, Brazil's nor Italy's, wanted a replay, but that was because the drawn-out, bloated competition had been so exhausting. The Italians fielded both Baggio and Franco Baresi though both were plainly unfit, Baresi having had a knee operation only days earlier, and both missed penalties in the shoot-out. Though Brazil had a dazzling strike force in the effervescent Romario and the lively Bebeto, they could in no way be compared with the superb Brazilian teams of the past. None of the same guile and technique in midfield and not a winger in sight till the powerful Villa was brought on late in the Final, for his first appearance in the tournament.

Two years later, at Wembley, Terry Venables' England team again lost a semi-final on penalties to Germany, but the truth of it was they were lucky to get so far at all, despite the huge wave of chauvinism that accompanied their progress. Bizarre refereeing decisions had saved them in the game against Spain, and their only rousing display was against the Dutch, whom they crushed 4–1, some kind of revenge for what had happened in the 1994 World Cup eliminators.

The 1998 World Cup was the eleventh I had covered, and the most taxing. This because the egregious President of FIFA, João Havelange – blessedly on his way out after 24 appalling years – had inflicted on us, now, a competition with 32 teams. This, working for the daily *Times*, meant the equivalent of a Tour de France without a bicycle, match after match after match to report, day after day after day. This until I found myself, in a phone booth on Lyons station, castigating a perfectly guiltless telephone operator back at Wapping who had told me that *The Times* had no one in that day. Suddenly, evoking all those tales of American tourists, I realised it was Saturday. Of course they were not in.

Bordeaux to Lyons – where the coach driver from the airport dumped us halfway and refused to complete the journey – on to a hotel in the fields outside Montpellier. A delightful place run by charming people, but murderously far away from a stadium which stood on the other side of town, where you searched desperately for a taxi after midnight.

Thank God, I did not have to cover England, with its 'minority' hordes of brutal, brutalised fans, ravaging Marseilles. A sinister, organised group of German neo-Fascists did still worse things in Lens, where they all but killed a poor gendarme. No real explanation for such gratuitous viciousness, unless you classed it as a resurgence of that dreadful German nihilism that characterised the Nazi years.

As for the England fans, here they were again, an alienated underclass that could express itself only through violence. A miserably untalented subspecies. Such a contrast with the cheerful Dutch and their jaunty band. Or with the French who so joyfully celebrated their win over Brazil in the Final. I came back to central Paris with scores of them in a packed metro carriage. They sang; they drummed on the roof of the carriage; but there was never a hint of violence, not even an expletive to be heard. England's fans drone away in mindless choruses of 'God Save The Queen' and 'Rule Britannia'. Something, as they say, must be done. Why should France and other countries be subject to the barbarian invasion? Ban all England's fans again – however unfair it may be on the decent majority – or, the worst-case scenario, ban England's teams from competing abroad.

It was not a World Cup of real quality, though the Final itself was a freak. Ronaldo played for Brazil when he shouldn't have been allowed to play at all, after a seizure the night before. The demoralised Brazilians were well beaten by a French team hardly to be compared with its best sides of the past; those of Platini, Giresse and Tigana. France were a team without an adequate centre forward. Stephane Guivarc'h's two dreadful misses against Brazil were almost bizarre.

It was a World Cup in which the tackle from behind was notionally outlawed, to be automatically red-carded, but in which the referees, common sense prevailing, seldom applied the letter of so Draconian a law – a law wanted of course by Havelange's successor as FIFA President, its ineffable ex-Secretary Sepp Blatter. Would one prefer to be shot or hanged? Blatter, forever wanting to fiddle with the laws, even favoured restoring the kick-in for the throw-in after over a hundred years.

A German journalist once said to me in Miami, 'Sepp Blatter has fifty new ideas every day; and fifty-one of them are bad!'

Blatter threw his weight about endlessly, unashamedly dictatorial, threatening referees with perdition if they did not expel players for tackles from behind. But the referees knew in their bones that the rule was wrong, that while a foul or dangerous tackle from behind deserved condign punishment, a tackle from behind that cleanly took the ball was perfectly valid and acceptable.

There had been much controversy just before the tournament started when Glenn Hoddle, the England coach, once such a sublimely talented, creative player himself, sent Paul Gascoigne home from training camp the very day after praising his physical condition. Whether or not the decision was right – and Gascoigne had certainly been indulging himself excessively – to do it in such a way was purely Pavlovian. Gascoigne, the eternal adolescent with the superb football brain, is a vulnerable creature at the best of times, and such alternating stimuli could have had the most dire results. Fortunately, he seemed to manage the disaster well. This was illusory.

Then there was Hoddle's strange attitude towards Michael Owen. The eighteen-year-old Liverpool striker was clearly the Gascoigne of his generation in terms of sheer, outstanding talent, with marvellous pace, the ability to know when to use it, superb opportunism and – so unlike Gascoigne – a balanced, precociously mature, disposition. Yet only a few months earlier Hoddle had gratuitously and deplorably criticised him publicly, not only as a player who had much to learn, but as one whose behaviour generally must be improved. Whereupon in England's game against Romania, despite the thrilling, winning goal Owen had scored away to Morocco, after being knocked out – Hoddle preferred Teddy Sheringham. Sheringham: a player whose antics in Portugal, when the players had been given a few days off, led to his making a humiliating, if stilted and plainly ghost-written, apology. And who, if it comes to that – and if Hoddle really is so concerned with general behaviour – had, with his friends, wrecked a hotel room in Oxfordshire the previous summer, with the help of a fire extinguisher.

Obdurate to a degree, Hoddle kept Sheringham – who had had a miserable season with Manchester United – trotting about the field to no evident purpose for almost three-quarters of the game. When Owen at last came on, he scored one of his typically exciting goals, but the game was lost. Against Argentina, when Manchester United's David Beckham deplorably got himself sent off for childishly kicking out (at Diego Simeone) as he lay on the ground after being fouled, Owen started the game. He procured a penalty that Alan Shearer converted and scored another of his marvellous goals, against an Argentine defence that had not conceded any for eight games.

England's ten men held out with enormous aplomb and resilience for some 75 minutes. Ultimately they went down only on penalties: that horrific abomination that Havelange had effectively inflicted on the World Cup even to the extent of deciding a very Final on penalties. England might not have won the tournament, but if things had gone a little differently, I think they would have made substantially more progress.

Hoddle's behaviour with Owen was so illogical, so patently self-destructive, that you wondered what lay behind it. Could a green eye somehow have been flashing? Controversial, too, was Hoddle's decision to induct his spiritual healer, one Mrs Eileen Drewery, who had been ministering to him since his early playing days. As one who is married to a healer and strongly believes in the potential of healing, I am perfectly ready to accept that Mrs Drewery has her manifold successes. But the publicity seemed to have strange effects on her.

In a newspaper article, she claimed she had 'a one to one with God', and had prevented Ian Wright from scoring the winning goal for England late in the World Cup eliminator against Italy in Rome, for fear of the consequences. She has not, I believe, told us whether she was responsible for Italy's Christian Vieri promptly missing an easy chance at the other end. The effect of her presence in the 'camp', one heard, was to divide the England players dangerously into two camps of their own, those who frequented Mrs Drewery and her healing, and those who, while sceptical of it, felt there was implicit pressure on them to avail themselves of it.

Italy, under the 65-year-old Cesare Maldini, went out on penalties for the third World Cup in a row – this time against the French – and made few friends. They should really have lost their opening game against Chile, but were saved after 84 minutes by the most dubious of penalties, awarded by an African referee who would subsequently be run out on a rail. There seemed no way the Chilean defender could have withdrawn his hand as Roberto Baggio – ludicrously and stubbornly underused by Maldini – tried to cross from the right. Baggio himself put away the penalty and, returning to the team after a long absence, was the star of the show. But Maldini later inexplicably preferred the much lauded but ineffective Alex Del Piero, to the detriment of his dull team.

On his appointment, Maldini had been hailed as the saviour of an Italian team reduced to drudgery by the four-in-line 'pressing' tactics of Arrigo Sacchi. It was conveniently ignored that Maldini was a high priest of *catenaccio*, which Sacchi had swept aside: the system that relied essentially on counter-attack. Maldini, father of the team's captain and left back, Paolo, did, it is true, reopen the way for talent, for the individual star, but even that did not last indefinitely. Long years in charge of the under-21 team, with whom he stubbornly stuck to *catenaccio*, despite the threat of losing his job, and never a club manager, he was catapulted into the top job at a time of his career when he should surely have been winding down.

That Croatia should have gone as far as they did without the excellent Alen Boksic is more evidence of the tournament's shortcomings. 'Boksic is Boksic!' said the Croatian defender Zvonimir Soldo with a sad smile, when one mentioned this to him in the clamour and dungeon-like depths of the so-called Mixed Zone, after France versus Croatia. Boksic in fact had to undergo a knee operation just before the tournament began. Yet even though this left Croatia with Davor Suker – hardly used all season by Real Madrid – as their one experienced international striker, they were able to reach the semi-final, thrashing Berti Vogts' ageing Germans *en route*. Wily Miroslav Blazevic was a cunning coach with long experience in France.

Recent years have seen profound changes in English football, by no means all of them for the better. It seemed an appalling sell-out to me when the Football Association made common cause with the major clubs to form the FA Premier League and thus spite the Football League. The whole *raison d'être* of the FA has surely been to hold the ring, to be above the conflict. Stanley Rous, for all his authoritarian faults, well understood that. It was sad to see the FA descend to the level of in-fighting personified by the late Alan Hardaker in his turbulent years as Secretary of the Football League. Hardaker had even established the League Cup as a would-be rival to the FA Cup, which might be described as the Mother of All Competitions. But even treating the competition as a rich father might have treated an ugly daughter, tempting clubs with the prospect of a Final at Wembley and a wholly illogical place in the UEFA Cup, the League Cup, in its myriad incarnations, has never attained the glamour of its senior and superior.

The birth of the Premier League meant a Faustian pact with television. Anyone who had studied American sport could have told you where that would lead; to a ride on the back of a tiger. I have always felt that the relationship was symbolised when a Super Bowl game, the most important in gridiron football and a kind of equivalent of the FA Cup itself, kicked off twice: once for television and once 'for real'.

Satellite television has poured immense wealth into the game, rewarding clubs and players with far more than their due, given the pedestrian nature of so many games, and despite the influx of so many foreign stars. But he who pays the piper calls the tune, and satellite TV's tune is a discordant one. Where the Italian clubs stood firm, insisting that, with the exception of dispensations before European matches, all games be played on the same day, with one game alone shown for pay TV at night, our football has capitulated. Games now are dotted all over the Saturday to Monday period, with pay TV threatening even to put an end to the grand tradition of Saturday football.

That the game has gained a belated popularity and modishness among the middle classes, long, long after it enraptured them in Europe and South America, has been scant consolation. Indeed, to those of us who endured the supercilious wonder of our contemporaries, who had to put up with the spurious moral claims of rugby football over soccer, there's a great irony about the bourgeoisation of the game. It was the working classes of this country who took it over and made it popular when the 'nobs' had turned their backs on it. Now, with much smaller, all-seater, stadia and rocketing ticket prices, there is a clear danger that the traditional supporter will be priced out of the game. Did not an administrator of Manchester United, the richest and most successful club in the country, say, a few years ago, that those not rich enough to watch the first team could watch the reserves?

Yet the game is vibrantly alive, after more than a hundred years. If there are ominous straws in the wind, such as the desire of Juventus to build a new stadium in Turin holding only 32,000, television being plainly and forebodingly in their minds, football has still conquered the world. Africa, for all the disorganisation that hampers its international teams, has long produced some of the best players in the game. Even the United States, whose own sports, largely shunned by the rest of the world, have been a kind of declaration of independence in themselves, now has more people playing soccer than any other sport, though it is still proving so hard to establish a successful pro league. Japan has its J League. Colossal crowds flock to see international matches in Iraq and Iran. In its sublime combination of surface simplicity and inner complexity, soccer looks good for another century at least; no small achievement in an age that technology has changed and is changing with such frightening speed.

For my part, I still enjoy watching it, still enjoy writing about it, still enjoy trying to play it. And, for all that it has done for me, I am still grateful.

Index